BIG PPI

MY STORY OF
BIG DREAMS
AND BIG HITS

DAVID ORTIZ

WITH TONY MASSAROTTI

St. Martin's Griffin
New York

www.stmartins.com

Design by Dylan Rosal Greif

Library of Congress Cataloging-in-Publication Data

Ortiz, David, 1975–
    Big Papi : my story of big dreams and big hits / David Ortiz with Tony Massarotti.
        p. cm.
    ISBN-13: 978-0-312-38344-2
    ISBN-10: 0-312-38344-4
    1. Ortiz, David, 1975–   2. Boston Red Sox (Baseball team)
3. World Series (Baseball) (2004)   4. Baseball players—Dominican Republic—Biography.   I. Title.

GV865.O78 A3 2007
796.357092—dc22
[B]
                                                        2007010172

First St. Martin's Griffin Edition: April 2008

10 9 8 7 6 5 4 3 2 1

For my mother, Angela Rosa Arias, who passed away in January 2002 and who gave me undying love and support, who taught me right from wrong, who remains my guardian angel and guiding light, and without whom I would not be who I am today. I love you and I miss you.

—David

For Mom and Dad

—T. M.

BIG PAPI

CONTENTS

ACKNOWLEDGMENTS

In September 2005, as the Red Sox were preparing for a late-season game at Tropicana Field against the Tampa Bay Devil Rays, the seeds for this project were planted. In between then and now, a host of people brought the flower to bloom.

Without them, the tale of Big Papi could not have been told.

From the start, David Ortiz embraced the idea of telling his story to the world with typical ease and warmth, both of which will serve as his true legacy to baseball fans and non–baseball fans alike. Ortiz's team of agents and marketing representatives, Fernando Cuza, Diego Bentz, and Alex Radetsky, similarly welcomed the idea of this book, taking large blocks of time to speak with the writer while structuring a plan that accommodated all involved parties; attorney Lee Galkin, in particular, worked painstakingly when it came time to finalize a contract. Scott Waxman and Farley Chase, both of the Waxman Literary Agency, negotiated in good faith between the author and writer, as well as with St. Martin's Press, which expressed a genuine eagerness in this project from the start. St. Martin's editor Marc Resnick and his staff (especially Rebecca Heller) demonstrated tremendous patience throughout the writing stages, working with both an author and writer who were unfamiliar with the process of an "as told to" account while agreeing to publish this work in both English and Spanish.

As is often the case, there were others, too, whose contributions might have gone unrecognized. Countless editors and aides at both St. Martin's and SFX Baseball, the agency which represents Ortiz, took time to review chapters, suggest changes, and offer their opinions. Similar contributions were made by Red Sox publicist John Blake and his staff, Major League Baseball spokesman Pat Courtney and his aides (particularly Michael Teevan), Major League Baseball commissioner Bud Selig, and Los Angeles Dodgers bench coach Dave Jauss, all of whom willingly offered their assistance. In some cases, those people were quoted. In others, they simply helped fill in the inevitable cultural and translation gaps that result in any bilingual work.

Beyond that scope, numerous others offered their support, cooperation, and insights, be they on Major League Baseball, the Dominican Republic, or Ortiz himself. Major leaguers Pedro Martinez and Torii Hunter, both All-Stars and onetime teammates of Ortiz, were remarkably gracious and helpful, responding to interview requests with eagerness and sincerity; to each, we owe a tremendous debt of gratitude. Minnesota Twins general manager Terry Ryan was both forthright and accomodating, consistent with his reputation as one of the most decent, honest, and grounded men in baseball. Boston Red

Sox general manager Theo Epstein, one of the youngest and most accomplished executives in the game, similarly demonstrated commendable humbleness while helping to assemble the timeline on which Ortiz traveled to Fenway Park.

A special thanks, too, to Red Sox owner John Henry, team president Larry Lucchino, and vice-president of public affairs Charles Steinberg (as well as the entire Red Sox organization) for their willingness to support projects like this and for their commitment to keeping the Red Sox one of the most successful and competitive franchises in all of professional sports.

Finally, a special thanks to the fans of Major League Baseball, particularly in Boston, where the game remains a passion as in no other place. In the end, that interest and intensity are what make projects like this worthwhile and meaningful, and allow David Ortiz to step into the batter's box, night after night after night, and be noticed for his remarkable accomplishments and feats.

In Boston, after all, it often seems as if the game is on the line with each and every pitch.

PREFACE

I n the heart of downtown Detroit, in a shoebox of a room where the best baseball players in the world were strewn about like collectible trading cards, David Ortiz gleamed like one of the brightest stars of Motown.

Nine months had passed since the unforgettable events of October 2004, yet the aftershocks were still rumbling throughout the subsequent summer as Major League Baseball gathered for what effectively served as its annual midseason convention: the All-Star Game. *Big Papi* had arrived. While reporters shot about like bees in a dark, cluttered function room that served as an interview space for representatives of the 2005 All-Star teams from the American League and National League, Ortiz sat behind a table that was not nearly big enough for the man or the assembled masses. He wore a powder-blue scally cap and matching blue-and-white striped shirt, and he wore designer, Gucci sunglasses that made him look, above all else, *cool*.

But after all of the dramatic events of the preceding autumn, after all of the twists and turns in a career that at one point seemed terminally ill, what had David Ortiz become if not the picture of cool?

"I don't know," Ortiz said when asked about his exploding success and popularity in baseball. "I guess people follow you and they really appreciate what we do on the field. They appreciate the good things they hear about you, I guess. That has a lot to do with it."

Said teammate Matt Clement, a right-handed pitcher also representing the Boston Red Sox at the All-Star Game and who was seated at the table next to Ortiz: "Obviously, you had to be under a rock to not see what he did in the playoffs last year. It shows how much the Red Sox are in demand. It shows the kind of presence he's become in baseball."

Indeed, in an era when baseball has had to endure congressional hearings and continuing skepticism, Ortiz's place among his peers was (and is) indisputable. Fueled by Boston's first World Series victory in eighty-six years—a historic achievement he was largely responsible for—Ortiz was named on more 2005 All-Star ballots than any player in the game. In and of itself, that achievement was impossible to overlook. The storied Red Sox never had produced such a celebrated player in their 105-year history, from Ted Williams to Carl Yastrzemski to Jim Rice and beyond. Not a single one of them ever had led the All-Star Game in fan balloting. Then came Ortiz, a six-foot-four, 260-pound slugger who was a teddy bear off the field and a grizzly in the batter's box, who delivered an impossible three consecutive home playoff victories on the final pitch thrown, who relished the moment, who remained as warm as the spotlight, and who stayed, through it all, astonishingly unaffected.

Even there, in Detroit, Ortiz's timing was impeccable. Baseball was in the midst of a growing steroids scandal and needed a hero unlike the ill-tempered Barry Bonds, who seemed to live in a perpetual state of annoyance. The All-Star Game, too, was being played in an American League city that required the use of a designated hitter, which meant that the position would be included on the ballot. In another year, in another city, Ortiz might have been listed as a first baseman or perhaps not at all—the latter is precisely what happened to him in 2004—leaving his place among the All-Stars open to interpretation or debate. But that was not the case this year, not in 2005, the season after Ortiz emerged as the most compelling and charismatic figure from a 2004 playoff season that forever would be remembered as one of the most improbable, remarkable, and extraordinary happenings in the history of organized team sports.

In the middle of it all stood a willing, unabashed, and undeterred David Ortiz.

"You've often heard me say that we're in the Golden Era of baseball. David Ortiz—Big Papi—symbolizes that Golden Era," said Baseball Commissioner Bud Selig. "He's been such a great player on a grand stage, but it's his personality along with his ability that has made him an important part of this sport. I have enormous respect for David Ortiz. He's conducted himself so beautifully off the field as well as on the field. I'm very proud of David Ortiz, for a myriad of reasons. It's everything about him. When you say 'David Ortiz,' the first thing I think is 'Big Papi,' and that's a great compliment to him. He stands as a great symbol for the success of this sport—and a symbol for all of the right reasons."

But then, too, what is his story if not one of perseverance, grace, and impeccable timing?

—

BEFORE READING ANYTHING FROM ORTIZ HIMSELF, KNOW THIS: BY all accounts, the man is what he seems. Ortiz can call people by the wrong name or by no real name at all, yet still make them feel as if he has known them all their lives. He will call a man "dude," "bro," or, of course, "papi," and most conversations with him inevitably conclude with a pat on the shoulder and a bright, warm smile.

Before and during his time in Boston, Ortiz never has really looked down on anyone.

Late in the 2005 season, after the All-Star Game and his ascension into baseball's elite, Ortiz was standing in front of his locker at the Rogers Centre, home of the Toronto Blue Jays, preparing for a road game later that night. There was a cluster of reporters at his locker, as there often was, and most wanted to know about Ortiz's unending heroics, about the Red Sox pursuit of a second consecutive world title, about whether Ortiz had positioned himself to make even more history by becoming the first true designated hitter in baseball history to win a prestigious Most Valuable Player award.

As usual, Ortiz accommodated them.

As it was, the 2005 Red Sox (unlike their 2004 brethren) were a terribly flawed team, short on that most indispensable of all things: pitching. Deep down, Ortiz knew that. Yet the Red Sox were still very much in playoff contention, still eyeing a world championship, largely because Ortiz was having the kind of season (again) that little boys dream about. Ortiz was on his way to finishing the regular season with a .300 batting average to go along with what were then career bests in home runs (47) and runs batted in (148), the latter of which would lead all major-league players. But those totals alone did not begin to measure the contributions of a man who was defying logic, time and time again, by delivering a succession of game-winning hits under the most demanding conditions.

Baseball, after all, is a game typically controlled by pitchers. The oldest adage in the game is that good pitching beats good hitting, always and without exception. That is thought to be especially true in late innings, especially late in the year, when the colder weather favors the pitchers and when the game becomes a test of skill and precision and determination. The hitters are always at a disadvantage because they have to *react,* a challenge that becomes psychological as much as physical. Standing on a mound, a pitcher has countless options at his disposal, depending on his arsenal. He might throw a fastball or a curveball, a slider or a changeup. He might pitch inside or outside, up near the letters or down by the kneecaps. Those variables create an array or combinations and permutations— fastball in, curveball away, slider down, fastball up—and can frequently clutter a hitter's mind, even under the simplest circumstances.

And if a game is on the line, if something more than just another chance at bat hangs in the balance, the weight of the outcome alone can devour a man.

As the Red Sox were preparing to play the Blue Jays, however, Ortiz was enjoying a most remarkable stretch. Beginning in the middle of August, Ortiz was taking a trendy baseball term—the "walk-off"—and making it a subheading on his résumé. In fact, it generally is believed that the term "walk-off" was popularized by, among others, Hall of Fame pitcher Dennis Eckersley, who ascended to greatness as a pitcher with the Oakland A's, though, oddly enough, the words to him had a negative connotation. An accomplished closer with a language all to himself, Eckersley recorded 390 saves during a fascinating twenty-four-year career that more than once seemed on life support. Still, his baseball life included some spectacular failures, breakdowns that Eckersley frequently would refer to as "walk-off pieces," because the defeat would require him, a most accountable being with whom all bucks stopped, to join all other players and *walk off* the mound in shame.

Somewhere in between Dennis Eckersley and David Ortiz, the walk-off became more a fashionable feat.

It was Ortiz, however, who elevated it into an art form.

In particular, in the final weeks of the 2005 season, Ortiz all but conducted a seminar in the art of clutch hitting. Beginning on August 16, when Ortiz tied a game at Detroit with a two-out, ninth-inning home run against fellow Dominican Fernando Rodney—Ortiz would add yet *another* homer in the eleventh inning of the eventual Red Sox victory—Ortiz was performing heroic baseball feats with such regularity that even a formal tally of his walk-off hits proved insufficient. For all of the glory that it possessed, after all, the walk-off did not include Ortiz's heroics in road games, when the home team always batted last. Nor could it account for those times, like the homer against Rodney in Detroit, when Ortiz tied a game or put the Red Sox ahead in the late innings, the former of which frequently possessed even greater value because they spared the Red Sox defeats when they could not afford them.

Slightly more than two weeks after saving the Red Sox in Detroit, Ortiz hit a true walk-off home run against Los Angeles Angels reliever Scot Shields at Fenway Park to propel the Red Sox to a critical 3–2 victory. And less than a week after that—the Red Sox were back on the road again—Ortiz hit two more home runs in a single game, the second homer breaking a 5–5 tie in the eleventh inning and carrying the Red Sox to yet another critical victory over the Toronto Blue Jays on September 12 at the Rogers Centre.

At a time of the season when many players cracked, when many broke from the pressure and fatigue of a long and relentless season, Ortiz was seemingly producing a nightly hailstorm of clutch hits, walk-off or otherwise.

By then, of course, the secret was out and a groundswell had begun. Reporters were gathering around Ortiz's locker on a nightly basis—before and after games—and all of them wanted to know: *Could Ortiz become the first true designated hitter in history to win the Most Valuable Player Award? Was it even conceivable that a DH could win an MVP?* Ortiz, for his part, already had spent considerable time pondering those questions, publicly answering them, saying that he was "trying to break the rules," which was his way of saying that he merely wanted to rewrite them.

The reporters persisted, at which point Ortiz noticed a familiar face in the back of the group and sought assistance from one of the very men questioning him.

"Jeremy, do you want to answer?" he asked.

The reporter—whose name was neither Jeremy nor anything remotely resembling it—politely declined and and broke into an amused, playful grin.

After all, what was in a name?

Before the Red Sox left Toronto, Ortiz lifted the Red Sox to another victory, hitting a game-tying, two-run home run off Toronto right-hander Josh Towers that gave Boston a 5–3 win. A few days later—albeit in the sixth inning—he hit a game-tying homer that forced a 2–2 tie in a game the Red Sox eventually won, 3–2, in extra innings. And less than two weeks after that, with the Red Sox on the verge of a potentially back-breaking defeat, Ortiz hit a game-tying home run—this one in the eighth inning—before coming up again in the bottom of the ninth and delivering a single that scored teammate Johnny Damon to give the Red Sox a pulsating 5–4 win.

After celebrating around their charismatic slugger for what

seemed like the umpteenth time in the span of just six weeks, the Red Sox, in unison, did what they learned to do regularly behind an unrelenting David Ortiz.

Together, following his lead, they *walked off* the field.

DAVID ORTIZ DID NOT WIN THE 2005 AMERICAN LEAGUE MOST Valuable Player Award, finishing second in a close race with New York Yankees third baseman Alex Rodriguez. Ortiz did not win the award in 2003, 2004, or, for that matter, 2006, though no one could dispute the following: In those four years, Ortiz led all American League players in home runs (173) and all major leaguers in RBIs (525). That was true despite the fact that Ortiz did not begin playing regularly for the Boston Red Sox until midway through 2003, his first season with the team, and, of course, did not measure the *timing* of Ortiz's contributions to a Red Sox team that heavily relied on him.

For instance, in 2005, in those clutch situations deemed "close and late" by STATS, Inc., Ortiz was the runaway major-league leader in home runs (11) and RBIs (33). Rodriguez, by contrast, finished with just four home runs (tied for twenty-ninth) and 12 RBIs (tied for sixty-sixth) in those situations deemed the most critical and demanding based on an array of criteria.

Translation: From 2003 to 2006, with or without a Most Valuable Player Award, the whole of David Ortiz was much, much greater than the sum of everyone else's parts.

But with Ortiz, of course, the on-field accomplishments are only part of the story. In 2004, on the night the mission-driven Red Sox clinched a return trip to the playoffs, Boston players celebrated in customary fashion in the visiting clubhouse at Tropicana Field, home of the Tampa Bay Devil Rays. To a man, the Red Sox uncorked one bottle of champagne after the next and doused one another with the bubbly. Seemingly dissatisfied with the weaponry, Ortiz lumbered into the adjacent bathroom and shower area, pulled a pair of swimming goggles over his head and attached a hose to a nearby faucet. Clearly a power hitter down to the very last detail, Ortiz then lumbered back into the middle of the room and sent his terrified teammates scattering, at which point he roared like a Dominican Shrek—his teammates had given him that nickname—and made an about-face back to his cave.

His gait, as always, was unmistakable. Once described by the Minnesota Twins general manager as if "walking on eggshells," Ortiz actually seems to walk as if he were always listening to music. His weight shifts heavily from the left to the right and back—all while his head and shoulders rhythmically sway from side to side, as if he were quite literally marching to the beat of his own drummer.

In Boston, on the field and off, people are all too willing to line up behind him. In 2006, thanks to the efforts of the Make-A-Wish Foundation, a teenage girl fighting ovarian cancer had the chance to attend batting practice and meet her favorite Red Sox player; she chose Ortiz. Later that same year, upon learning that Ortiz never had been to Maine, Governor John Baldacci sent Ortiz forty-one lobsters, one for every home run he had hit to that point. At the souvenir stands in and around Fenway Park, shirts and memorabilia bearing Ortiz's number 34 have sold more consistently than any other, validating his place as the most marketable and appealing of the personalities on a Red Sox club that might be the most powerful corporate enterprise in New England.

In the clubhouse, the trust in Ortiz is so great that teammates have empowered him to control the clubhouse music, an honor far more prestigious than it might seem. In recent times especially, locker room music has been such a flash point for friction between teammates that many clubs require their players to wear headphones. Many clubs, including the Red Sox, can cite instances in which fights took place (or nearly did) over the style of music that was being played, the volume at which it was being played, or the sound of any music at all.

But in Boston, a baseball crockpot that always simmers like perhaps no other, in Papi they trust.

The rest of the world? It, too, has come to embrace Ortiz in recent years. In D'Angelo sandwich shops throughout the northeastern United States, customers have been greeted by a large, life-size cardboard cutout of Big Papi; the same has been true at the Papa Gino's pizzerias. Ortiz has had national endorsement deals with Reebok, XM Radio, AT&T, Sony PlayStation, and Vitamin Water—and rest assured that others are on the way. At one point during the summer and fall of 2005, travelers flying from Boston to Florida could do so on the Song Airlines jet cleverly nicknamed the "Big Papi." Shortly after the historic events of October 2004, Ortiz's picture appeared on the front of a box of Wheaties (the Breakfast of Champions) while he proclaimed, to all of America, that he was joining a long line of American sports heroes at DisneyWorld. His national popularity has reached such heights that Ortiz is now regarded as the face of baseball, and he rivals New York Yankees shortstop and all-American boy Derek Jeter as the most marketable and influential personality in the game.

For a player born outside of the United States, his popularity is unprecedented.

"I hope people appreciate what he's doing right now," cerebral Red Sox outfielder Gabe Kapler said of Ortiz's magnificent performance during Boston's comeback against the New York Yankees in the 2004 American League Championship Series. "It's not that easy."

Said Red Sox manager Terry Francona time and time again

during Ortiz's first four years in Boston: "It's hard to imagine anyone being more important to their team that he's been to ours."

NOT LONG BEFORE, DAVID ORTIZ WAS A MAN WITHOUT A TEAM. Dissatisfied with Ortiz's performance, the Minnesota Twins released their rights to him in 2002, effectively placing him out on the curb for anyone else to pick up. Ortiz was just twenty-seven years old and about to join his third team, the Red Sox, who considered him only as one of many possible solutions to their problem at first base. One of the primary reasons Ortiz selected Boston was because he simply wanted what most everyone else wants: a chance.

In retrospect, what is Ortiz's story if not one of opportunity? What is it if not a success story of a young boy who grew up in an impoverished Dominican Republic, hoping and praying to be discovered? What is it if not one of a loving mother and a committed father, of the influence they can have on their children? What is it if not one of persistence and perseverance, of confidence rising above self-doubt? And what is it if not a story of fate, about a man who finally ended up in the right place at the right time and under the right circumstances, despite all of the roadblocks along the way, despite all of the failures and setbacks that might have derailed a dream?

What is it if not a story of hard work, a historic account of a figure who is truly Ruthian?

But then, David Ortiz's spirit always has been one of his greatest assests.

And the story is really one that only he should tell.

—Tony Massarotti

BIG PAPI

THE BIRTH OF
BIG PAPI

To be honest, I still laugh about it sometimes. I'll be out there on the field, warming up for a game or something, and somebody from the other team will come over and ask me: "What's up, *Papi?*" I might not even know the guy, might not even recognize him, but he knows me by my nickname. So I'll say hello back—"Wassup, dude?"—and then get back to my running or stretching or whatever. But inside, I'll be laughing.

I'm really not sure how it started, bro. I have no idea. After I got to Boston and started playing for the Red Sox, I would walk around the clubhouse and talk to guys, and I starting calling them *papi*. Some of my teammates did it, too. Someone like Manny Ramirez would walk by a reporter or someone whose name he didn't really know, and he would say things like, "How you doing, *papi?*" or "It's a beautiful day, *papi!*" and people would laugh. In the Dominican Republic, we use the word all the time, like Americans would use "buddy" or "pal," but it's more like "daddy" or "pops." It's just the way we talk. And in Boston, before we knew it, everybody on the team was calling everyone else "papi," and it wasn't too long before the name somehow belonged to me.

David Ortiz.

Big Papi.

Wherever I go now, bro, that's what people call me. I'm serious. Whenever I come out of the dugout before a game, if it's in winter ball or spring training or the playoffs, the fans all start screaming it. Even in the Dominican Republic, where anybody can be *papi,* that's what everybody calls me. Before the 2006 season, when we had the World Baseball Classic for the first time, I couldn't go anywhere without people calling out my name. There were teams there from the United States and the Dominican Republic, Puerto Rico, Venezuela, and Cuba. There were teams and fans from everywhere. And no matter where I went, no matter who we were playing against, the people all knew my name from seeing me on television or in the newspaper, or wherever.

It's funny, bro.

And it took me a little while to get used to it.

Since I got to Boston—since 2004, especially—a lot of things have changed. My life is totally different now. I'm still the same person—still my mom's baby—no matter how different things get. It can be hard for me now to go places, especially when I'm home in the Dominican, but I'm happier than I've ever been. All my life, I've had good people around me, people who gave me good advice and tried to teach me things. My mom. My pop. My wife, my family, and my friends. I've always been the kind of person who tries to focus on the good things, who tries to take the positive out of something.

My mom was the same way, and my pop is, too, and my parents always tried to teach me to get better at things, to improve, to work at them and to keep trying, no matter what happens. That's what we should all try to do, bro—to keep getting better, no matter what we do.

So starting again this year, in 2007, that's my goal: to get better.

Since I got to Boston—even before—I feel like I've been getting better every year. People always ask me how that happened, if there's some secret or something, and I always tell them the same thing: It's confidence and hard work. In 2002, my final year playing for the Minnesota Twins, I hit 20 homers in about 400 at-bats, and I thought that was pretty good. In 2003, my first year in Boston, I hit 31 homers in about 450 at-bats. Since that time, when the Red Sox started playing me everyday, I've hit 41 homers (in 2004), 47 homers (in 2005) and 54 homers (in 2006). Basically, my RBIs have been going up, too. I even missed some time last year late in the season, so I know I can be better. Maybe I can hit 60 homers. Maybe I can hit 70. Maybe I can help the Red Sox win another World Series.

It sounds crazy, right? But let me tell you: If you set your mind to it, you can accomplish almost anything. You need the confidence and you need the support, but you can do it. Trust me.

The team—I think we're going to better this year, too. We had a lot of changes last year, a lot of new players, and we had a lot of injuries, too. We had a lot of guys who were playing in Boston for the very first time, and some of those guys had never played in the American League before. It takes a little while to come over to a new league, like those guys did, and to learn the pitchers, make adjustments, get used to everything. I know because I've played my whole career in the

American League and it still happens with me. Every year, there are new guys in the league and new pitchers to learn, things like that. But the longer you're around, the more you know and the less you have to learn, and the easier it all gets.

Look at someone like Mike Lowell, bro. He's a smart dude who's been around awhile, but he never really played in the American League before 2006. He hit .280 with 20 home runs and 80 RBIs last season—which is a good year—and I bet you he'll be even better this year. I feel the same way about our young pitchers, guys like Jonathan Papelbon and Josh Beckett. Papelbon is nasty, bro, and he's been nasty since the day he got to the big leagues. How much better can that kid get? I remember once when we were in Toronto in 2005, the dude pitched three innings in relief and he didn't give up a hit or a run. It was a game we had to win. It was late in the year and we were trying to make the playoffs, and we were having all kinds of problems with the bullpen. The kid came into the game—he was a *rookie*, bro—and it was like he'd been pitching in the big leagues his whole life. I remember the game because I hit a home run in the eleventh inning and we won, 6–5—it was my second homer of the game—and Pap got his first major-league win. I remember the reporters coming up to me after the game and asking me about him, and I remember telling them that Pap reminded me of Roger Clemens. And he does, bro. As long as that kid stays healthy, he's going to do great things.

I only wish I had that kind of confidence when I was a rookie.

Beckett, too, dude. You just watch. He's got great shit. He won sixteen games for us last year and he's only going to get better. He's only six months older than Papelbon, I think. He's still learning. Beckett pitched his whole career in the National League before coming to the Red Sox, so he didn't know the hitters or know the league, and the whole season was a learning experience for him. The American League is tough, bro. It's a lot different than the National League. You've got big dudes like me in the middle of the lineup and you can't make mistakes over here. It's just different. A pitcher can get to the end of the lineup in the National League and he can pitch around guys, save pitches, do things like that because the other pitcher is coming to bat. But you can't do that kind of stuff in the American League, and it takes time to learn.

You have to have patience with people, bro.

Trust me.

I'm proof.

Even though we missed the playoffs last year, let me tell you: We didn't have a terrible year. We had a lot of injuries, especially late in the year, and we have a lot of talent. One of the good things about playing in a place like Boston is we're always going to have talent, no matter what, and that's a big difference from a place like Minnesota, where I played the first four or five years of my career. In Boston, we have to compete against the New York Yankees every year and we know the Yankees are going to be good, too. Our owners and our general manager make changes every year—they've made some since the end of last season—and they're always trying to make us better. After the end of last season, they went out and invested a lot of money to improve our team. They spent more than $100 million just to get Daisuke Matsuzaka, a pitcher from Japan who should be a big help to our staff for years to come. Our front-office people have hard jobs, bro, but we have to have confidence in them, too.

Making the playoffs is something we want to do every year, but even when you miss the postseason, October can still be valuable. You can make good use of the time off. The baseball season is long and it can wear you down, and by the fall of 2006 we had been to the playoffs three years in a row. In 2004, when we won the World Series, the off-season was like one big party. Wherever we went, everybody wanted to talk about the Red Sox. It seemed like there was always someplace to go, somewhere to celebrate, and I think we all felt that way going into spring training and into the early part of 2005. It was like the season never ended. And then we made the playoffs again in 2005, and even though we got swept by the Chicago White Sox in the first round, it was like spring training came fast. We had the World Baseball Classic and then the season started, and then all of a sudden we were right back there in August and September again, trying to make the playoffs.

Last winter, finally, I think we all got to catch our breath, get some rest, prepare for the season like we really wanted to. And because the Yankees kicked our asses a little bit, because they beat us by eleven games and we missed the playoffs and finished in third place, maybe that was a good wake-up call for us. Nothing ever comes easy. You have to work for everything you get because your competition is working, too. You have to work hard just to keep up and you have to work harder to get better, or we all know what's going to happen.

You're going to get beat.

And I don't know about you, but I don't like to lose.

LET ME TELL YOU WHAT I'VE BEEN DOING SINCE THE END OF LAST season: I've been working out. After the season ended, almost right away, I started going to the ballpark to get ready for this season. I bet you a lot of my teammates (and opponents) did the same thing. The baseball season doesn't officially start until April, but we show up at spring training in February. I usually start playing winter ball even earlier than that. And if you want to make it through a season that long, if you want your body to hold up, you have to work at it in October, November, and December.

I want to tell you something funny, bro: Anytime I go somewhere, people expect me to be fat. I'm serious. Last year, after the season ended, I went out to buy a new shirt at this store someone recommended. I walked into the place and one of the guys there recognized me, and we started talking. I tried on a couple of shirts and the dude is looking at me and he said, "Can I tell you something?" I said sure. So the guy tells me that he thought I was bigger, that he thought I was *fat,* that he watches the game on television and he was surprised how different I look in person.

Know what I told him?

"I get that all the time."

Seriously, bro, I'm not joking. Every time I go someplace where the people have never met me before, they all tell me the same thing: I look fatter on TV. I'm a big dude—I'm six foot four and between 255 and 260 pounds—but I try to take pretty good care of myself. In baseball, you have to. Like most guys, I'm in the weight room a lot during the season and I try to eat right, but I'm a big dude. Even my teammates give me shit about it sometimes. But I wear a really big uniform that must make me look fat on TV, so every time I meet someone for the first time, they look surprised that I'm not this big, fat guy.

I always joke with them: "Who do you think I am, Kevin Millar?"

(Trust me, bro. Millar would say the same thing about me.)

I'm not kidding about the uniform, bro. I like it baggy. I think my shirt is one or two sizes too big and my pants are a lot bigger than that. I have a 40-inch waist and a 34-inch inseam—so my real pants size is 40–34—but the ones I wear in the game have a 46-inch waist and a 40-inch inseam. They must make me look fat, but I like the uniform to be loose so I can move my arms and legs. And then I hear from people like the guy at the store and I wonder how big I really look to the people who are watching on TV.

My pop, he's in pretty good shape. My mom wasn't heavy, either. But I'm a big dude and I'm over thirty years old now, so I decided after last season that I was going to start taking even better care of myself. I started working out with a new personal trainer and I changed my diet, and I stopped eating as much pasta and rice, things like that. If you're not careful, bro, that stuff can stick to you. My trainer told me that the workouts won't mean anything unless I change what I eat, too, so I changed everything at the start of the off-season. While the baseball playoffs were going on, my trainer had me lifting in the morning and running on the treadmill in the afternoon. I never did much running before, but I told him I wanted to lose ten or fifteen pounds before the start of the season.

That was the goal, bro. That's what I told my teammates, too. I wanted to get stronger but be in better shape, and so I started working out harder than I ever did before.

The baseball? That doesn't usually start until December, bro. For a while there, I don't even pick up a bat. I get my swings in every day during the season, so I like to take a little break after the year. I usually stay in the United States in October and early November, and then I go back to the Dominican, where the weather is warmer. By the time January comes, I'm hitting for at least part of almost every day, and I still work out, eat right, stay in shape. I try to keep doing that right through spring training. But once the season starts and we start playing games—and we start traveling from one city to the next—it gets a lot harder to stay in the routine.

But that's why it's so important to do it all when you have the time.

Like everybody, I get tired sometimes. That's when it really gets hard. The baseball season is long—we play just about *every day*—and the games come fast. Sometimes it feels like you wake up, play, go to bed, and wake up again. The routine wears you down. You hear a lot of players say sometimes that they get more tired mentally than physically, and that's what they mean. You just don't get any breaks. The average person doesn't understand a lot of that because they see us play the games, but there's a lot more to it than that. For every hour we spend on the field, we have to spend at least an hour preparing. Maybe it's more like two hours. We might play every day for three weeks in a row. I remember once in the 2005 season, because of rainouts, we played thirty games straight. It was late in the season and we were tired, and that was *before* we had to play all those games in a row. By the time it was over, we were wiped out. We had nothing left. That was the year we played the White Sox in the playoffs. We were a very tired team, and we lost in three straight.

Looking back, I don't know how we even made it that far, but I think that tells you something about the guys we had on the team. They were tough. They kept playing. We did the best we could.

When you get a little older, like me, that's why the preparation becomes even more important. After the 2006 season, I turned thirty-one years old. I'm still in the prime of my career, but I'm not twenty-five anymore. Every year now, I have to prepare myself for it and work hard before the season begins, because I need all the strength I can get once the games start. As you get older, life gets easier in some ways; in other ways it gets harder. Baseball is the same. You don't have the same strength and energy when you get older, but you also learn to save it. You know when you need it. And you learn to control your body, your emotions, so that you can stay as sharp as possible for as long as possible.

I'm not going to lie to you, bro.

Playing baseball is hard work.

But if you ask most of the guys playing in the major leagues, we'll all tell you the same thing.

We love what we do.

I'VE BEEN IN BOSTON FOR FOUR YEARS NOW AND I PLAN TO BE HERE a lot longer. That's something you should probably know. Early last season, the Red Sox signed me to a four-year, $52 million contract extension that will keep me with the team through 2010. The team holds an option for 2011, too, which means I could be in Boston for the next five years. I've learned that things can change quickly in baseball because the game is a business first, but I love playing for the Red Sox and I love the city of Boston, and I think the city and the fans love me back. That means a lot. I hope I finish my career here. My wife and kids live with me in Boston and we spend most of our time here, year-round. I go back to my home in the Dominican Republic for a while each winter, but my kids are getting a little older now and they're going to school, so we've decided to plant our roots in Boston, too.

In Boston, everywhere I go now, people treat me like I'm one of them. It's one of the best things about living here. Last winter, when the Boston Celtics opened the basketball season, I went to the game with my wife, Tiffany, and a couple of our friends. We had seats under one of the baskets and they showed us on the scoreboard at halftime, and the place went crazy. They asked me to be part of the halftime show, when the Celtics mascot—some dude named "Lucky" who's dressed up as a leprechaun—sets up a trampoline and does some wild and crazy dunks, things like that. So the dude, Lucky, tells me to stand near the trampoline and hold the ball in the air, and he comes running down, jumps on the trampoline, grabs the ball, and does a flip in the air, then dunks it.

I have to admit it, bro.

It was pretty awesome.

The place went crazy again—I know they were cheering for Lucky—but I have to say: It's nice to feel part of something like that. Not long before the game at the Garden, I was involved in this charity event where I played Wiffle ball with some kids in Weston, a suburb of Boston. A little while after that, I donated some football jerseys to one of the high schools in the city, and I even put on one of the jerseys when I gave them to the school. It was an unbelievable feeling, just like the one I had about a month or two after that, when I was in the Dominican to donate $200,000 to a children's hospital in Santo Domingo, the Plaza de la Salud Hospital de Niños. We raised that money in a lot of ways, by auctioning off my record home run balls from the 2006 season, through donations made by the Red Sox and my teammates, from a hitting clinic that I did for kids in the Boston area, and from a fundraiser and party we held in downtown Boston. All of that stuff really makes you feel good, bro. You feel like you can make a difference. You feel like you're doing the right thing.

That's why I want to keep helping. I feel like I'm as much a part of Boston now as I am of the Dominican Republic. My parents always told me to remember who I was, to help others, so that's what I feel like I'm doing now.

Since I came to Boston, things have changed so much. I really don't know where to start. It's hard for me to go back to the Dominican sometimes because some of the people there always want something from me, but I think that's true of all

Dominican players. I'm sure it's the same for Pedro Martinez and Vladimir Guerrero, Miguel Tejada and Bartolo Colon. Those guys are all great players. We're all Dominicans and we love our country. But there are times when going back there can be really hard because the people expect so much from us, because they want to know us so bad that we can't go anywhere or do anything.

Let me try to explain.

A couple of years ago—after the 2005 season, I think—I went back to the Dominican after the season, like I usually do. I can't remember if it was December or January. But there is this little park near my apartment in Santo Domingo, and it's a place I go with my friends to just hang out, listen to music, talk about things. Music is something I really love. We can spend hours out there just hanging out and killing time, relaxing and listening to music. It's one of the things I really like to do when I go back to the Dominican. The baseball season can be so long sometimes, so hectic, that you really appreciate those times during the winter when everything slows down. That's when ballplayers get to live like normal people again, when they get to go out and do the things that most people take for granted.

While we were hanging out, some dude recognized me and wanted to say hello. So I went over to the guy and met him, shook his hand, tried to be nice to him. I expected him to do the same, but he wouldn't let me go. He wanted to keep talking, hang out with us, be my friend. My guess is that he probably wanted or needed some money, which always makes things a little uncomfortable for me. What am I supposed to do? I want to be polite to people and be friendly to everyone, and I tell my friends the same thing. Be nice. Don't be rude. People usually just want to say hello and let you know that they see you on TV and watch the games, that they appreciate the way you do your job and the fact that you look happy.

And I tell them: I *am* happy. Baseball is supposed to be fun. That's why I play.

And then we all go on our way.

In the Dominican, it's just a little hard sometimes. I don't know if I can really explain it. Baseball players are so big there—they become such heroes—that they forget we are all just people. I'm sure they all mean well, but sometimes—like this dude in the park—they start to hang around all the time. It can make you a little worried. So my friends had to go over to this one guy and tell him—politely—that I just wanted to hang out with my friends for a while, that I was just another person, that I wanted to do my own thing. And the reason it's hard is because I feel *badly* about it, because I would love to help every person I meet and solve everybody's problems

But I'm sure I don't need to tell you, bro.

The world doesn't work that way.

Since I got to Boston—and since we won the World Series in 2004, especially—I've had to deal with a lot more of that stuff. And sometimes, when I start to feel like I'm complaining about it, I remind myself: *I'm the same way!* I remember one time when I was in the Bahamas with my wife, Tiffany, and we saw Evander Holyfield, and I couldn't believe it. I was like, *"Holy shit, Tiff! It's Holyfield!"* She couldn't understand what I was getting so excited about. There was another time when I saw Denzel Washington and I felt the same way. And anytime I see a rapper, or someone whose music I listen to, I get excited and then I try to remind myself: *That's how Red Sox fans feel about you.*

In Boston, for the most part, the fans have been great. Last Halloween, my wife took the kids out trick-or-treating and left me at home, and I was grilling in the backyard with some of my boys. That's one of the other things I like to do. There weren't many kids in our neighborhood, so I told my wife I'd take care of the trick-or-treaters. This woman brought her kids by and we gave out candy, took some pictures, did all of that stuff. It was fun. And then, all of a sudden, before we knew it, there were all these kids and parents coming to the house. We went out front to look and there was this line of cars all the way down the street and around the block—I'm not kidding, bro—and it was like, "Where did all of these people come from? Who goes trick-or-treating in their cars?" Someone must have called someone on their cell phone and told them that we were giving out candy and taking pictures, and all of a sudden there are all these people at the house. In a situation like that, there is just no way we can keep everybody happy.

And that's when I start to feel bad again.

Aside from times like that, the people in Boston have been great. I might be out to dinner with Tiff or something and people will come up to us, just to say hi and shake my hand. That's something we don't mind. People here care so much about the Red Sox that you really feel like they care about *you*, and that's something you don't get in a lot of places. You really do feel like you know them and that they know you. It's an unbelievable feeling. And then they move on and they give you back your privacy—your *space*—and it's like they're saying to you, "Hey, I just wanted to say hello and let you know how much I appreciate what you do, but I don't want to bother you too much." That really makes you feel good. It lets you know they respect you as a ballplayer *and* as a person.

And that's really all that any ballplayer can ever ask for.

AFTER THE 2006 SEASON ENDED, A LOT OF PEOPLE ASKED ME HOW I felt, if I was disappointed, where I thought the team was going. I'm not going to lie to you. It's always disappointing when you lose, when things don't go like you thought they would, but the frustration doesn't last too long. It goes away. And when it does, you realize that sometimes you can only get better when you fail because that is what drives you. That's how you learn.

With the Red Sox, we had a lot of questions when the season ended, but I was confident that our front office would do the things we needed to do to make us better. That's one of the really nice things about playing in Boston. After I signed my last contract extension, Tiff and I decided to buy a house in the Boston area because we want our kids to go to school there and beause that's where we're happy. We belong to Red Sox Nation now and we belong in Boston. As long as I'm playing, that's where we want to stay.

Like I said, right after the season I started working out right away, trying to get myself in better shape for 2007, trying to get better. There's always room to improve. The clubhouse at Fenway Park is really empty at that time of year, but that can make it a good place to go and get work done, to focus. I work out two times a day, most times, and I try to be careful about what I eat, when I eat, what I do. And then I go home and take my two girls grocery shopping or play with my son, D'Angelo, and maybe I go in the backyard and grill some dinner for me and Tiff and the kids.

One day, right after the season ended, I was in the clubhouse after a workout just talking with some of my friends when they asked me how disappointing the season was with the way things went for the team. By that time, the games were over for a few weeks and I had a little time to think, to get my head straight, to see things more clearly. During the season, when you're so focused on the games and trying to win, that can be a lot harder to do. We ended up winning eighty-six games and finishing in third place—the Toronto Blue Jays won eighty-seven games and finished just in front of us—and I did something no Red Sox player ever has done. I felt like I was still getting better as a player and as a person, that I was still learning things and growing. That's really all you can ever ask. As disappointing as the season was—and it was—sometimes you need to be reminded that there are other people out there working hard, too, and they want to win as bad as you do. You have to work and fight for everything you get because they're probably going to do the same.

For me, that's the way I try to look at things. That's what works. Just because you take a little step backward one year, that doesn't mean you can't go forward again the next. You just have to learn how to deal with it. So when people ask me now about dealing with failure, about bouncing back from a season like the one we had last year, I usually try to tell them all the same thing and give them the kind of message my parents always gave to me:

I can handle it, bro.

I've been through worse.

My mom and pop taught me that much.

BOTTLECAPS AND
BROOMSTICKS

I think every father hopes that his son will grow up to be a ballplayer. I was one of the lucky ones, bro. I actually made it.

I can tell you now that it wasn't easy, that it took a lot of hard work, that I am proud of the things I have done. God gave me the gift to play baseball—to hit, especially—and I feel like I have taken advantage of that. People watch me play and see me hit home runs, and sometimes they think it is as easy as just stepping into the batter's box and taking a swing. Let me tell you, bro: It isn't. It is one thing to have a gift, to be able to play baseball at a high level, but it is another thing to get to the big leagues and compete against the best players in the world. That takes hours, weeks, months, and years of commitment, of time in the batting cage and in the gym, of making mistakes, of learning lessons and making adjustments.

I think that is all probably true in anything we do, not just baseball.

And even then, you need so much more.

For me, that is where my family and friends become important—my father and mother, my sister, my wife and kids. My friends. My coaches and teammates. My agents. My fans. Even my opponents, who sometimes can help by saying the littlest things, like "Hang in there," or "Keep fighting." Baseball is a hard game to play, so no matter what uniform you wear, you have something in common with the guys in the other dugout: We all fail. The game is built that way. And so even when you are competing against somebody, when you watch him succeed, you can't help but have respect for what the other guy has done. We all know how difficult it is. We all know what it takes to succeed and be consistent. We all know there is no easy way around it, especially in baseball, because we play every day for six months a year—eight months, if you count spring training and then, if you're lucky, the playoffs. Then the season ends and we all go home—to Florida or California or, for me, the Dominican Republic—and it all starts again. The hours in the gym. The time at the batting cage. A lot of guys even decide to play winter ball, just so they don't spend too much time away from the game.

I'm one of those guys that doesn't like to spend too much time away from the game. I take a little time off after each season, but then I get right back to work. I like to spend a lot of time hitting because it makes me more comfortable in the batter's box and helps build my confidence. That all goes hand in hand. Any baseball player will tell you that the game can really beat you down, that it can kick your ass no matter how good you are. That's why confidence is so important. Growing up—and even after I got to the big leagues—there were a lot of times I failed, and others when I wanted to quit, and the littlest things sometimes seemed like the biggest setbacks. I used to think that maybe other people didn't believe in me, that maybe a coach or a scout or a manager thought I wasn't good enough. And then I realized that people can only doubt you if you doubt yourself, and in baseball, especially, doubting yourself is an easy thing to do.

And it's the easiest way to fail.

In my case, that's where my father comes in. My pop was a ballplayer, too, so he understands how the game works. He taught me lots of things along the way, and there are times when I don't think I really understood him. But when I look back now at all of the good things that have happened to me in the last four or five years, at all of the things I've accomplished on the field and in the major leagues, I think my father had a lot to do with it. My mom, too. I can't tell you how many times my pop pulled me aside and gave me encouragement, told me that I was going to make it to the major leagues no matter what anyone else thought. My pop was always good like that, bro. Even after he and my mom split up, he stayed involved in my life. He kept his eyes on me. People ask me sometimes about my dad and I always tell them, "My main man took good care of me." I still talk to my dad a lot, and he sometimes comes to see me play at Fenway Park, where I play my home games as a member of the Boston Red Sox. There have been times at Fenway when I've crossed home plate after hitting a home run and I've pointed to my father in the stands, just to let him know that I remembered he was there. That I appreciated his help. That I recognized all he did for me and all he taught me.

But I'm getting a little ahead of myself.

I WAS BORN IN SANTO DOMINGO, THE CAPITAL CITY OF THE DOMINI-
can Republic. There are roughly nine million people who live
in the Dominican Republic, who call it home, who grow up
there, and who dream the biggest dreams. Baseball is one of
our passions. To this day, you can drive to most any place on
the island and find children playing on the ball fields or in
the streets, hoping to improve their skills and praying to get
noticed. Most of the fields are overgrown and rough, and the
ground is so bumpy that even the best major leaguers could
not possibly field a ground ball there. But that is where we go,
day after day after day, all with the idea of reaching our
biggest hopes.

If you were born and grew up in the Dominican Republic,
you are born to play baseball. And let me tell you, bro, that
was especially true for me.

My father's given name is Americo Enrique Ortiz, though
most people who know him call him either Enrique or Leo.
My father never played in the major leagues, never really had
the chance, in part because he was a man committed to his
family. Early on in his life, that was a choice he made. My father was a city boy, raised in San Juan, not too far from Santo
Domingo. He came from a family of seven children, with very
little money, and he eventually moved to Santo Domingo because he wanted to make something of himself. He loved
baseball more than almost anything in the world—anything
but his family—and he went to Santo Domingo because he
wanted to pursue his dream of becoming a pitcher. He might
have been on his way when something happened that forced
him to change the way he tought about things.

That something was me.

Even now, more than thirty years later, I think about it all
and wonder: What if things had been different? I still have
good friends who I played ball with growing up, guys who

were good players but never made it to the big leagues. I'm not sure why. But even now, we'll be talking sometimes about my career and how things have happened for me, and they remember things that I don't. They'll tell me that they remember my pop always showing up at my games, no matter what, and leaving work early to be there. They remember my pop running onto the field when I hit a home run in Little League. And then they tell me that they wonder if they could have made it to the major leagues if they had a pop like mine.

That's when I realize it, bro.

I'm lucky to have a father like him.

When he was young and moved to Santo Domingo, my pop decided to live with a friend of his who was married to a woman named Aurora Arias. It was during that time that the woman introduced my father to her sister, Angela, an outgoing and happy woman with a great personality. My father has told me a million times that he liked her right away, and they quickly began dating. They fell in love. And when Angela Arias became pregnant, when she and my pop decided they would get married and begin building a life together, my pop also decided that his days as baseball player were over. He decided that his dream was nothing more than that—a dream— and he believed he had the responsibility to be both a good husband and father.

He was twenty-one.

My pop always has downplayed his abilities as a baseball player, but everything I ever have heard about him told me he was a good player. Today, there are still people in Santo Domingo who know me primarily as Enrique's son, who come up to me on the street and remind me of the sacrifices my pop made so that I could be who I am today. They tell me my pop was a right-hander, that he had the kind of fastball that could have delivered him to the big leagues. When I was young, a tall and big-boned boy who had yet to grow into his body, I remember standing beside my pop and listening to people ask him: "Is he a pitcher like you? Can he throw like you did?" I look back at those moments now and recognize that my pop had a life before I came along, that he had a future and he had plans.

That he, like anyone else, had goals and hopes and dreams.

Many people believe that baseball is a religion in the Dominican Republic, and in some ways it was the two together that brought me where I am today. Not far from Santo Domingo, in the town of Higüey, there is a basilica known as Nuestra Señora de la Altagracia, or Our Lady of High Graces. It is the most famous church in the Dominican Republic. People will travel for miles to go there, as Pope John Paul II did in early 1979. And that is where my pop went roughly four years earlier, during the summer of 1975, when he asked God for guidance, for the strength to be a good father and husband, for the blessing of a happy, healthy child.

For a son.

My pop has told me the story so many times that I sometimes feel like I know it better than he does.

Doesn't everybody feel that way when their pop starts telling stories?

"I prayed," my father told me. "I said, 'God, I am going to leave this game that I love and I do not need to explain why. Angela is due to have our first baby. I am soon going to be a father. Maybe you can bless me with a boy. And maybe someday he could be a major-league player.'"

See?

Even before I came along, my pop must have been a good man.

After all, God answered him.

Not long after my pop's visit, I was born David Americo

Ortiz Arias in Santo Domingo on November 18, 1975. I have been to La Basilica, as we call it, many times during the course of my life. Even now, well into my career as a major-league baseball player, I make the trip to Higüey each winter, just before the start of spring training, to thank God for what he has given me, for the abilities to succeed in the major leagues, for allowing me to recognize the truly important things in life and the people who have made sacrifices to help me become who I am.

I thank him mostly for allowing my pop's wishes to come true.

My family lived in Santo Domingo until I was about fourteen or fifteen and I have an apartment in Santo Domingo now, not too far away from where I grew up. I always liked the city. Even though we lived in Santo Domingo, my mom and pop had a house with a pretty big backyard—at least it felt big to me—where me and my younger sister, Albania, would play after school. We never really felt like we were poor, but we also didn't know any better. My pop sold auto parts and my mom worked as a secretary at the Department of Agriculture, and she spent some of her extra time trying to make money any way she could, by buying clothes and re-selling them, whatever it took. She was always ahead of the game. I remember my mom going to other parts of the Caribbean to sell them clothes from the Dominican, then buying the native clothes there and coming back to sell them in Santo Domingo, or wherever. She would go to places like Curaçao and sell them our clothes, then come back and sell clothes from Curaçao to the people in the Dominican. I don't think I ever realized the kinds of things my parents did so that Albania and I could have the things we needed, but most kids don't. Growing up takes so much work that you don't have time to worry about anything else.

Now, when I look back, I know better. That's why I try to help where I can. A lot of people in the Dominican are poor and can't afford the most basic things, like health care. It's tough, bro. Most Americans have no idea. I have three kids and I worry about them a lot—just like my parents worried about me—but what about the people that can't take care of their kids? What do they do? In 2006, when I broke the Red Sox record for home runs in one season, I donated some of the baseballs to charity. I finished that year with 54 homers, best in the league, and we used some of the last few baseballs to raise money for the Plaza de la Salud Hospital de Niños, a children's hospital for kids in the Dominican. We all like kids, I think. We should all try to help them. And for me, in a place like the Dominican, I think the best way for me to do that is to help them get the things they need, the care they deserve, especially in a place where it can be so hard to grow up.

I think a lot of the other players who grew up in the Dominican, like me, feel the same way. Life can be hard there, bro. It's difficult. People are poor and they have a lot of needs, so the best way for us to help is to give back.

Growing up, in a lot of ways, I guess my family was the same as anyone else's. My mom gave us a lot of the love and my father went out and worked, making most of the money. I remember times where my pop wouldn't come home at night because he was busy driving all over the Dominican, but if you think about it, I guess that's not much different from how me and my wife, Tiffany, do things now. In the major leagues, we play half of our games on the road, so there are a lot of nights when I'm not at home. The other times, we play at night. So our kids go home to Tiff and she takes care of them, and I do my part in other ways. Parents are a team, too, though I didn't understand that at the time.

That's the way life works, bro.

You have to learn it as you go.

My mom—I don't think I've ever heard anybody say a bad word about her. She was a great person. She wasn't a pushover—trust me on that—but I don't know if anyone could ever love her kids as much as she did. I remember times where I would sit down at the kitchen table and have something to eat, and my mom would just sit there, smiling, happy to just watch her son eat. Even after I grew up, my mom would stick her head in the bathroom while I was in the shower just to make sure I was washing my back the right way. Can you believe that? I told Tiff that story once and she got this look on her face—it was before we were married—and it was like, "What have I gotten myself into?" She told me right then and there that she wasn't sticking around to help me wash my back. I told her I didn't expect her to.

And I laughed out loud.

My mom could be tough, too, but my pop handled most of the discipline, at least when it came to the big stuff. My mom would yell at me and Albania, discipline us and things like that, but I always knew we were in trouble by the tone of my pop's voice. My mom and pop usually called me David, though in Spanish it's pronounced more like *Dah-veed*. But when my pop was mad, or when he really wanted to get my attention, I could tell just by the way he changed his voice. *Dah-veed* would become *Dah-VEED*, and that was when I knew that my man meant business. I didn't mess much with my pop then. That's all it took for him to get my attention.

Like I said, we stayed in Santo Domingo until I was about fourteen or fifteen, when we moved to an area outside the city called Haina. It was a lot different than Santo Domingo. Our house was on the end of a small street, half of a side-by-side, two-family home. Facing the house, we lived on the left, our neighbors on the right. The house was the color of an avocado, with no backyard, and the entire first floor was maybe the size that a garage now is in most American homes. We had a small living area on the first floor and the kitchen was toward the back of the house. Our bedrooms were upstairs. There really wasn't much room—or much to do there but eat and sleep—but, again, I didn't know any better. The specific area we lived in was called Invi-cea, which was like a lot of other places in the Dominican. Most of the people were pretty poor, at least based on what I know now, but we never wanted for much. The streets weren't paved; they were mostly made of dirt. We didn't live far from the high school, where I played both basketball and baseball, and most of the fun we had was out in the street, in front of our homes, where kids and parents would get together and hang out, listen to music, and have fun.

And, of course, play baseball.

Thankfully, one of the great things about baseball is that you do not need much to play. All you need is a bat and a ball—not even a glove—and a whole lot of imagination. After I joined the Boston Red Sox in 2003, I remember our ace pitcher, Pedro Martinez, telling stories about how he played ball in the streets. Pedro is one of the greatest pitchers in history and one of the most successful players ever to come out of the Dominican, so his words meant something to everyone—in the United States or in the Dominican. I remember Pedro telling American reporters that when he and his friends needed a baseball, the kids would find a doll that belonged to someone's sister, then snap off the doll's head and rip out the hair. I still laugh at that. On more than one occasion, that is what I did with the dolls that belonged to my sister, even though I knew it would upset her and that there eventually would be hell to pay.

But really, bro, what kind of choice did we have? Like I said, you don't need much to play baseball, but you need a bat and a ball. If something was round—or even close to round—we probably used it as a ball. When you're that age, you can get into a lot of trouble if you're not careful. You need to put your attention into good things and find productive things to do with your time. For us, that was baseball.

So I broke off a few doll's heads, bro.

Does that make me a bad guy?

We found other things to use for baseballs, too. Sometimes, my pop would reach for a pair of socks only to learn that one was missing, usually so that the kids in the neighborhood had a "baseball" to use in the afternoon game. I learned early that my pop's socks soaked up water, that a ball hit into a puddle or used on a rainy day wouldn't last for long, so we found ways to solve the problems. I remember taking any plastic bags we could find—trash bags, wrappers, whatever—and stuffing them into my father's sock as tightly as we could. We would then tie off a knot and wrap the slack around the ball. And just like that, we had a baseball.

And a waterproof one, too!

Sometimes, we didn't even need a real ball to play. As long as it was something we could throw and hit, we could play baseball with it. I remember times where we would use a bottle cap for a ball because it was easy to make the ball curve or rise, dip or turn. Have you ever tried to hit a bottle cap? It's not easy, bro, I'll tell you that. After I got to the big leagues, I heard some of my teammates tell stories of how they played Wiffle ball growing up, using a ball with holes that made it easier to throw curveballs and breaking pitches. I tell them that we played Wiffle ball, too, but instead of a ball we used a bottle cap. And I don't care how much a Wiffle ball curves, it has to be easier to hit than a bottle cap. But I think back to some of those games now, at how I learned to hit, and I have to believe it helped me develop my hand-eye coordination, things like that. I'm not kidding. I've always been able to hit a curveball, and I think one of the big reasons is because I learned how to hit a bottle cap with a broomstick when I was growing up.

Think about it.

I mean, if you can hit a bottle cap with a broomstick, you can pretty much hit anything, right?

In most cases, we didn't have bats in those game, either. There are a lot of reasons I don't get back to Invi-cea much anymore, but I make it back there once in a while. I still see kids playing ball on the same streets that I did, but they usually play with something that looks like a tennis ball, using real bats and real gloves. We had none of that. Along with the doll's heads and socks that we stole from our sisters and fathers, we took mop handles and broomsticks from the house to give us the last piece of equipment we really needed: our bats. I have seen some of those old pictures of American boys playing stickball in places like New York City, and I guess our games were pretty much the same thing, Dominican-style. And when it came time to field our position, to catch a doll's head or a rolled-up sock, we used our bare hands.

Who needed gloves?

You have to understand: Most days, baseball is how we passed the time. I might wake up and go to school every day during the school year, but I couldn't wait to get home and to meet my friends in the neighborhood, to start playing ball again. Sometimes, we even snuck out of school early. In the late afternoon and early evenings, our parents and neighbors would come out and sit on the curb or stand on the sidewalks, watch our games, and sometimes play with us. It was just what we did. For all that we didn't have—even if we didn't know it—we always had our baseball games, those moments when all of our worries seemed to go away and when anything seemed possible.

That's what baseball is for people in the Dominican.

It's something to look forward to.

And something to help you forget about everything else.

BY THE TIME MY MOM AND POP SPLIT UP, IT WAS PROBABLY FOR THE best. My parents were arguing a lot and it wasn't too comfortable for me and Albania. Something like that is always toughest on the kids. You feel like you should do something, but you don't really know what. You start to think that maybe you did something wrong. You wonder how you can fix a problem that really has nothing to do with you, but you really don't understand that those kinds of things are between only your mom and pop. How could you? You couldn't possibly know something like that until you get married.

So when my parents finally split up, I think Albania and I were actually relieved. It was something we didn't have to worry so much about anymore. My parents' splitting up isn't really something I like to talk about, but I think it worked out for the best. My pop ended up getting remarried and had another child—my half sister, Yacili, who is now a teenager. My pop still took an interest in what we were doing, still made sure that we stayed out of trouble even if he wasn't living in our house anymore. Some nights, I can remember him driving all the way out to our place from the city, where he lived, just to check up on us and make sure we were taking care of business, doing the right things. He could have just called, bro. But he *came*.

I guess the easiest way to say it is that my pop might have stopped being married to my mom, but he never stopped being my father.

Does that make sense?

By the time I got a little older, into my teens, I needed my dad. I'm not sure I knew that at the time. Believe it or not, I was actually a little shy as a kid and I didn't like confrontation. (I still don't.) I think that's part of what made things so hard in our house when my mom and dad were arguing, though I'm not sure my personality would have made that much of a difference. Something like that would be hard on anybody. It was hard on me.

But when it came to my baseball career, my pop was the best. He was the best advisor I ever could have had. My pop was always pretty calm and had a nice way of explaining things to me, especially when I got down. He always had time for me. From the time I first started playing ball, my pop was always there for me when things got tough, when I failed, when I thought I wasn't going to make it. He always gave me confidence. I don't know if my pop was the same way as a player or if he just learned that as he got older, but however he learned it all, he took the time to make me a better player, a better person, to teach me to keep working hard and to keep trying, to believe in myself and have faith in my abilities.

If I did all of that, he told me, I would succeed.

Before I go on, you need to understand something about baseball players in the Dominican: They're like movie stars. Americans have lots of things to be interested in—baseball and football, basketball and hockey, movies, art, and the theatre. In the Dominican, we have baseball. The players who succeed in the big leagues become the biggest celebrities in the country because the game means that much to us. I think that is true of most of the countries in the Caribbean. The people in Puerto Rico, Venezuela, and Cuba—baseball is a passion to them. That's why the World Baseball Classic was such a big thing when it finally happened in the spring of 2006. The rest of the world got to see how much baseball means to us, to our people, to our culture. In the Caribbean, we play baseball all year. And so when one of our own makes it to the big leagues, when he succeeds, the whole country is proud of him. Everybody feels a little bit of the success.

Understand? In the Dominican, a Hall of Fame pitcher like Juan Marichal, especially, is a hero. Marichal was born in Laguna Verde in the Dominican and he was the first Latino pitcher ever inducted into the Hall of Fame at Cooperstown. He pitched from 1960 to 1975—that's sixteen years—and he won 243 games, most of them with the San Francisco Giants. He won twenty games in a season six times, bro. He was one of the true greats. Marichal helped open the door for people like Pedro Martinez, one of my teammates in Boston and now a pitcher for the New York Mets. Pedro has won three Cy Young Awards during his career as the best pitcher in his league, and he's probably on his way to the Hall now, too. But when Pedro won his first Cy Young in 1997 with the Montreal Expos, he tried to give the award to Marichal, who wouldn't take it. Marichal never won a Cy Young during his career, but Pedro wanted to show him respect for making so much possible for so many other Dominican players.

That's just how Pedro felt.

That's how we all felt.

Marichal is just the beginning. Felipe Alou, who has been in major-league baseball for about fifty years as a player and manager, is also a hero in the Dominican; his son, Moises, is in the major leagues now. And as time has gone on, as the Dominican has developed more and more ballplayers, people have started to realize that we have some of the best baseball players in the world. If you look at any big-league team now, there are probably several Dominicans on the roster. For a country our size, that is quite an accomplishment. Players like Pedro, Sammy Sosa, Vladimir Guerrero, and Miguel Tejada have all been All-Star players—and they're all from the Dominican.

So is Albert Pujols. And then there are guys like Alfonso Soriano, Jose Reyes, Adrian Beltre, Bartolo Colon, Armando Benitez, Robinson Cano, Rafael Furcal, Manny Ramirez . . . The list goes on and on. I couldn't possibly name them all. And we all grew up at roughly the same time, dreaming the same dream, wanting to make it to the big leagues like Marichal did.

All from a country of nine million people, only a little more than all of New York City.

Think about that.

Could New York City alone produce as many great ballplayers as the Dominican does?

I'm telling you all of this so that you can understand how it all works in the Dominican, just how important baseball is. Most of us begin playing when we are little kids. We play through grade school and into our teenage years, though by then most everyone knows if he has a chance or not. The best players end up getting recruited, almost like good high school players here in the United States, but it's still a lot different. In every part of the Dominican, there are scouts who look for talent, who have connections to big-league clubs and get you a tryout. We call those guys *buscones*. They're almost like street agents. Sometimes the *buscone* is a former player, or maybe he is a scout or a former coach. Maybe he is none of those things. Maybe he is a guy who just lived in the area and loves baseball—knows baseball—and has friends who work in the big leagues that will ask him to look for players.

In that way, baseball in the Dominican has changed. Years and years ago, there were only a few teams that understood how much talent there was in the Dominican. The big one was the Los Angeles Dodgers. The Dodgers developed players like Pedro Guerrero and Ramon Martinez, who was Pedro Martinez's older brother and pitched a no-hitter once. And because of that, because of the success of those players, there were a lot of kids who grew up in the Dominican wanting to play for the Dodgers. So the Dodgers had lots of people in the Dominican working for them, scouting for them, keeping an eye out for players like me or Manny, Vladimir (we call him Vladi), or Miguel. And if a scout or a buscone could find a player the team liked—and if the player got signed—the team might give the scout or the buscone some money, like a finder's fee.

Of course, the players got money to sign, too.

By the time kids like me were old enough to be noticed, the Dodgers weren't the only team bringing in players from the Dominican. Everybody was. Lots of teams were using talent scouts and buscones to find players in hopes of finding the next Marichal or Martinez. And because there was money in it for the buscone, a lot of them would start recruiting kids with talent and work them out together, develop them until they were ready for a tryout. The buscone might see that he has a pretty good player who can play shortstop, so he might call up a friend with, say, the New York Yankees because the Yankees were looking for one. He might pick up the phone and say, "Hey, I've got a kid here you might want to look at— he's the next Miguel Tejada," and the team would come down to see the kid play, maybe sign him to a contract.

Me?

I was supposed to be the next Fred McGriff, who hit almost 500 home runs while playing in the big leagues.

At least that's what they told me.

I was a teenager when I started to work out with one of the buscones in what we called The Program. That's how we described it. When people talked, they might say, "David Ortiz is in The Program in Haina," or "Pedro Martinez is in The Program in Manoguayabo," and everybody knew what that meant. Most of the kids from the same area played together and were in the same program, and there was usually some-one in the area that ran the workouts. Sometimes it was a bus-cone. Sometimes it was a scout. Sometimes it was at a field that might have been paid for by a major-league team looking to get known in the Dominican.

One of those fields is in Haina, not far from the house I lived in with my mom and sister. I think the Tampa Bay Devil Rays pay to have their name on that field now, but I don't remember there being a name on it when I was a kid. I just re-member going there and working out, waiting for somebody to tell me that they thought I was good enough to play in the big leagues.

Waiting for my chance.

In the Dominican, you cannot sign with a major-league team until you are sixteen years old. Those are just the rules. I guess Major League Baseball doesn't want teams to sign play-ers when they are too young, though that didn't stop guys from working out with buscones, from trying out for scouts who might want to know when a player was going to be old enough to sign. That's just how it worked. The younger a player was, the more value he had. That was just how the big-league clubs felt. If they drafted a kid who was sixteen, they had plenty of time to put him in their minor-league sys-tem, to develop him, to coach him and help him improve. There was always more potential for a sixteen-year-old than a nineteen-year-old, so major-league clubs always looked for the most talented kids who were also the youngest.

Of course, a lot of kids started to lie about their age, just so that they could sign and have a chance. All of us needed the money, bro. A kid who was nineteen might say he was seven-teen, and most of the time the teams had no way to check. Af-ter a while, the teams didn't care to. There was so much competition for players in the Dominican that teams were willing to sacrifice some things to sign a good player, and age was one of them. Big-league players joke a lot about the real age of the guys from the Dominican and some of the stuff they say is true. But there are guys, too, who sign earlier than they're supposed to because maybe their family needs the money or they can't wait until they turn sixteen. So it worked both ways, at least until September 11, 2001, when the terrorist attacks in America changed the way we had to apply for visas and fill out paperwork to play the coming season.

A bunch of guys (like Ramon Ortiz, who was pitching with the Los Angeles Angels at the time) were forced to disclose their real ages.

But nothing ever really happened because of it.

As for me, I was sixteen when I signed, but it wasn't as easy as you might think. I was playing in The Program when I met this one scout, a man named Edmundo Borrome. He worked for the Florida Marlins. Borrome came to one of our workouts, and when he saw me hitting, he told the buscone that I was going to be the next Fred McGriff. How about that, bro? I was sixteen years old and someone was comparing me to Fred McGriff because I was a big, left-handed-hitting power hitter and I could hit the ball to the opposite field, and when I finished my swing my hands were up high, like McGriff's. So Borrome took me out of the program and took me to a place where the Marlins were working out players—the buscone must have made a few bucks—and I thought that was my first step to becoming a big-league player.

It was.

And it was also my first step back.

I spent four or five months working out with a bunch of other kids that the Marlins had an interest in even though Florida hadn't even started playing major-league games yet. Florida was an expansion team that played its first season in

1993, but the Marlins were trying to develop minor-league players before then. The Colorado Rockies were, too. The Rockies and Marlins were added to baseball in the early '90s, which is when I came along. A few years later, in 1997, the Devil Rays and Arizona Diamondbacks joined the major leagues, too. Those were good things for everyone in baseball, but especially for the players in the Dominican. More teams meant more players, and more players meant more jobs. There was more opportunity for all of us, which increased the chances for everybody.

When I was in the Marlins camp, I played more baseball than I ever had before. We worked out almost every day so that we would be ready to go when we were ready to sign. I don't think I ever had played that much baseball in my life. I think I was sixteen at the time, so I was still growing. I was living at home. One of my cousins used to pick me up every morning and drive me to the workouts, and my pop would pick me up late in the day, after work, and drive me home. I think that was during the summer before I turned seventeen. In between, we worked out all day, in the heat, but that's what we were used to. The weather didn't bother us much.

For whatever reason, I was one of the only first basemen in camp. That was a good thing, in some ways, because it meant that I didn't have a lot of competition. So if a team was looking for a first baseman, for a guy who could hit home runs, I was an easy decision. The bad part for me was that I had to be on the field a lot, which means I was working more than anyone else on the field. There might be three guys at second base, five guys at shortstop and four guys at third base—and they all needed to get their work in. So the coaches and instructors would hit infield practice for everybody, which meant that I did a lot of catching and throwing. And because of that, it was only a matter of time before something happened.

My elbow got sore.

Real sore.

And it hurt so much that I had to stop throwing.

Right about then, the Marlins sent me home. I couldn't do much at the workouts, so they told me to shut it down. I was devastated. I remember going home and I was so disappointed that I didn't want to eat. I didn't want to do anything. My pop came over and he could tell I was down, and that's when my pop was at his best. I remember thinking that I had just lost my chance to play in the big leagues, that I was never going to get another chance again. My elbow hurt and I felt sick to my stomach, and I wanted to cry. I thought it was over.

My pop, as usual, gave me a pep talk.

"*Dah-veed,*" he said, "you are going to play in the big leagues someday. Maybe it won't be with the Marlins, but that is their mistake. There are other teams to play for."

See what I mean, bro? My pop, he always had a way of reminding me that there was still work to be done, still something to accomplish. If somebody thinks you're not good enough, it doesn't mean they're right. Maybe they just made a mistake. Maybe they'll regret it.

Growing up, I was always an emotional kid. I was like my mom in that way. My pop always was able to calm me down and keep me focused, and he taught me how to control my emotions. The older I got, the more I advanced, the more I realized how important that would be.

On the day the Marlins sent me home, I also heard from this buscone named Hector Alvarez, who was watching me when I was working out with the other guys for the Marlins. His nickname was Machepa. The buscone who ran the workouts was a guy named Louis, and Machepa thought Louis made a mistake by sending me home. I remember leaving the field that day and Machepa pulling me aside, and I didn't think anything of it because I was so upset at the time. But after I got home, after I calmed down, I remember talking to my dad about him.

As I was leaving, here's what Machepa told me: "Of all the kids out there, you're the best one. You have a chance to play in the big leagues. If I wanted to take you someplace to work out, would you come?"

Before I answered him, Machepa told me that I had to ask my pop about it. He gave me his phone number. My pop and I talked about it and we called Machepa, and before long I was playing ball again. Machepa ran The Program in the city, in Santo Domingo, and spent time training me for a couple of weeks. We did everything but throw. Because my arm was sore, Machepa wouldn't let me pick up a ball, bro. We worked on my hitting, on my conditioning and even on my fielding, but rested my elbow. Before too long, the pain in my elbow went away and I felt like I was back to being 100 percent healthy.

I didn't know it at the time, but Machepa already was talking to scouts about me, about how I could hit. I had no idea. Machepa had a lot of friends in baseball, and there were a lot of people who respected his opinion. One of the guys Machepa spoke with was a guy named Ramon de los Santos, who actually pitched in the big leagues for a short time. Ramon made it to the majors with the Houston Astros in the 1970s—in 1974, I think—and he was working as a scout for the Seattle Mariners when Machepa called him. The way I've heard the story, Machepa did not compare me to Fred McGriff, but he told Ramon that I was something special.

"This kid, when you watch him swing the bat, you're going to forget about everything else," Machepa told Ramon.

Know how Ramon answered him?

"I've got to see that," he said.

At the time, the Dominican Summer League was going on. The summer league is a time when all of the prospects play against each other, kind of like rookie ball. Some of them are signed and some of them aren't. But because there are so many players, the big-league clubs send down their scouts and general managers because it is a good way to see a lot of the talent in the Dominican at the same time. A general manager could come down and scout his own players—the ones his team already had signed—and he could see new players, too. He could see players in other organizations so that teams might be able to make trades, things like that. It was a good way for big-league clubs to come down and evaluate players, see new ones, try to sign players, and make deals.

One day, thanks to Machepa and Ramon, they brought me over to one of the summer-league games for batting practice. I'm pretty sure Jim Beattie was there for the Mariners. Beattie pitched in the big leagues with the New York Yankees and Mariners, and he was Seattle's farm director and director of player development in the early 1990s. Machepa told Ramon Beattie that I really wasn't ready to throw yet, but that I could hit. He told them to focus on my hitting. And I remember taking batting practice with them watching and feeling like I had another chance to make it again.

On November 28, 1992, almost two weeks after my seventeenth birthday, I signed a professional contract with the Seattle Mariners. The Mariners gave me a $7,500 signing bonus, I think, which was about what a player like me got at the time. I remember thinking it was a lot of money. My pop handled most of the negotiations and took care of the money, and he did some really nice things for me. He bought me some equipment. And he bought me a big radio that I could play at the house. I liked music. I still do. And my pop said he wanted to get me something I needed and some things I like because he wanted to make sure that I spent my time doing the right things. For a kid like me, outside of baseball, there was the chance to get into trouble in the Dominican. There were always bad kids around and lots of bad things to get into, and so my pop wanted to make sure I was happy so that I put my energy into the right things.

Back then, I thought the hard part was over. When the Mariners signed me, I felt like I was going to make it. I forgot about my sore elbow and the Marlins, Louis, and everything else. I was going pro, bro. I remember thinking that I was on my way to the big leagues, that the Marlins had made a mistake, that my dad was right.

I remember thinking that I was going to make it.

STEPPING OUT OF THE BOX:
PEDRO MARTINEZ

In baseball clubhouses, as in real estate, the corner lots frequently have the greatest value.

And so, in the home clubhouse at time-dipped Fenway Park, one of the more distinguished stalls in baseball is nestled behind a support pole and wedged behind a nearby couch. It is truly a corner space. The stall cannot be seen from the main clubhouse entrance, which is one of the primary reasons it holds such appeal. The players who have dressed there have done so in relative obscurity.

Frequently, they have needed to.

For seven seasons, Pedro Martinez resided in that stall. Before him, it was Bret Saberhagen. And before that the stall belonged to Roger Clemens, arguably the greatest pitcher in baseball history—let alone the history of the pitching-starved Boston Red Sox—and winner of an unprecedented seven Cy

Young Awards as the best pitcher in his league. Saberhagen's career included two Cy Young Awards and Martinez's career had produced three by the time he left Boston, bringing the total of Cy Young Awards housed in that space (at one time or another) to an astonishing twelve. In Martinez's final years with the Red Sox, that fact helped explain why the locker also included a black leather recliner in a room otherwise filled with white, padded folding chairs.

A king, after all, requires a throne.

But by the time Martinez returned to Fenway Park in the final days of June 2006, much had changed in the history and government of the Boston Red Sox. Boston was not solely run by pitchers anymore—David Ortiz now ruled the Red Sox clubhouse from a different corner—and Martinez was now a member of the New York Mets, having left the Red Sox to sign a four-year, $53-million contract following the 2004 season. In his absence, Martinez's former locker was given to right-handed pitcher Keith Foulke, a reliever whose career never quite reached greatness. The more celebrated pitchers on the Red Sox now sat on the wall opposite Foulke, where veterans Curt Schilling and Tim Wakefield stored their belongings.

And in the opposite corner of the clubhouse from the reliever, similarly tucked into a more private corner, rested Ortiz, who was becoming one of the most celebrated performers in all of major-league baseball.

So, as Martinez and his cousin, Franklin Paulino, arrived at Fenway in a glistening white Hummer and walked toward the unfamiliar visiting clubhouse on the night of June 27, the scene was striking. The man who once ruled the Red Sox clubhouse stepped in from the parking lot and through a brick portal, walked down a concrete ramp and along a cramped concourse beneath the third-base grandstands, before finally arriving in the decidedly smaller visitor's clubhouse. It was a much longer walk than the one he was accustomed to. Martinez walked in the door to a locker that, while tucked around a corner, was remarkably ordinary. The space was not especially large. It was not particularly well hidden. And there was no recliner fit for a king.

"He's our number-one figure right now—him and Albert [Pujols]," Martinez said during a visit that was to serve as his homecoming to Boston. "It's well deserved. My time was my time. I'm still pitching and everybody looks up to me, but as a public figure, he's bigger. He's great in the community and he sets the best example of all. He's grown up under my wing."

He was David Ortiz.

In major-league baseball, especially, there is a kinship among Dominican players. Martinez might play for the New York Mets and Ortiz for the Red Sox, and Albert Pujols might play for the St. Louis Cardinals. But they are all Dominicans first. The bond is difficult for many major-league players to fully understand, save those rare major leaguers who have forged careers in foreign countries like, for instance, Japan. Only then do others realize that Dominicans do not speak their language. Only then do they realize that such foreigners are unfamiliar with the most basic things, like a menu. Only then do they realize that some of their very teammates look around the room and see nothing but strange faces, save for those select few who look the same, who nod knowingly, who come from the same place and speak the same language and feel the very same pressures that the displaced do.

More than anything, that is why the foreign players so frequently cling to one another.

In Boston, especially, minority and foreign-born players frequently saw assimilation as a struggle, a viewpoint that was often difficult to dispute. Though Jackie Robinson broke baseball's color barrier with the Brooklyn Dodgers in 1947, the

Red Sox did not integrate until twelve years later, in 1959, with a player named Pumpsie Green. They were the last major-league franchise to do so. As recently as the early 1990s, Boston's roster included a paucity of African-American players and, as a whole, minorities generally played a lesser role, at least with regard to the team's public image and marketability. There were exceptions—colorful and charismatic Cuban-born pitcher Luis Tiant was adored in the 1970s—but even an accomplished player like African-American slugger Jim Rice (who could be reserved and standoffish) never was truly embraced as he should have been. Things began to change in earnest only in the mid-1990s, when African-American first baseman Mo Vaughn became de facto captain and spokesman of the Red Sox and emerged as a force in the Boston clubhouse and in the local community.

As it turned out, Vaughn was in his final season in Boston when the Red Sox acquired Martinez in a trade with the Montreal Expos, though no one could have known at the time that the intersection of their careers would be so brief. No one could have known, too, that Martinez would replace Vaughn as a central figure both on and off the field, that the colorful, charismatic, and supremely talented pitcher—more than once, Red Sox broadcaster and analyst Jerry Remy compared Martinez to Tiant—would emerge as the team's greatest personality and asset at a time when the face of the Red Sox was undergoing fantastic changes that hit the entire New England region like a gust of crisp, fall air.

Vaughn was black. Martinez was Hispanic. And the Red Sox, finally, were growing in ways and directions that increased their appeal and made them all the more interesting and entertaining.

"I can't be any happier to come back and be well received like I am," Martinez said in 2006 upon returning to Boston for the first time since his departure. "That's how they received me on the field when I was here and in the streets when I was walking around.

"In the seven years I was here, I got to see Boston take a different spin," he continued. "In the stands, they were waving the Dominican flag and that was a great feeling. . . . The atmosphere in the stands was probably the biggest change, the mix that got into Fenway Park, not just on the field, but in the stands—how the atmosphere changed, not just from the boos and cheers, but to the music and making it fun."

In retrospect, those changes have even greater meaning.

Even before David Ortiz arrived in Boston, it seems, Fenway Park was preparing for him.

Ortiz and Martinez, too, had some knowledge of each other before becoming teammates with the Red Sox, though, by then, everyone in the Dominican knew Pedro. Martinez arrived in Boston via a trade with the Montreal Expos in November 1997, subsequently agreeing to what would become a landmark seven-year, $90-million contract, a deal that reached such a total thanks to the inclusion of an unthinkable, $17.5 million option. (The Red Sox eventually picked that up.) The Red Sox were conducting their spring training workouts in Fort Myers, Florida, where the Minnesota Twins, too, were holding their spring workouts. And while Martinez was coming off a brilliant 1997 season in which he won the National League Cy Young Award—the first of his career—he was just establishing his place in both the history of Dominican and Major League Baseball.

Pedro Martinez was becoming a superstar to baseball followers.

And he was becoming a role model to Dominicans everywhere.

During his seven years with the Red Sox—during his seven

springs, especially—Martinez very much regarded himself as a pied piper to young Dominican players. Upon signing with the Los Angeles Dodgers as a free agent in 1988—Martinez's older bother, Ramon, was playing for the Dodgers at the time— Martinez, like so many other foreign-born players, had some difficulty adjusting to the new culture. He later determined that one of the biggest adjustments was the food; he lost weight because he was not eating properly. And so as he matured, as he grew older and wiser, he solved the problem by bringing his older sister, Luzmaria, with him to the United States, where she would prepare his meals and take care of his home.

By the time Martinez arrived in Boston, his sister's cooking was becoming well known among most Dominican players. During spring training, for instance, Martinez would invite other Dominican players—be they with the Red Sox or the Twins or anyone else—to his home for lunches and dinner. His sister would cook. Martinez would send Paulino to pick up someone like Ortiz, to drive him to and from the home or condominium he had rented in Fort Myers, and then have Paulino drive the player home at the end of the day.

For Ortiz and many Dominican players, Martinez was a mentor, guardian, and nurturer.

The Dominicans, like most, believe in taking care of their own.

"Being here, he would miss the Spanish food," Paulino said of Ortiz. "So he would come over."

Later, by the time Martinez had signed with the New York Mets and Ortiz had established himself among the most popular and productive baseball players in the world, Ortiz had virtually no needs. Their relationship might have changed. By the middle of the 2006 season, when the Mets visited Fenway Park, Martinez was two seasons removed from a Boston clubhouse where Ortiz was now regarded with the utmost respect and admiration; it was Ortiz who had become the teacher, mentor, and guardian. Yet as the two saw each other on the field prior to the series opener between their teams, Ortiz immediately walked over to Martinez and embraced the slight, smaller pitcher. Awkwardly, Ortiz leaned over placed his head on Martinez's right shoulder, the larger man seeming to act like a grandchild in the smaller man's arms.

Recounting the episode in the small, cramped and archaic visitor's clubhouse at Fenway Park, Pedro Martinez beamed proudly.

"If you noticed, he wouldn't raise his head above mine. He put it in my shoulder," Martinez said. "In the Dominican, that's a sign of respect."

Respect was something Pedro Martinez demanded.

For himself and for all Dominicans.

BY ALL ACCOUNTS, THE STORY GOES SOMETHING LIKE THIS: ON THE day he was released by the Minnesota Twins, Ortiz was dining out at Vesuvio, an Italian restaurant specializing in seafood in that region of Santo Domingo known as Jaragua. Ortiz had not seen the release coming. He'd had a productive 2002 season for the Twins, who had made the playoffs for the first time since winning the World Series in 1991, and there was a general belief in the Minnesota organization that the Twins had rebuilt their baseball operation effectively and were about to begin a new, successful era.

And then, on December 16, just nine days before Christmas, Ortiz received the word that he had been released.

As always, economics played a role in the decision, something that was becoming more and more common in baseball; Martinez, too, had ended up in Boston as a result of the game's financial imbalances. In 1997, his final year with the Montreal

Expos, Martinez had earned a base salary of roughly $3.5 million, a significant amount to pay for a team like the Expos, who had been nearly last in attendance and, thereby, revenue in baseball. And while Martinez was just twenty-six, having just blossomed into an award-winning pitcher who went 17–8 with a National League-leading 1.90 ERA and remarkable 305 strikeouts in 241⅓ innings pitched—while he was entering his peak years—the reality was that the Expos were all but forced to explore trading him. Martinez's salary was due to increase through that mechanism known as salary arbitration, the vehicle that allowed major-league players with at least three years of experience (but fewer than six) the right to be paid at a rate commensurate with their peers. And there was simply no way the Expos could afford to pay him, in the short term or the long, because the pitcher's salary essentially was set to double.

Adding to urgency was this: Though Martinez was under Montreal's control for another season, 1998, he was eligible for full free agency at the end of that season, at which point he would certainly leave the Expos to sign a multiyear, multimillion-dollar contract with a team that could both afford and celebrate his considerable talents. So, with Martinez under their control for one more season, the Expos faced a choice: Trade Martinez then, when his value was highest, or hold on to him and lose him a year later, when they would get virtually nothing in return.

For Montreal officials, of course, the decision was really no decision at all.

And so, less than three weeks after the conclusion of the 1997 World Series, Expos general manager Jim Beattie—the same man who served as the farm director and player of development for the Seattle Mariners when Seattle signed seventeen-year-old David Ortiz—traded the best pitcher in the

National League to the Boston Red Sox for minor-league pitching prospect Carl Pavano and a player to be named, the latter of whom would become promising right-hander Tony Armas. And while baseball officials, like most business leaders, were fascinated by that most alluring of all things—*potential*—neither Pavano nor Armas would come close to matching Martinez's career accomplishments, at least in the short term. By the end of 2006, in fact, the pitchers had fewer career victories combined (109) than Martinez alone had amassed after the trade (141).

The moral of the story was clear: A bird in hand was better than two in the bush.

In the case of Ortiz, the decision was not so clear. At the conclusion of the 2002 season, in which be batted .272 with a career-high 20 home runs and 75 RBIs, Ortiz was eligible for salary arbitration for the second time in his career. He was coming off a season in which he earned a base salary of roughly $950,000, and his projected 2003 salary rested somewhere in the neighborhood of $2 million; the latter number seemed prohibitive for a Twins organization that recently had its existence threatened. For all of the growth in major-league baseball over the years—Martinez, for instance, was traded from Montreal to Boston at a time when baseball was *expanding* from twenty-eight teams to thirty teams—competitive and economic imbalance had created a situation where the rich were getting richer and the poor poorer. During increasingly sensitive labor negotiations between Major League Baseball (which typically represented the owners) and the Major League Baseball Players Association (the MLBPA, or players union), the disparity became such an issue that baseball officials hinted at the eradication or *contraction* of those clubs that might most easily be erased.

At the top of the list: the Expos and the Twins.

While such a scenario never played out, the Twins nonetheless continued to face difficult, annual decisions. Though the team had a wonderfully successful 2002 season— Minnesota's attendance nearly doubled from 2000 to 2002—a small payroll forced the general manager of the team, Terry Ryan, to rely heavily on players whose production far surpassed their salaries. Minnesota had room for a handful of star players with big contracts, but the club had little choice but to cut those players who *might* prove to be good values, who *might* blossom, who *might* allow the Twins to succeed in a league and world where they did not have the revenue to compete with big-market teams from, among other places, Boston and New York.

So, in the weeks following the most encouraging season of David Ortiz's career, the Twins—as the 1997 Montreal Expos did with Martinez—actively sought to trade Ortiz. But because Ortiz had not yet reached his potential, because his salary was about to grow, because the rest of baseball knew that the Twins were faced with a difficult decision, Twins GM Ryan found no takers for a young man who *might* be on the verge of blossoming into a slugger.

Unable to find a taker for Ortiz—and unwilling to absorb what they deemed to be a far too risky cost—the Twins cast Ortiz back into the water as if he were a fish not quite big enough.

Not long after, Ortiz was seated near the door at Vesuvio when Paulino entered, at which point the two immediately exchanged pleasantries and engaged in a conversation. The conversation turned to baseball, naturally, and Ortiz told Paulino the news: He'd been released. He was looking for a job. Did he happen to know anyone who could help?

Martinez was seated toward the rear of the restaurant when Paulino and Ortiz joined him.

"David was crying at the restaurant," said Martinez, who has always had a flair for the dramatic. "That was when he told me he just got released. He had a [new] baby at that time and we needed help [at first base]. We had Brian Daubach, but he didn't have a good year [in 2002]."

The Red Sox, in fact, were undergoing a major transformation from old to new. Despite having both Martinez (20–4) and Derek Lowe (21–8) finish the season as twenty-game winners—and despite finishing with a very successful record of 93–69—the 2002 Red Sox missed qualifying for the postseason by six games; they finished 10½ games behind the first-place New York Yankees in the American League East. Unlike the Twins, who were forced to watch every penny, the Red Sox had one of the highest payrolls in baseball and the ability to take million-dollar gambles. The club had just hired a hip, young general manager—the intelligent, hardworking and shrewd Theo Epstein—and less than a year had passed since the Red Sox had undergone an official, dramatic change in ownership. The Red Sox were being run by new people with new philosophies and new objectives, and one of the few certainties was that Pedro Martinez remained one of the building blocks.

Nearly everything else was open for debate.

Knowing his place in the Boston organization—and the power he wielded—Martinez wasted little time. He called Jack McCormick, the Red Sox traveling secretary, and left him a message urging him to call back. Martinez also called Epstein and left a similar voice message, telling him that he had run into Ortiz, that Ortiz was available, that the Red Sox should seriously look into signing a player who was entering his peak years, who was starting to mature as a hitter, whom Martinez felt would be a valuable and fitting addition to a Boston club that had deteriorated only a year earlier, in 2001, when the star-studded Red Sox failed to meet expectations and dissolved into blaming and finger-pointing in the bubbling cauldron that was baseball in Boston.

David Ortiz, Martinez believed, would be a good fit.

But the story does not end there.

ALONG WITH ACQUIRING ORTIZ, GENERAL MANAGER THEO EPSTEIN made a number of other acquisitions during the winter of 2002–03. All of them were designed to maximize value, giving the Red Sox the biggest bang for the buck. For while Epstein now ran the Boston Red Sox, he was raised as a baseball executive with the San Diego Padres, a team in a relatively small market that, like the Twins, was forced to make decisions primarily based on cost efficiency and effectiveness. In 2002, despite Pedro Martinez's assertions, first baseman Brian Daubach had not given the Red Sox a bad year. Rather, Daubach had given the Red Sox almost precisely what he had provided in the two prior seasons—from 2000 through 2002, he batted .259 while averaging 21 home runs and 75 RBIs—but his salary had gone up. In 2002, thanks to salary arbitration, Daubach earned a base salary of $2,325,000, nearly ten times what he had earned only two years prior ($295,000). But while his salary increased nearly tenfold during that time, his production did not.

So, as Terry Ryan and the Minnesota Twins did with David Ortiz, the Red Sox effectively released Brian Daubach following the 2002 season. The most significant difference was that Daubach had played the entire 2002 campaign at age thirty, leading the Red Sox to believe that Daubach had reached his full potential as a player.

With Daubach dismissed, the Red Sox opted for a committee approach at first base. The team had traded for Jeremy Giambi—the younger brother of accomplished New York Yankees slugger Jason Giambi—whom Epstein referred to as "a big part of our solution at first base." Epstein's subsequent maneuvers delivered to Boston both outfielder–first baseman Kevin Millar, third baseman Bill Mueller, and Ortiz, all of whom would serve as complements and depth to the right-handed-hitting Shea Hillenbrand, whom the Red Sox believed they could use at both third base and first.

In Boston, the logic was simple: Build a balanced portfolio with several elements so that no loss is too costly, then adjust accordingly if one of the stocks soars.

Nearly two months into the season, the situation had not truly resolved itself. Giambi was injured much of the time and failed to perform at others. While Millar's ability to play the outfield earned him playing time, Mueller and Ortiz were getting squeezed out. Ortiz found himself in a situation almost identical to that in Minnesota—where he was regarded as nothing more than a part-time player—and his frustration brought him to the point where he was ready to demand a trade.

At that point, too, Martinez remembers trying to help.

Said Martinez: "I didn't think that was fair when Jeremy Giambi was getting most of the playing time."

Before too long, he would not be alone.

In late June 2003, the Red Sox had an interleague series with the Phillies, something that had made playing time even more difficult to come by. Because the games were being played in Philadelphia, the teams had to operate under National League rules; neither club could use a designated hitter. One less spot in the batting order made it even less likely that Ortiz would play, especially now that he was regarded almost exclusively as a designated hitter, and not to be trusted in the field.

Until that point, Martinez had done what he could in hopes

of getting Ortiz into the lineup. Shortly before the middle of May, Martinez went into then-manager Grady Little's office and asked that Ortiz be in the lineup for games in which Martinez pitched; according to Martinez, Little agreed. Martinez subsequently went on the disabled list on May 16 and did not return until June 11, pitching just three times between May 15 and June 20. In each of those games, however, Ortiz was indeed a member of the starting lineup, something that satisfied both Martinez and, to a lesser extent, Ortiz.

Then came the Philadelphia series.

Though Martinez pitched against the Phillies on June 21, Ortiz was not among those Red Sox players to start the game. Philadelphia's starter that night was left-hander Randy Wolf, a fact that might have given Little cause for sitting the left-handed-hitting Ortiz, though Ortiz had played under similar circumstances just five days earlier, Martinez's previous start, in a June 16 meeting between the Red Sox and Chicago White Sox. Chicago's starter that night was Mark Buehrle, also a left-hander, though Ortiz finished the contest (a 4–2 Chicago victory) having gone 0 for 4 with a strikeout.

In Philaelphia, according to Martinez, Ortiz was expecting to play against Wolf. Martinez was expecting the same. According to Martinez, Little's initial explanation for Ortiz's absence was the player had left the ballpark early on a preceding night, before the game was over, violating a team rule in the process. Martinez's account was dramatically different, insisting that Ortiz had *not* left the ballpark early because Martinez and Ortiz had spent that night eating dinner together after leaving the ballpark.

"Somebody complained that David left [early], but the game was over," Martinez recalled. "The next day [and after the contest against Wolf and the Phillies], I get really upset. David was supposed to be in the lineup and [leaving early] was an excuse that Grady gave me. I snapped. I said, 'Grady, don't give me any of that bullshit.' He looked at me he said, 'Hey. Don't blame me. It's not up to me.' And I said, 'Well, you're going to play him when I pitch; you're going to start playing him in my games.'"

By consequence or circumstance—Hillenbrand already had been traded and the deteriorating Jeremy Giambi would soon be lost for the season—Ortiz's playing time soon increased dramatically. He started in Martinez's next start, on June 26, against the Detroit Tigers at Fenway Park. He started the next one, too, on July 2 when the Red Sox visited the Tampa Bay Devil Rays. And he started the one after that, on July 7, against the Yankees at historic Yankee Stadium.

All told, following the series in Philadelphia, Ortiz made fifteen consecutive starts in games started by Martinez after having appeared in a mere three of the pitcher's first eight, leading up to Martinez's start against the Texas Rangers on May 15. And it was during that span, beginning in July 2003, that Ortiz became a regular contributor to the Red Sox, that he started to produce, that the Red Sox began to discover they might have stumbled upon something far greater than just the Dominican version of Brian Daubach.

"All of a sudden, David went *boom, boom, boom*," said Martinez, referring to the noise Ortiz began making with his bat. "And he became who he is."

Of course, it wasn't really that simple.

Ortiz still had numerous strides to make.

But in the eyes of Pedro Martinez, the career of another Dominican superstar had just been launched.

MINOR
DEALINGS

When you're seventeen years old, you think everything is going to be easy. You think you're ready to play in the big leagues right away, that you just need a little time to show a team what you can do. You never think that you can fail, that you might not end up in the big leagues and play baseball for the rest of your life. The idea never even enters your mind.

And then you show up at your first camp and see that there are a lot of other players just like you. And after a while you realize that most of you aren't going to make it at all.

I learned early on that there was a lot more to making it to the big leagues than I thought, no matter how good I was. The baseball was just part of it. I had a lot to learn and a lot of growing up to do. The first year I played for the Mariners, in 1993, I played in the Dominican Summer League, where a lot of players from the Dominican Republic start their careers. It makes a lot of sense. At seventeen, It was going to be a while before I was ready to play in the minors, never mind the majors, so the Mariners knew they had to take it slow with me. That was the best way for any young kid. I played in sixty-one games that summer, and I batted .264 with 7 home runs and 31 RBIs. But at the beginning, all you are trying to do is learn the game, play as much as you can, try to understand what the organization wants from you little by little. That way, once you start playing in the minors for real, in the United States, you have a much better idea of what a team is going to expect from you.

And when you're someone like me, who's coming from another place, every little bit helps. Moving and being away from home for the first time is a big adjustment for any player, even if you're from the United States. And if you're someone like me, if you're from the Dominican Republic or anywhere else, you have to learn a lot of other things, too. You need to learn the food and you need to learn the language, the culture, the things most people take for granted. That can be tough. That's why, if there are any other guys on the team just like you, you end up spending a lot of time together at the beginning. You have the chance to go through some of those things together.

You know what was a big deal for me? The food, bro. I'm not kidding. I'm a big boy and I like to eat. Up to that point in my life, I had spent my whole life in the Dominican eating my mom's food. My mom used a lot of spices when she cooked, like a lot of people do in the Dominican, so that's what I was used to eating. When I got to the States, everything tasted sweet to me. The food wasn't as spicy and there wasn't as much flavor. I remember Pedro Martinez saying once that he had a lot of trouble eating when he first came over, that he lost weight and it was a problem. Pedro isn't a big guy, bro, so he needs all the food he can get. If he's not eating right, it's a problem. It was a problem for me, too, but I don't think I had as much trouble as he did. Maybe I just got hungrier.

While I'm at it, let me tell you something else, too: In the Dominican, we don't look at people as being different colors, different races, things like that. We are all just people. Sometimes, people ask me now about racism and things like that, and here's what I tell them: In the Dominican, there's really no such thing. I'm serious, bro. In the Dominican, there are people whose skin is light, dark, and anything in between. Nobody gives it a second thought. At least that's how I was raised. So when I got to America and started playing ball with all different kinds of people I never gave it a second thought. That's one of the really nice things about baseball, bro. No matter where you're from or what you look like, if you play the game, you have something in common. You're a team. Everybody has a job to do. And that's all that really matters. That's all that *should* matter.

You know how I learned about racism, things like that? When people asked me. Until that time, I really had no idea. When people ask me questions about it now, I think they expect certain answers from me because I'm dark-skinned. Because of that, it's like they expect me to have certain opinions, like I'm supposed to think a certain way. But I never really looked at it that way. Like I said, it's not my personality. I like to treat everybody like a person and I expect them to do the same to me. At the end of the day, isn't that all that really matters?

But that's one of things when you move to a new country, bro. You have to learn the culture, the people, the way they think, everything. A lot of times, you have to learn the language, too. All of that stuff is not easy.

By the time I got to rookie ball, my English was pretty good, so that wasn't too much of a problem. Most things really weren't. I think that's where my personality has always helped me. I like people and I think they like me, so that always makes things a little easier when you have to go through a transition. But there were a lot of things I learned at the beginning, things I didn't know about. There are things I'm still learning now. But when you're young, especially when you're seventeen or eighteen or nineteen years old, there are a lot of things that just are the way they are, and they can be hard to understand if you don't have a lot of an experience.

Let me give you an example:

When I first started playing in the minor leagues, it was with a team in Peoria, Arizona, where the Mariners had one of their Single-A teams. A lot of people think there are only three levels in the minor leagues—and I guess there are—but it's a lot more complicated than that. Most players, before they get to the big leagues, have to play in Single A, Double A, and Triple A depending on how good they are, how fast they make it through the system. Some guys can jump two or three levels at a time if the organization thinks they can handle it, but most guys go one step at a time. And at the beginning, especially, there are different levels of Class A, just so a team can make sure you're not being rushed.

A team like Peoria is considered *low* Class A, or Rookie League. It's where teams send their youngest and most inexperienced players (after a place like the Dominican Summer League) to develop. After that, a player usually goes to *mid-* or to *high* A ball, a place like Wisconsin or Fort Myers, both A-ball affiliates I played at while with the Mariners (Wisconsin) and, later, the Twins (Fort Myers). So by the time a player like me reaches Double A, chances are that he has already played for a few teams, like I did, especially if he was traded. Counting the

Dominican Summer League, I was in the minors for more than four years before I finally got to Double A, which is why the best thing you can have going for you, as you come through the minors, is obvious.

You need patience, bro.

But how many twenty- or twenty-one-year-old guys do you know who are patient?

In my first year with Peoria, I didn't play great. I hit .246 with 2 homers and 20 RBIs in just 53 games, but, like I said, there were a lot of adjustments to make. Even if you're not putting up great numbers, you're learning from the experience, even if you don't really know it. That's how it works when you're young. I was just eighteen years old when I played my first year in Peoria, so I was just starting. I was still *growing*. I came back that year expecting the Mariners to send me to their team in Wisconsin, the Timber Rattlers, who were in the Midwest League. The Timber Rattlers played in Appleton, which isn't too far from Green Bay, and I really had no idea where that was. I didn't know anything about Appleton or Green Bay. But I knew it was the next step *up*, the next place for me to go in my development, the next stop for me before I made it to the big leagues.

When you're that age, that's all you're focused on.

Just before the start of that season, the Mariners told me I would be spending the year at Peoria again. I didn't know what to say. I was pissed off, upset, hurt—all of those things. When you're eighteen, like I was at the time, your mind starts going fast. *What does something like that mean? Does that mean I'm not going to make it?* You feel like someone is quitting on you before you even got a chance, and that's what pisses you off more than anything. You feel like you haven't even started yet and somebody is already telling you that you have to stay back another year, like they tell some kids in school.

Even if that's not really what's happening—and it's usually not—that's what you feel like.

For me, there were other things that made me wonder about how the whole thing worked. Just before my second year in Peoria, the Mariners made a big trade with the Yankees that turned out to be one of the best deals in their history. Seattle sent a designated hitter named Ken Phelps to New York for an outfielder named Jay Buhner, and Buhner went on to have a really good career in Seattle. He was a good outfielder who hit a bunch of home runs, and there was one year, I think, where he almost won a Most Valuable Player Award. At that time, the Mariners organization had a lot of good, young players, so Buhner only made them better. They had Ken Griffey Jr. and Randy Johnson, and they ended up getting Alex Rodriguez to the big leagues, too. They were loaded, bro. They made the playoffs a few times and even got to the American League Championship Series, but they never made it to the World Series.

Anyway, at about the same time the Mariners got Jay Buhner from the Yankees, Seattle picked up Buhner's brother, Shawn, in the draft. I had never heard of Shawn Buhner and I don't think anybody else had, either, but the Mariners took him in like the twenty-eighth round, probably as a favor to Jay. I really don't know that for sure, but that kind of stuff happens all the time in baseball, even now. Look at a guy like Mike Piazza. The Los Angeles Dodgers grabbed Piazza really late in the draft one year, just as a favor to Tommy Lasorda, who has spent his entire career in the Dodgers organization as a manager and an executive. I think Piazza got picked in the 62nd round, even later than Shawn Buhner got picked when Buhner was in the draft, and it was only because he was Lasorda's godson—or something like that. Then Piazza got into the Dodgers system and ended up becoming one of the best catchers in the history of baseball, and the Dodgers looked like the smartest people in the world when really they just got lucky.

But in baseball, that's the way it is. The game is so hard and so unpredictable—you never know what's going to happen—that it's hard to evaluate real talent, especially in young players. You just don't know what you have yet. Sometimes all a guy needs is a little luck and some guidance, and that can be the difference between a guy who makes it and a guy who doesn't. That's why you have to be patient with young players, wait them out, build their confidence and give them a chance. You never know when you're going to draft the next Mike Piazza or trade away the next Jay Buhner, so teams have to be careful. And when it gets late in the draft, when there aren't many players left—the draft goes fifty rounds every year and there are thirty teams, so that's 1,500 new players *every summer*—you'll see teams draft their manager's son, or something like that. Really, the club is just doing a favor for its manager, giving his kid a chance to play for a while. But what if the kid pans out? I mean, a lot of guys who are the sons of big-league managers have been around the game for a long time. They know how to play. Maybe they are just a little late to develop, but if the player ends up being better than anyone thought, now the team just got a steal.

And when you get to the fiftieth round of the draft, bro, when there aren't many players left, what does a team have to lose?

In baseball, most players who are taken after the first ten rounds or so never make it. I'm not sure what the percentages are, but the later you're picked, the worse your chances are. There are a lot of reasons for that, but the biggest one is talent. The good players always get taken in the earliest rounds of the draft. But the other thing that comes into play sometimes is money, how much a team spent on a guy after drafting him. I mean, if a team signs a first-round pick and gives him a signing bonus worth millions of dollars, they're going to be careful with that kid. They're going to take their time and make sure they protect their investment. That kid is going to get a lot of attention and a lot of chances, and he's going to get the best coaching and instruction. That makes a lot of sense if you're the team, but it can be really frustrating if you're somebody like me.

Like I said, bro, I signed for $7,500, which isn't much.

If I didn't pan out, the Mariners weren't going to lose much.

And I felt that unless I started proving myself from the beginning, a team like the Mariners might quit on me and I might never get the chance.

That's the hard part of being a prospect, bro.

You can work hard and do all of the right things, but you can't make anybody give you a chance.

Anyway, let me get back to Shawn Buhner. He was drafted out of college, I think, so he was a little older than me. He was a first baseman, too. So when it came time for the Mariners to decide which player they were going to send to Wisconsin, to their A-ball affiliate in Appleton in the Midwest League, they chose Buhner over me. There were a lot of reasons for it at the time, even some things I didn't know. If you get to be a certain age, you can be too old to play in the rookie league, so a team has no choice but to send you to the next level. That's what happened with Buhner. But at the time, I was a teenage kid from the Dominican who couldn't understand why I wasn't going to A ball, and that bothered me. I thought Jay Buhner's brother was getting special treatment, that he was getting a chance I would never get, and I felt like I was being taken advantage of. Looking back, I really don't think I understood what was going on, but at that age, especially, you put so much pressure on yourself to be successful that sometimes you don't see straight.

Still, you need to understand, bro. *I thought I belonged there.* The way I remember it, it was late in spring and we were just getting ready to break for the start of the season when the Mariners gave me the news. I had my bags, thinking I was going to Wisconsin, and all of a sudden I was staying in Peoria. I was mad as hell. I didn't know how to deal with it. People can teach you all they want about dealing with adversity, but when you're that age, it's tough. You just don't know how. So I unpacked my stuff and did the same thing I always did whenever I got pissed off or frustrated.

I called my pop.

Like I've already told you, bro, my pop was really good about calming me down when I got frustrated or upset. It was like that time in the Dominican, when I got sent home from the Marlins camp because my elbow was sore. My pop told me that there was nothing I could do about it, that all I could do was to go out and play my best. He told me that I needed to go out and show the Mariners that they made a mistake, that I belonged in Wisconsin, in a mid-A ball, and that I didn't belong in Arizona anymore, that I didn't belong in rookie ball. He told me that I was talented and to believe in my ability, and that everybody has to prove himself, no matter what he does.

So what could I do, bro?

I had to play in Peoria or I had to stop playing altogether.

That year, from the beginning, I was killin'. I don't know if it was because I was pissed off or more focused, but I felt like I had something to prove. The rookie league season is pretty short, so if you can get hot, you can stay hot for a whole season. That's what happened with me. I think I finished that year batting .332 with 4 home runs and 37 RBIs in 48 games, and I think that's when I probably started to get people's attention. My 37 RBIs tied for the league lead and I led the league with 18 doubles. You put up numbers like that, you hit .332, people are going to notice you, no matter what level you're at. That's one of the nice things about baseball. Whether you're at Single A or Double A or Triple A—or if you're in the big leagues—a .300 average is still a .300 average. The numbers don't change that much. So what happens, when you put up numbers like that, is that the team bumps you up to the next level. They give you another challenge. They make the competition tougher and they start asking you to do more, and it's up to you to prove to them again that you belong there.

That's the lesson you learn.

You want to hear something funny? Until I got to the minor leagues, until I started playing professionally, I didn't really know or understand the numbers, at least not the way I do now. I mean, growing up in the Dominican and playing in the streets with a broomstick, you don't worry about your batting average or things like that. You just go out and play because you enjoy the game and you have fun. Then you get into a professional organization and you start competing with other guys, and that's when you start to understand that everybody is getting measured, that the numbers are like your grades in school. They mean something, bro. The better your numbers, the better your grades, the better it is for you. That's when you really start to understand competition, that there are a lot of other guys out there who want the same job you do, that you have to keep producing or someone is going to go right past you.

After that season, like all young players, I went to Instructional League, which is another way for teams to develop young players, give them more attention, work on their skills.

All of it is important, bro. Baseball is like anything else. You have to play a lot and get as much experience as you can because that's the only way you're going to get better. It can take a long time. But the more times you step into the batter's box, the more times you field a ground ball, the more it becomes second nature, almost instinct. You don't really have to think anymore about the mechanics of your swing or your footwork around the bag. It just happens naturally. That's what experience is. It's when you do something so many times, over and over again, that you don't even have to think about it.

And when that happens, you have complete confidence.

That year, in instructional league, I'll never forget something that happened to me. A lot of people knew that I was pissed off at the beginning of the year, that I thought I deserved to be in mid-A in Appleton, playing for the Wisconsin team. But after I went out and had a great year, after I put up the numbers, I remember one of my coaches coming up to me in instructional league and telling me something. I think the guy's name was Jim Skaalen. Skaalen pulled me aside and put his arm around me, and I'll never forget what he said: "If they don't send you to Wisconsin next year, I'm going to quit."

Can you believe that?

I think it's one of the nicest things anybody has ever said to me.

I haven't seen Skaalen since that time, bro, but let me tell you: I'd like to bump into him someday, just so I could say thank you. Like I said, confidence makes all the difference in life, especially in baseball, and I can't tell you what it meant to me to hear one of my coaches say that. When you're that age, you have a lot of doubt in yourself and there's a lot of pressure. Even if you go out and have a good year—even if you put up the numbers—you still need to hear somebody say it. You still need to hear somebody tell you that you're doing a good job, doing it the right way, that you're making *progress*. That's really all you're looking for. When it gets right down to it, we all know that it takes awhile to get from the minor leagues to the big leagues, that you have to have patience. But if you don't feel like you're making progress, if you don't feel like you're getting *closer*, it can be really frustrating because you can feel like you're not accomplishing anything, like you're not succeeding.

And then, even if you do feel like you're playing well, you need to hear it from the people making the decisions because they're the ones who decide whether you stay or you go, whether you're going to keep getting chances or not.

That's where a coach can make all the difference in the world, bro.

That's when you really appreciate the good ones.

And the next year, just like Jim Skaalen promised, I got promoted to the Midwest League.

There's something I forgot to tell you: If you go back and look for David Ortiz on the roster of the 1996 Wisconsin Timber Rattlers, you're not going to find him, bro. He didn't exist. Back then, my name was David Arias.

Some of my boys still bust me about that now—guys like Torii Hunter—but until I started playing professionally in the major leagues, I always went by Arias. That was my mom's last name before she married my pop. In the Dominican, it's not unusual for people to put their mom's last name after their pop's, and I didn't learn until later that people do it the other way around in the United States. So when I was a kid, when I went to high school and got drafted, even when I started playing for the Mariners and the Twins, my full name was David Americo Ortiz Arias. So I went by David Arias.

It wasn't until I got to Minnesota that I changed my name to David Ortiz, mostly because some of the people who worked for the team told me it would be the best thing to do. As citizens of the Dominican Republic, we have to file paperwork every year so that we can play in the United States and earn a living here. It's the same for players from places like Venezuela or Colombia. Every once in a while, something gets messed up or the paperwork doesn't match up right, so somebody ends up coming late to spring training. In my case, to avoid problems, the Twins told me one year that I should change all my paperwork to David Ortiz because that was my pop's name and that's how they did it in the United States. So one year, before the season started, I went into Santo Domingo and filed all the paperwork to change my name from David Arias to David Ortiz.

Looking back, it was probably a good thing. I was playing with the Twins in 2001 when the September 11 terrorist attacks took place, and after that the whole world started to do things differently. Baseball changed things, too. Because the American government got more strict about their policies in letting people into the country, it got a lot harder for some Dominican players to get their paperwork right, starting during spring training in 2002. There were some guys who had done the same thing I did, using their mom's name growing up and their pop's name in the big leagues. That created a lot of confusion. But because I had already taken care of all my paperwork, because I made sure that everything lined up, I didn't have a lot of the problems that some other guys did. I really didn't have any problems.

By then I was David Ortiz.

And I was staying David Ortiz.

But in 1996, at least, I was still David Arias. I opened the year in Single A with the Wisconsin Timber Rattlers, but even then it was a little frustrating for me. When I first got to Wisconsin, they had this other dude there—his name was Scott Smith—and they told me that he was going to open the year as the first baseman. It was unbelievable, bro. I finally got promoted, got to another level, but I had to sit behind someone else at the very beginning. I was a little pissed off again. But then the team worked it out so that both me and Smith got to play—he moved to the outfield—and after that, I didn't have to worry about it anymore. They put me in the lineup and I started killin' right away; nothing else really mattered much. That's another thing about baseball: If you hit, you play. Nothing else matters. There aren't a lot of guys who can hit for average and power, so no manager is going to sit a guy down because he's too slow or because his defense isn't good enough.

Want to know something? With me, none of that other stuff mattered, either. A lot of people see that I'm a big dude and think that I can't run, but it's not true. I run fine. I don't steal bases like Jose Reyes—he's another Dominican guy and plays for the Mets, and he's *fast*—but I'm really not that slow, bro. Once I get going, I move OK. I'm not like a lot of guys, who get on the bases and the manager has to run for them late in games. I feel like I can go from first to third or second to home, and most managers have let me run, even late in games.

Know what else? When I played for Wisconsin, I was voted the best defensive first baseman in the league. I'm not kidding. I was twenty years old and I was pretty good around the bag. A lot of people wouldn't believe that now. A lot of that stuff about my defense didn't start until I got to Minnesota, when the Twins told people that I didn't play good defense and that I would have to be a designated hitter. So then I started playing less at first base, and when that happens you're not going to get any better. Fielding is like anything else. You have to practice it to be good at it. The best experience is the experience you get in games, so if you're only the designated hitter most of the time, it's almost impossible to become a good defensive player.

Now? I'm a designated hitter almost 100 percent of the time. I played some at first base when I first got to Boston, but now I don't play there very much at all. Our manager, Terry Francona, usually plays me at first base only during interleague games, when we have to play in National League stadiums and can't use the designated hitter. He used me there during the World Series in 2004, too, and I even made a big play in Game 3, throwing out a runner [Jeff Suppan] at third base to help get Pedro Martinez out of a jam.

But even back in 1996, with Wisconsin, teams wanted me to focus on hitting. I think everybody recognized that I had most of the tools to be a good hitter, starting with my feet. To me, that's where hitting starts. If you have good footwork, a good lower body, it's a lot easier to get your hands in the right place. That's why, even now, I try to focus on my feet if I start struggling and get into a slump. I know that if I just close my front foot a little, it helps stop my hips from opening up too fast, and that's usually when a hitter can get into trouble. But if you stay back on the ball, if you trust your hands and don't open up too fast—we call that "pulling off" the ball—you can keep your bat through the strike zone longer and you increase your chances for good contact.

In my first year at Wisconsin, I ended up playing in 129 games and we had a pretty good team. In 485 at-bats—that was the most I'd ever had in my life—I hit .322 with 18 home runs, 93 RBIs, 89 runs scored, and 34 doubles. I had a big year. I led the team in almost every offensive category and I was near the top of the league leaders in just about everything. I played in the Midwest League All-Star Game and I got voted the Most Exciting Player in the league, and I really felt like things were starting to happen for me, like I was putting myself in a position to succeed. I was pretty sure that I wasn't going to be at Wisconsin again the following the year, that I was going to get bumped to high-A ball or even better, and that I was going to take the next step in my career.

I was right, too.

But it wasn't with the Mariners.

Not long after the '96 season, the Mariners told me that I'd been traded, that I was the player to be named in a trade they made during the season with the Minnesota Twins. The Mariners were in contention and they needed a third baseman, so they got Dave Hollins from the Twins for a player to be named. Hollins was a pretty good player who had some good years—he was a tough competitor, from what people tell me—and it was the kind of trade that happens a lot in baseball. But when you're that age and you get traded for the first time in your career—I learned about the deal just before my twenty-first birthday—you think that maybe you did something wrong, that maybe somebody didn't want you anymore.

In my case, over time, I learned it was the opposite.

Someone *wanted* me.

That's the thing about being traded, bro. It's all how you look at it. My pop was good at making me realize things like that, too. During the season, I guess the Twins' general manager, Terry Ryan, was at our games scouting one of his own teams when he saw me play. So when it got to late in the season, when the Mariners needed a third baseman and the Twins had one to deal, my name came up. Ryan probably said something like, "Hey, what about that Arias kid?" and the Mariners agreed to the deal. I was still in Single A at the time. I had a long way to go to get to the big leagues. So a team like the Mariners figures there is still a long way to go, that I have to go to Double A and maybe even Triple A before I make it to the big leagues. And that's a lot of time for things to go wrong. There's still a long way for a kid like me to go. So they make the trade thinking the odds are in their favor.

Seriously, bro, go back and look at a lot of the trades that are made late in the season between teams who are in contention and teams who aren't. A lot of times, a team can get a veteran player for a kid at Single A, and most big-league clubs aren't afraid to trade minor-leaguers who are still young, who have a long way to go in their development. It makes perfect sense. I mean, if a kid gets to Triple A and he's still playing well, now he's *close* to the majors and everybody knows about him. Everybody probably wants him because he's passed a lot of tests, played well at Single A and Double A and Triple A. But if he's still in Single A, if he's still young and early in his development, he has a lot to prove. There's no way of knowing if he's going to make it. Teams will trade away a player like that before they'll trade a kid at Triple A.

Even then, if a team has to give something up, it can be worth it. If you're a team that has a chance to win the World Series, you have to take a shot, bro. Those chances don't come along all the time. It takes a lot to win in baseball—pitching and hitting and defense—and it takes luck, too. Your players have to stay healthy. They have to produce. The ball has to bounce the right way and you have to hope that maybe the other team makes some mistakes, because it's not like you're out there playing by yourselves.

I mean, the other guys want to win too, right?

For me, I had to look at it the right way. I had a good year. Another team wanted me in a trade. Even though I was in another system, I still had to play well, still had to move up, still had to deal with the same challenges. That much didn't change. At the time, all I wanted to do was to get to the big leagues. It really didn't matter who the team was. The only bad part about leaving Wisconsin was that I'd made some friends there, met some people, built some relationships.

And I didn't know it at the time, bro, but I'd also met my wife.

MOST PLAYERS WILL TELL YOU: THEY LIKE TO KEEP THEIR FAMILY lives private. I'm no different. My wife and my kids are the most important people in the world to me, right there with my mom, pop, and sisters. Sometimes, people think that because we're ballplayers, our lives are different. They're really not. The things that are important to you are important to us, and sometimes it feels like they're even more important. We spend so much time away from home sometimes that we want to make sure nobody interferes with us when we're with our wives and kids.

But how I met Tiffany is a pretty good story.

In a place like Appleton, there aren't too many places to hang out after games. And as a baseball player, because you play most of your games at night, you usually want to go out after the game, maybe get something to eat and hang out with friends, just to relax. When you're twenty years old, that's especially true. You want to meet people, bro. You want to go dancing, listen to music, and have a good time. You can always sleep in the morning. So, after games, a lot of guys would go out to bars and restaurants, places like that, to just kill some time and have some fun. There was this place not too far from the stadium where I used to hang out a lot—I don't even remember the name of it—and I liked going there because they had music and dancing, things I liked to do when I was growing up in the Dominican.

Looking back, I guess I picked a good place.

Because that's where I met Tiff.

At the time, there was a group of us that used to hang out together. I mean, I spent time with people I don't even remember. But there was this girl named Abby who was dating one of the guys on the team, I think, so she came out with us one night and she brought some of her friends. Tiff was one of them. So we started talking and hanging out, dancing and having a good time. I think we liked each other right away. And by the end of the season we were spending a lot of time together, which was probably a good thing because of what happened at the end of the baseball season.

I'm not talking about the trade, bro.

I'm talking about the playoffs.

Let me explain: In the minor leagues, the baseball season usually wraps up at the end of August or the beginning of September. Then you either go to the playoffs or to the instructional league, or, if you're playing at Double A or Triple A, maybe you get to spend a few weeks in the big leagues. It depends on how long you've been around, how much you've developed, things like that. Every team wants to make the playoffs, but when you're in the minor leagues, especially at the low levels, making the playoffs means that the season gets longer, and that can create some problems.

For me, it meant that I needed to find someplace to live.

My lease was up.

In a place like Appleton, bro, you don't have many choices. It's not like we made a lot of money at that time and could just pay for a hotel room for a week or two. You had to find ways to get by. Tiff and I had been spending some time together by then, so she offered to let me live at her house, which isn't as simple as it sounds. She wasn't much older than me, bro. She lived with her mom. So Tiff decided to go up to her mom one day and say, "Hey, Mom, one of the guys on the team needs a place to live and I told him that he could stay here," and I don't think her mom was too happy about it at first. I mean, who would be? Her daughter is hanging out with this ballplayer who plays for the minor-league team in town, and now she wants him to stay at their house for a little while because he doesn't have a place to live.

Then a big dude like me walks in the door and her mom must be wondering what she got herself into.

Know what happened? Me and Tiff's mom, we hit it off right away. I think she really liked me. The first day I stayed there, I woke up and came into the kitchen, and she had this big breakfast for me. She treated me like her son. I was twenty years old and I didn't have a place to stay, and she took me into her house like I had lived there my whole life.

I really don't need to tell you too much after that. Tiff and I didn't get married until 2002, but we have three kids now, two girls and a boy. My daughters' names are Jessica and Alexandra and my son's name is D'Angelo, who we named after my mom, Angela. During my career with the Twins, and even after I got traded to Boston, our family used to spend a good part of the off-season in Wisconsin, where we bought a house. That was important to Tiff because she wanted to stay near her mom and her family. Tiff tried to make me a Green Bay Packers fan, too—now that I'm in Boston, I've really started to like the New England Patriots—and I've been on the sideline at Lambeau Field, met Brett Favre, things like that. After we'd been in Boston a couple of years, once the kids started to go to school, we bought a place there and sold the place in Wisconsin. We spend a good amount of our time now in Boston, but I still go back to the Dominican for part of every winter to see my family, get in shape, and train for the season, maybe play a little winter ball.

In Boston, during the season, I like to do most of the same things I did in the Dominican and in the minor leagues. I like to cook out on the grill, and I like to take my kids to the supermarket with me when I go grocery shopping. I think the kids like to come with me because they know I'll buy them whatever they want at the store, but that's part of being a pop. My mom and pop always did things like that for me, made me feel like I was part of what they were trying to do, gave me love and kept me laughing.

As a husband and a pop, now I get to give that back.

It's funny how life works that way.

THE
MINNESOTA YEARS

Life is unpredictable, bro. You can spend your whole time in one place—and you can think everything is good—but you never really know until you go somewhere else. Then you can understand the difference between the good things and good things, which is basically what happened to me in my final year with the Minnesota Twins.

In a some ways, it was my best year there.

In some ways, it was my worst.

God has his own way of doing things, so maybe he was trying to tell me something. Maybe he was trying to teach me. The year got off to a bad start from the beginning. It was New Year's Day 2002 and we had just celebrated Christmas, and I was driving with my pop when I got a call from Albania's boyfriend. He told us that we needed to come right away. He told us we had to hurry. I think I've told this story a million times now, but it still bothers me when I talk about it. A reporter from *Sports Illustrated* asked me about this during the summer of 2006, when I was having one of my best years for the Red Sox, and I remember telling him that it took me eight minutes to get there after I got the call. Eight minutes, bro. That's not a long time.

But that's how long it took for me to find out that my life had changed.

That I'd lost my mom.

That we all had.

Like I've told you before, my mom was a really warm person. She was full of happiness and she was always helping people, giving them things, making them feel good. That's just the way she was. I think that's part of the reason it was so hard for all of us when she died. Back home, people tell me all the time that I'm just like my mom, that I have her personality because I'm friendly and easy to talk to. I think that's part of the reason why fans see me the way they do, why they feel like they can talk to me. That all comes from my mom. That was a gift from her.

Every New Year's Day, my mother would go to see her brothers and sisters in Haina. That was one of her traditions. We all spent New Year's together in Santo Domingo, and in the morning my mom called this friend of hers, a guy who used to drive her places, and asked him if he would take her to Haina. The guy didn't want to go. He said he was tired and had been all out night, but my mom talked him into it. He said he would do it only because it was my mom who asked him. If it was someone else, he said, he would have just said no. I think that tells you how much people loved my mother.

So my mom left to go see her brothers and sisters while I was taking my dad home. A little while later, Albania's boyfriend called and gave the news to me and my pop: She had been in a car accident. So my pop and I started driving toward Haina, where we moved when I was a teenager and where I went to high school, and the car was on the side of the road when we got there. The car hit a dump truck, and my mom was killed instantly. We're pretty sure she had no pain. The driver survived, but for a while we thought he was going to die, too. I haven't talked to him in a long time, bro. I'm not sure what he's doing now.

My pop, my sister, me . . . We were devastated. I don't know how else to describe it. My mom grew up in a family of seven kids and she was the youngest. She was the baby of the family. They all loved her and all watched out for her, the same way she watched out for me and Albania. When my mother was nine years old, her mom died. She was only forty-six. It was during the holidays. Now here we were again, during the holidays, and my mom was the one who was gone. She was forty-six, too. People sometimes say that everything happens for a reason, but I'm still not sure why we lost my mom. I guess God wanted it that way, but she didn't have to go.

Everyone in the family, they all struggled when my mom died. My aunts. My uncles. My sister and my pop. I felt like I had to be the strong one, like I had to take care of everybody.

That's what my mom would have done.

When *Sports Illustrated* asked me about it, almost five years later, this is what I told them:

"I had to act like, 'Hey, let's hang in there.' I got to take the heat. I lose my mother, that I love, the person that gave me the most love ever. But I never quit. I acted strong in that one moment that was terrible. But I've got my pain. I deal with the situation. After that, I don't think I have faced anything worse than that, anything more painful than that."

What can I say, bro? I still think about my mom. I think about her all the time. Not long after my mom died, I got a big tattoo of her face on my right arm. She's still there, still watching out for me. People ask me sometimes why I point to the sky after I hit a home run, and I tell them that I'm thanking God, but I'm also thanking my mom. She taught me so much. She gave me so much love, helped me become a good person. I owe so much to her for the things she did for me, the sacrifices she made.

You know what else? In some ways, I think she's still helping me. For a long time, I had trouble forgetting about my mom, about the way she died. Now I try to remember the good times and the good things. I try to see everything as a positive, to take the good out of things. Life is too short to focus on the bad things all the time. You have to remember the most important things in life, like taking care of your family. That's what counts, bro. Your friends and your family and the people you love, the people you care about. Nothing else really matters.

Since my mom died, I tried not to worry about the little things so much. I try not to worry about baseball. My mom had been gone for about six weeks when I went back to spring training with the Twins in 2002 and my salary was up to about $950,000 a year. All the things that happened to me in baseball didn't seem like such a big deal. All I wanted to do was to stay healthy and to get the chance to play because I knew I could hit. I knew I could produce as long as someone gave me the chance.

That was my attitude going into spring training.

That was going to be my attitude from now on.

But I should probably start at the beginning.

WHEN YOU'RE YOUNG, EVERYTHING ABOUT THE MAJOR LEAGUES can be intimidating. Everything is new. You have to learn the most basic things all over again—how to get to the stadium, where to park, where you fit in—and it's a big transition. You want to do everything the manager says and you want to impress him, even if it's not your best way to succeed.

I don't feel that way now, but I'm older and I know better. I've been in the big leagues for almost ten years now. But I was just twenty-one when I got to the majors for the first time, and I was still a little shy and sensitive. The Twins manager at the time was a lot older than the players—his name was Tom Kelly but everyone called him TK—and that made it hard enough. TK was kind of a hard-ass and he felt like he had to teach us the game. He treated us like we knew nothing, and it was hard to like him. I think he liked it that way. If you screwed up, you were gone, and that's a hard way to do anything, especially play baseball, especially when you're young. A lot of us felt like we couldn't make a mistake.

Before we go on, let me tell you a little more about TK. He was the manager of the Twins for sixteen years, from 1986 to 2001. The guy has seen a lot of baseball and he knows even more. Kelly was managing when the Twins won the World Series in 1987 and again in 1991, but I don't know much about that because I wasn't in the organization. I didn't come along until later, until after the Mariners signed me, until after they traded me to Minnesota. By then, the Twins were a bad team. They couldn't beat anybody, bro. The first year I got called up, in 1997, the Twins won 68 games and finished in fourth place. The next year, we won 70 and finished fourth again. After that, we won 63 and 69, and we finished in last place both times, behind bad teams from Detroit and Kansas City. We were bad, bro, and we weren't getting any better.

Let me tell you something else: When I first got called up

to the big leagues, the Twins didn't have anybody who could hit the ball out of the park. I think they finished that year [1997] with fewer home runs than any team in the American League, so they should have wanted to have a guy like me in their lineup. I got called up in September. I started the year in A ball [at Fort Myers] and had a big year. I hit .331 with 13 homers and 58 RBIs in 61 games at A ball, then hit .322 with 14 homers and 56 RBIs in 69 games at Double A. I was killin'. I only had 42 at-bats at Triple A before they brought me up to the big leagues, and I hit .327 (with one home run) in 49 at-bats before the season ended. I was Minnesota's minor-league player of the year and I led the organization in hits (187), doubles (41), total bases (328) and RBIs (130). I tied for the lead with 32 homers. Going into the winter—and into 1998— I thought I was ready to play in the big leagues every day, especially for a team that needed a guy who could hit with power.

The next year, things started to go wrong from the beginning, even if I didn't understand it all at the time.

For all of the stuff people have said about TK, here was the thing that really bothered me: Once he put something in his head, that was it. There was no other way of doing things. With a big son of a bitch like me—and with a lineup that didn't have much power—the last thing you'd want me to do is swing like a little son of a bitch. That's obvious, right? Bro, I'm six foot four and 260 pounds. I'm a big dude. Most managers want a guy like me to swing from my ass up there because I can hit the ball out of the ballpark. When I got to Boston later in my career, teams would start shifting their defense on me and playing everyone to the right side because I pulled the ball a lot. So every once in a while, just to mess with them, I'd push a bunt down the third-base line and get an easy single. Manny Ramirez was hitting behind me and I figured it would help the team to have Manny hit with me on base, so I didn't see anything wrong with bunting.

You know what the Red Sox told me? They said they wanted me to swing. Terry Francona was the manager—we called him Tito—and he told me they wanted me to hit the ball out of the ballpark. He told me they appreciated what I was doing, but they wanted me to swing from my ass.

But in Minnesota, with TK, it was the opposite.

After a while, it got a little frustrating. I felt like I couldn't say anything because I didn't want to get myself in trouble. TK was the manager, bro. I was the player. My job is to play for him. TK had a lot more experience than me—he had more than all of us—and we couldn't say shit. That's just the way it was. We knew we had to keep our mouths shut.

But seriously, bro, I can't tell you how many times I got yelled at from the dugout because TK didn't like what I was doing. The Twins wanted us to hit the ball to the opposite field because that was the best way to hit for average, and the best way to do that is to try to jam yourself, to feel like you're bringing your hands in toward your body. The idea is to keep your hands back, but it's a hard way to hit for power. A big guy like me can do it—I basically try to jam myself now—but I always felt like the Twins weren't teaching us the right way. They wanted us to give up power to get a single to the opposite field, especially with two strikes, and that didn't make much sense to a guy like me. I'd hit home runs all my life, dude. I'm a big man. I want to get my arms extended and swing from my ass—even once in a while—but TK and the Twins didn't want me to do that. So I started changing my swing and my approach, and I had trouble being the same hitter I was in the minors.

I didn't even have a year in the big leagues and I was already getting messed up.

In 1998, I made the Twins out of spring training and I was playing mostly first base. I got off to a good start and hit .299 in April with 4 home runs and 17 RBIs in twenty-two games, which was a pretty good pace. I was striking out a lot, but I was also drawing walks and hitting for power, doing all of the things I'm supposed to do and the things I basically do now. It was a good beginning. I kept right on hitting into the early part of May, when I went 3 for 4 with a double in a game against the Yankees. I was batting .306. My on-base percentage was .375, and I was slugging .531, and I was still just twenty-two years old. But after that game with the Yankees, my right wrist was bothering me and the team sent me for X-rays, which showed that I had a fracture of the hamate bone at the base of my hand. It's a common baseball injury, especially for power hitters, because, when you swing, the knob of the bat hits against your wrist. And when it happens over and over and over again, the best way to fix the problem is to go in and remove the bone that causes the problem.

The bottom line?

I needed surgery.

And I was going to be out awhile.

When I came back to the lineup in July, I started hitting again, right away. In my second game back, at Cleveland, I went 2 for 4 with a home run. The next day, I went 3 for 5 with another home run—my fifth of the season—and 4 RBIs. I was killin' again. My average was up to .321 and I was slugging .587, and I was pretty sure I was on my way to a big year. Maybe I could even have won the American League Rookie of the Year Award. But then I started to struggle a little in July and August—like a lot of young players do—before I got hot again in September. All in all, I thought I had a pretty good year. I finished the season with a .277 average, 46 RBIs and 9 home runs in 278 at-bats—about a half season's worth. If

I had played full-time—and if I hadn't hurt my hand—I might have hit 20 homers with about 90 to 100 RBIs. That's what my numbers projected to, and that's not bad for any player, let alone a twenty-two-year-old rookie.

Again, going into the winter, I felt pretty good about myself.

And then, in the spring, of 1999, a funny thing happened. I didn't make the team.

I KNOW I'VE SAID THIS ALREADY, BUT I'LL SAY IT AGAIN: NO MATTER what you do in life, the most important thing you need is confidence. For me, confidence has always been number one. Everything in life is a learning process. You need experience. You have to learn about everything in life and, the sooner you learn it, the better off you are.

But when you're a young player trying to make it in the big leagues, it isn't that easy. Teams don't want to wait for you to develop. There are other players in camp trying to make it to the big leagues, just like you, so you feel like you can't make mistakes. You need to have managers and coaches who give you confidence, who support you, who stand behind you. Even now, I try to remember that. If I'm in camp with the Red Sox and there's a young guy who's trying to make the team, I try to give him some support or some encouragement because that's what he needs. In the spring of 2006, when I was with the Red Sox, I remember taking batting practice one day against this kid we had in the minors, a left-handed pitcher named Jon Lester. The kid was a pretty good prospect, I guess. Lester threw me a pretty good curveball that I swung at and missed, and I remember yelling out to him, "Hey, good job, nice pitch." I think he just kind of nodded. But I could tell that he appreciated it, that it meant something to him to know that someone like me, who was having success in the big leagues, thought he did something right.

With the Twins, I never felt like I got that kind of support, especially from TK.

I felt like they spent more time tearing us down than building us up.

The spring of 1999 wasn't a good one for me. I hit .137 and had just one home run, and I struck out 12 times in 51 at-bats. I struggled and I'm not sure why. Like I said, I had a pretty decent year in 1998, so maybe I thought I was going to be on the Opening Day roster. But as the spring went on, I started hearing things that made me kind of upset. The Twins said I needed to work more on my defense, that I was lazy. They told me my attitude had changed, that I had a bad attitude now, and that I needed to work. Can you believe that shit? Bro, let me tell you: Anybody who knows me knows I've never had a bad attitude. Never. I'm a pretty happy dude. I try to focus on the good things in life. But every time I made a mistake, I felt like TK was riding my ass, making an example of me. That's a hard way to play, especially when you're twenty-three, when you're trying to make it, when you're trying to convince yourself that you belong.

You always need people to support you, especially when you're young.

You don't need them screaming and yelling at you all the time.

Near the end of camp, the Twins told me I was going to start the year in Triple A. I was pissed off. I thought I had a pretty decent season the year before and now I was going to open the year in Triple A, and I'm going to tell you the truth: I didn't want to go back. I knew I deserved to be on that team, but the Twins told me I needed more time in the minors. How much more did I have to do there? The Twins told me I'd never had a full year at Triple A, that I needed more time. Every time I went down to the minors I started killin', but that wasn't good enough for them. I needed time in the big leagues. I just needed more time to learn there, more experience. But the Twins wanted to send me back down, and I didn't see the point.

Let me back up here for a minute and try to explain something to you: When you're a kid and you come to this country from somewhere else, when you're different, you can be intimidated. I was signed as a free agent because Dominican players couldn't be picked in the draft, and when I got to minor-league camp most of the other guys were draft picks. Just something like that can make you feel different. Most of the guys you play with are cool because we're all on the same team, all trying to get to the same place. But you wonder sometimes about the people making decisions, about whether they are going to spend more time working with the draft picks than they are with some kid they signed for $7,500. You wonder if you are going to get the same chance. And that doesn't even get into the fact that you speak a different language, are used to eating different food, are away from your family and your friends. That's a lot to overcome, bro. Sometimes, as a kid, you're better off if you don't notice so much.

Most Americans don't look it that way because the United States is their home. Everybody here is like them. But I can tell you that most every player from outside the United States has felt that at some point whether they've admitted it or not. There's no way around it. This isn't our country. We're not from here. We don't know the people, the culture, or the customs, and it takes us years to catch up.

And then, when you feel like someone won't give you an opportunity along the way, you don't know what to think.

So you start to doubt yourself.

With TK, I learned after a while that he was just the way he was. I don't know if he didn't like young players or what, but he made it hard on all of us. A year after spring training in 1999, when I got sent back to the minors, Todd Walker had almost the same experience I did. Walker was a California dude. He went to college [Louisiana State University] and was a high draft pick. He hit everywhere he went and batted .339 with 28 home runs and 111 RBIs at Triple A in 1996. Walker could kill, bro, and we all knew it, but that was about the only thing we had in common, at least on paper. Walker and I were from different places, different countries, different backgrounds. He went to college and was drafted. I signed out of high school in the Dominican. But we both had trouble with the way things went with the Twins, which was probably good in some ways.

At least I know I wasn't the problem.

Like I said, we didn't have much power when I got to the Twins, but Walker was our best hitter. He didn't hit for a lot of power—he hit, like, 11 or 12 home runs, I think—but he hit a lot of doubles (41) and stole some bases, hit for a high average. On that team, we needed any offense we could get. Walker was twenty-five that year, I think, and he hit .316 with a bunch of steals (19), too. He had a damned good year. He made the club again in the spring of 1999—while I went to the minors—and he batted .279, which was still pretty good. He didn't hit as many home runs (6) or knock in as many runs (46), but he still stole bases (18) and hit for average. He was twenty-six, bro. The league was making adjustments on him and he was learning how to make adjustments back. That's all part of the process. Sometimes you have to take a little step back to go forward again.

The next year, in 2000, Walker got off to a slow start. He hit only .243 in April and he wasn't hitting for much power, but that's the way the game goes. It's a long season. You're going to have streaks and slumps, especially when you're young, because you're still learning how to deal with it all. I was with the team then and we played a series against the Seattle Mariners (my old organization) in early May when Walker got called into the manager's office and they told him he was going back to Triple A. Walker was mad as hell. We all were. The dude hit .316 and .279 in his first two full seasons in the big leagues, and now he was going to Triple A because he had a bad month? He didn't understand it. None of us did. We thought it was bullshit.

Let me tell you something about those guys on the Twins: Those guys were all my boys. They were good dudes, bro. Walker, Torii Hunter, Brad Radke, A. J. Pierzynski, and Jacque Jones—we all grew up together. Corey Koskie. Cristian Guzman. I don't know where to stop. We were like a family. We liked playing together and we liked being with each other, and we had a lot of fun, even when we lost. We would have won in the big leagues, too, but we didn't have enough time to play together. Little by little, they started getting rid of us— me, Walker—because they thought we couldn't play. Last year, there weren't many guys left. I think Torii and Radke were the only ones.

Looking back, we should have known when Walker got sent down that maybe we were in the wrong place. I mean, bro, he could *hit*. He still can. When you have a player like that, who proved he could hit in the big leagues over two years, why would you send him down after a bad month? Why would you do that? Is that how you're going to build a guy's confidence? Is that how he's going to believe in himself? I don't understand it, bro. I don't understand what they did to him. I don't understand what they did to me during the spring of 1998.

Sometimes, I still get mad about it.

———

MY POP KNEW I WAS HAVING TROUBLE. I WAS TALKING TO HIM A lot on the phone and he could tell that I was down. My mom knew, too. I was having a bad spring. The manager was riding my ass. And like I've said before, my pop always knew when I needed a little pep talk just by the sound of my voice or by the way I talked.

It's a good thing he came, even if I didn't know he was going to be there.

By the end of that spring, I think I was talking to my pop on the phone almost every night. I was down, bro. I didn't know what to do. A couple of days before the Twins sent me back to Triple A, my pop called me and said, "Stay there, I'll be there in a couple of hours." I was confused. I said to him, "Where are you, Pop?" He told me he was at the Miami airport. He already had flown over from the Dominican and he was going to drive to Fort Myers because he wanted to see me and talk to me. He must have known it was serious, that I needed his help. He was always good at reading me.

For a couple of days, my pop stayed with me in Fort Myers. I had this condo on the south end of town, near Summerlin Road, one of the major streets down there. We were getting near the end of camp and that was always a tough time, especially for a team like the Twins. There were a lot of young guys there. It wasn't like playing in Boston, where you know who the starters are going to be and where guys have signed long-term contracts. We all felt like we had to make the team, and I guess that's the way the Twins wanted it. They liked it that way. They didn't want us to get too comfortable, to get too lazy and go through the motions. But if you ask me, I think it had the opposite effect. I think we all tried too hard.

I think we put pressure on ourselves. And I think they destroyed our confidence.

At least, that's what I think it did to me.

A couple of days after my pop arrived, I got called into TK's office and the Twins told me I was going back to Triple A, that they were giving the first baseman's job to Doug Mientkiewicz. I was devastated. I was pissed off, upset, you name it. I didn't know what to think, where to go, what to say. The Twins told me I could have a couple of days to get my things together before I reported to the team, but I was so bullshit that I wanted to tell them to go to hell. I didn't want to report at all. I wanted to quit. I thought I belonged in the big leagues and I couldn't believe they were sending me back.

When I walked out of the clubhouse that morning, my pop was there waiting for me. He knew I was pissed. He took me by the arm and he said, "Hey, let's go have breakfast," and we went to this diner not far from my condo on Summerlin. He let me yell for a while, and then he started cracking jokes. Ten minutes after we sat down, my pop had me laughing.

That's what your parents do for you, bro. They keep you balanced. They give you support. My mom and pop were always good like that, even after they got divorced. They always cared about their kids.

I've been in the big leagues for a while now, but let me tell you something: That day in spring training was one of the worst of my career. When you're that young, you always think the worst. You overreact to almost everything. I thought my career was over, bro. I thought I was never going to make it back to Minnesota, that the Twins didn't like me, and that they didn't want me there. I was sure of it. And then my pop started talking, started explaining things to me, and after we had a few laughs, I started listening to him.

Know what my pop told me that day? That life is not all flowers and roses. That there were bumps in the road. That it was easy to get knocked down but it was hard to get up. He started going over all of the things that had happened in my life, all of the successes I had after the Marlins sent me home from one of their camps because I had a sore arm. I was sixteen then. He told me that being sent back to the minors was going to make me a better player and a better person, tougher and stronger. He told me it was one of the things I had to go through, that sometimes I had to take a little step back to take a bigger step forward.

I was twenty-three, bro.

My career hadn't really even started yet.

And I was going to quit?

The next day, I was still in bed when my pop knocked on my bedroom door. He wasn't going to let me cry about it. He stuck his head in the room and told me, plain and simple: "Time to go to work." I got my shit together and went to the ballpark, and I think the Twins were surprised I showed up. I think they thought I would take couple of days, get my head together, then come back. I didn't waste any time. As soon as I got to minor-league camp, I remember hitting three home runs in a game against the Cincinnati Reds—one to left field, one to center, one to right. My pop was there to watch. My pop always taught me to hit to all fields, and that's something I'm still good at now. He taught me to do everything. After camp, I spent almost the whole year in Triple A and hit .315 with 30 homers and 110 RBIs, my best year in the minors. I was killin' again. The Twins called me up in September—I should have been there earlier—and I really didn't play too much. I don't think I had a hit in twenty at-bats, but I wasn't too upset. I did what I had to do to get back there.

After that year, I never really went back to the minors

again. But when I look back now and think about what I could have done, how lucky was I? I was pissed off the Twins were sending me back. I was convinced they didn't like me. I was ready to quit and walk away from baseball—for good— and the only thing that stopped me was that my pop was there to calm me down, to talk to me, to straighten me out. My main man gave me good advice. But what if my pop wasn't there? What if I had walked out? What happens to someone who doesn't have parents like that, who care for their kids, who really talk to them and straighten them out and point them in the right direction?

I was lucky, bro.

Like I've said a million times, my main man took care of me.

I PLAYED THREE MORE YEARS IN MINNESOTA, BUT THINGS NEVER really went right there. There were a lot of reasons. I made the team in 2000 and spent the whole year in the big leagues, and I finished with a .282 average, 10 homers, and 63 RBIs in 415 at-bats. They weren't great numbers, but they weren't bad, either. It was a start.

By that time, the Twins had decided that I was going to be a designated hitter, which pissed me off a little, too. Mientkiewicz spent almost the whole year in Triple A—he didn't really hit in the big leagues in 1999 the year before— but we played Ron Coomer at first and Koskie at third. That didn't leave much room for me. I got my share of at-bats, but I didn't play all the time and I sometimes sat against lefties. There were times it got frustrating. A lot of players get reputations sometimes, and once you get one, it's hard to get rid of it. With me, they said I couldn't play defense and that I couldn't hit lefties. So I had to get my playing time as a DH, which was better than sitting on the bench. But sometimes you wonder how you're ever supposed to get better at something if they never let you do it.

Seriously, bro. How was I going to become a better fielder if I never played the position? And how was I supposed to get better at hitting left-handers if I only played against righties? It's tough, dude. Baseball is a long season. If you take a little time off, it's like starting all over again. I don't think I played thirty games at first base in 2000, and that's a hard way to get better. Then the manager puts you in the game and you haven't played there in two weeks, and you're supposed to make plays like you've been there all year? Hitting is the same way. If you face righties all the time, that's what you're used to seeing. Then you face a lefty and he makes you look bad, and everybody says that you can't hit lefties.

See what I mean?

How can you prove them wrong if you never really get the chance?

By the 2001 season, I barely played first base at all. But at least I was getting to hit—and I got off to a good start. I homered against Detroit on Opening Day and I hit another a few days later, and a little more than a week into the season I was batting almost .400 with 3 homers and 10 or 11 RBIs. I was killin'. I didn't expect to keep up that pace, but nobody does. I was happy to be swinging the bat again and happy to be hitting for power. I finished the month batting .309 with 5 home runs and 16 RBIs, pretty good numbers for a guy who was still just twenty-five.

A few days later, we were in Kansas City playing against the Royals and I was having a pretty good day. I singled in my first two at-bats, and I was standing on second base with the bases loaded in the fourth inning. Jacque Jones came up and singled to right field, and because there were two outs, the third-base coach waved me home. Jermaine Dye was playing right field for the Royals at the time, and he has a good arm, and the ball beat me to the plate. I slid and tried to get my left hand in behind the catcher [Hector Ortiz] to avoid the tag, but I was out at the plate. And I guess I was paying so much attention to getting my left hand on the plate that I didn't notice I had put my right hand on the ground, under all of my weight. Remember: I'm a big dude, bro. And my right wrist couldn't support the weight.

My wrist broke.

At the time, I wasn't sure what happened. I just knew my wrist hurt. I used to tape my wrist before most games—it was the same hand I had surgery on in 1998—and I started to feel pain in my wrist. The tape got tight. My wrist started to swell up and it started to hurt, but I didn't say anything because I didn't think too much of it. We had another rally in the next inning against Kansas City's starting pitcher, a right-hander named Brian Meadows, and Matt Lawton was on third with one out when I stepped into the on-deck circle. Koskie was hitting in front of me at the time, and I started to take my practice swings when he got in the batter's box. And when I started to swing the bat, just practicing, my wrist hurt so much that I couldn't do it. I couldn't swing. Koskie's in the box and we're about to score—and I'm 2 for 2—and all I can think to myself is: "What the fuck?"

Koskie ended up striking out.

Two outs.

My turn to hit.

At the time, if I knew my wrist was broken, I wouldn't have hit. It wouldn't have made much sense. But again, we were a young team and we were all trying to prove ourselves, and we were never the kind of team to score a lot of runs. In the week leading up to that game, I didn't have any RBIs. Not one. Now we had a man on third, with two outs, and my chance to knock in the run was coming up. You think I was going to pass that up? No way, bro. No chance. I got in the box against Meadows and my adrenaline started pumping, and all of a sudden I felt like I could swing the bat. Meadows threw me a pitch that I could handle and I got my bat through the zone, and by now you can guess what happened.

I homered, bro.

I hit one way the hell out of there.

When I was jogging around the bases, my wrist started to hurt again. It hurt like hell. I was in so much pain that I couldn't even high-five the third-base coach when I went by, so I gave him my left hand instead. I got back to the dugout and people started asking me what happened, and I told them that I hurt my wrist when I slid into the plate. TK pulled me out of the game and they replaced me with Brian Buchanan, and they sent me to the hospital for an X-ray, MRI, all of that bullshit. I remember sitting in the car on the way over there and thinking, "Please, God, don't let this be anything big." I was worried that I'd done something bad.

After I'd been there awhile, the doctor came over and told me my wrist was broken. For the second time in my career, I needed surgery. The doctor asked me how I hit that homer with my wrist in so much pain, and I told him I wasn't sure. I just went up there to hit, bro. I started to concentrate on something else. But after I hit the homer, my wrist hurt more than it did before.

When I had the surgery, the doctors inserted a pin in my wrist. The pin is still there. I still can't move my right wrist as much as my left, and I never really got right again that year. I missed almost three months of the 2001 season—I didn't come back until July, after the All-Star break—but I hit only .207 the rest of the way. I hit some homers and finished with 18, almost double what I had the year before, and I hit them in only 303 at-bats. But my average for the year was only .234 and I struck out a lot, and I just couldn't get the bat through the zone. It took me almost a year before I started to feel right again.

Until that point, I had never really been injured much. I had the sore elbow when I was a kid and I broke my hamate bone in 1998, but this was the first time I really had to deal with something major like that. A lot of times, with injuries, the doctors or the team will tell you that you'll be six to eight weeks, two months, whatever. Then you can come back and play again. But the time you miss means that you basically have to start the year all over again, and it takes awhile before you start to get all of your strength back. I don't care who you are. I don't care what the injury is. It takes awhile for your body to feel healthy again.

And for me, when it did, I had other things to worry about.

IN MINNESOTA, WE ALWAYS FELT LIKE WE HAD TALENT. WE JUST FELT like we needed the chance to learn the game, to get better. That happened for all of us in the summer of 2002.

Let me start by telling you this: Until people explained it to me, I didn't know what "contraction" was. There was a lot of talk about it, about what contraction was, that baseball could eliminate teams that were struggling financially, but it never happened. I don't know how much of it was bullshit. I had a lot of other things to worry about over the winter because of my mom and her car accident, so I didn't spend too much time thinking about what might happen to the Twins. If I didn't play for the Twins, I'd play for someone else. We all would. That's just the way I felt.

But if someone was going to tell us that our team wasn't good enough to make it in the big leagues, then we felt we had to prove to them that we could. Are you kidding? When you get into a competitive situation, you try to motivate yourself any way you can.

By the time I got to spring training, a lot of things were different. For a lot of reasons, I decided to go to camp early to be with some of the guys and to spend some time with Tiff. She and I weren't married yet, but we were planning to get married soon. Jessica was already five years old and Alexandra was almost one, and we spent part of the time apart during the off-season while I went home, played winter ball, and did all of that. Tiff liked to stay home in Wisconsin, to be closer to her family. We did that routine a lot, even after I started playing for the Red Sox, until we decided to buy a place in Boston. That made more sense then. We knew we were going to be in Boston for a little while and the kids could stay in school there, and we still had our place in the Dominican.

But back then, when it came time to go to spring training, it didn't hurt to go early. The weather was better than in Wisconsin. We could all be together. And I could start getting ready for the season.

I didn't play great in winter ball, but like I said, I had a lot of other things to worry about. I was thinking about my mom a lot. I played in about thirty games and batted .255 with 3 homers and 18 RBIs, but none of that seemed too important at the time. Part of the reason I left the Dominican early is because I wanted to be with Tiff and the kids, and part was because I just needed to get away from the Dominican, to forget about how my mom died, to try to get back into my routine. It was hard, bro. We weren't scheduled to start spring training until the end of February, but I knew some of the guys were going in early, to start working out at the complex. So I decided to go in and be with them, to get my shit together, to start focusing on the season.

That was a big help.

At the time, we had a great group of guys with the Twins. We were all like brothers. Doug Mientkiewicz and Brian Buchanan were there—I used to call Buchanan "Buck Wild"— and they helped me right away, just by being there. The reporters who covered the team came up to me and asked about the winter, about my mom and about being around the guys and I remember telling them that my teammates were like my family. They gave me strength, bro. Along with Tiff, they helped me get by. We had a lot of young players on the Twins and a lot of us came through the minor leagues together, so it meant something to be at the big leagues together. We struggled together. We made it together. We played jokes on each other and helped each other, and that was the best part of being there.

"As soon he walked in, he opened up his big mouth," Buck Wild told one of the reporters who asked him how I was doing after my mom's death. "He's got a great personality and gets along with everyone. He's a great teammate to have."

Know what else that dude said?

"I think of him like he's my brother. When he's not going good, I worry about him. When he's going good . . . I worry about him more."

I felt that way about those guys, too.

We all pulled for each other.

Let me tell you something else: The baseball season is long. Chemistry is very important. You have to like the guys you play with—you have to respect them, too—because you see each other more than you see your families sometimes. That's why it can be so hard to win. With the Twins, there were a lot of reasons we started winning in my last couple of years there, but I really believe that chemistry was one of them. We all got along. We had fun. We played jokes on each other and nobody took it personally, and that's the best way to deal with the failure. You laugh, bro. Everybody is going to lose games at some point. The best teams are the ones that can deal with it.

With the Twins, we had a good time and always acted the same, whether we were winning or losing. Our expectations changed a little as we got older, but we tried to act the same way. Corey Koskie was one of my teammates there, and his locker was right next to mine, and Koskie used to play jokes on everybody all the time. He played them on me. I remember one time, when I was in the shower, he put peanut butter in my underwear. Can you believe that shit?

I don't know why, but I didn't even notice until I put on my clothes. I had to go right back in the shower again. I told Corey I was going to kill him, his family, and his dog, but he couldn't stop laughing, bro. He was the type of guy who, if you messed with him, he'd get you back worse.

With all of my teammates, that's the way it was. They used to make fun of my clothes. They used to make fun of the way I walked. I came to the ballpark wearing this good-looking suit one time—you should have seen it, I was killin'—and Corey put it on when I wasn't there. He walked into the wives' room wearing that suit and they all started laughing because he looked ridiculous.

But it's like I told him: It's not my fault if the clothes don't look good on *you*.

On the field, a lot of things were changing. We won 85 games the year before and we had a bad second half, and we felt we were all a year better, a year older. TK wasn't managing anymore—he had decided to give it up—and that didn't bother me because I always thought he didn't like me very much. I think a lot of guys felt that way. The new manager was Ron Gardenhire, who used to be our third-base coach and who had been with the organization for a long time. That's how the Twins did things. Minnesota wasn't like a lot of other places where they changed managers all the time. And when they did, they usually hired someone from the inside, a coach who had been there and who knew the people, who put in his time and waited for his chance. That was Gardy.

When camp started for real, everybody told me they were sorry to hear about my mom. Gardy told me that, too. In a lot of ways, I felt like the 2002 season was going to be a new beginning for me, a chance to play every day again after missing so much time in 2001. My wrist felt better. I felt like I was back to normal. And even though my mom was gone, we had a new manager and we thought we could start winning some games because we were starting to get older and we were starting to get experience.

In 2001, even though we missed the playoffs again, we had a good year. We went 85–77 and it was our first winning season since 1992, before all of us got there. We had one of the best records in baseball in the first half of the season, then played really bad in the final month or two. My injury didn't help. We didn't have a lot of power, so we had to play a style with pitching and defense, but even that wasn't enough. In baseball, you need to do a little bit of everything to win because the season is long. If you don't pitch, you need to hit. If you don't hit, you need to pitch. There aren't that many times during the season where you're doing everything right, but the good teams pick each other up.

In 2001, for the first half, that's what we did.

In the second half, that stopped.

In 2002, we got off to a pretty good start again. We went 16–11 in April, but I wasn't around at the end of the month because I got hurt again. Can you believe that shit? My left knee started bothering me and it was affecting my ability at the plate, and somewhere in the middle of the month we decided that I should have surgery. It wasn't anything big; they just poked a few holes in my knee and cleaned me out. (I had bone chips.) But I had to miss time again and it was tough. I had, like, three home runs and seven RBIs in the first week of the season, but then my knee started getting worse. I couldn't play through it. So I had surgery and went on the disabled list, and Matt LeCroy became the full-time designated hitter while I was out. LeCroy and I were platooning to start the year—I played against righties and he played against lefties, which I wasn't happy about—but at least we were winning. Everything is always a little easier to take when you're winning.

When I had surgery, I didn't know how long I'd be out. I thought it would be for a while. But maybe a week or two after my surgery, the trainers told me that I could start working out again, that I could get my leg in shape and be playing soon. It was unbelievable, bro. I'd never had arthroscopic surgery, so I didn't know what it was about. But before I knew it, my knee started to feel better again. I thought it started to feel strong. I think I missed only about a month, but I still wasn't the same player when I came back.

Remember what I told you about my wrist? That took about a year, bro. The big injuries do. My knee wasn't that bad, but I still wasn't right when I came back. I didn't hit one homer in May. I didn't hit one in June, either. I didn't hit a homer for forty-three games, which is a long time for a dude like me. When I came back from hurting my wrist, I couldn't get the bat through the zone, but I hit some homers at the end of the season. This was different. Our hitting coach at the time was a guy named Scott Ullger, and I remember him saying that hitting was like building a house. You needed to have a good foundation or you weren't going to build anything, and your foundation was your legs. For me, my left leg was the important one because that's where I put all my weight. That's where I built my foundation. It was going to take awhile for my knee to get back to normal, for me to feel right, for me to build my foundation again.

I just needed to get my legs back under me.

Just after the All-Star Game, I started hitting again. I started hitting like crazy. I hit one homer before the break and another one after, and then I hit six more in about a week. I was killin'. In July, I went 30 for 79—a .380 average—with 8 home runs, 7 doubles, and 20 RBIs. My on-base percentage was .462. My slugging percentage was .772. Those were the kinds of numbers I could put up in a short period of time, and those were like some of the numbers I started putting up for the Red Sox when I got the chance to play every day. My confidence was high, bro. I felt like I could hit anything.

When I finished my streak, I had hit in nineteen straight games from the end of July into early August. I had 8 homers and 18 RBIs. My average for the season was back up to .289 and I was starting to hit again like I did in the minors, and we were winning a lot of games. In July, the Twins went 19–7 and we took control of the American League Central. Nobody else was really even close to us after a while. We went 29–24 over the final two months of the season, playing a lot better than we did down the stretch in 2001. We were so far ahead that we clinched the division in the middle of September, which is pretty early in baseball. But that gave us a lot of time to get our shit together, to get rested and get our pitching ready for the playoffs.

As for me, I cooled off a little in September, but I still had an okay month. I batted .273 for the month and hit 4 homers, but I got 99 at-bats and was playing almost every day. Then I started splitting time again and my average started to drop in

September, and I finished the year hitting .272 with 20 home runs and 75 RBIs in 412 at-bats. Those weren't the numbers I put up in Boston, but they weren't that far off, either. People ask me sometimes what changed when I came to Boston, what made me such a good hitter, and I tell them two things: confidence and the chance to play every day. They go together, bro. You can't have one without the other.

Know what else I tell people? Do the math. Take the numbers I put up in 2002, and what would they be if I got 600 at-bats, like I do in Boston? I'll tell you what they'd be: 29 homers and 109 RBIs, which is a pretty good for anybody. I was still twenty-six. I was still learning. I was still figuring it all out.

I should tell you one other thing: Late in September of 2002, after we clinched the division, we played a game against the Cleveland Indians at our home field, the Metrodome. The Indians went ahead on a home run by Ellis Burks in the top of the ninth inning, 5–4, and we tied the game in the bottom half. So we had to play extra innings and the game was tied at five when we went into the bottom of the twelfth, and I came up with one on and one out against some dude named David Maurer.

Know what I did, bro?

I homered.

I hit one out and we won the game, 7–5.

I didn't know it at the time, but I'd just hit the first walk-off home run of my career.

I couldn't have known there would be so many more.

WE DIDN'T WIN THE CHAMPIONSHIP WITH THE TWINS IN 2002, BUT we had a good run. We played the Oakland A's in the first round of the playoffs and we came back to win the first game, 7–5. We were down early, 3–0 and 5–1, and we came back and won on big homers by Koskie and Mientkiewicz. The A's won the next two games—Game 2 and Game 3—and I didn't do much in the series to that point. I didn't play in the second game because the A's started a left-hander, Mark Mulder, so Gardy put LeCroy in the lineup. We went into Game 4 knowing we had to win or it was over.

In Game 4, we faced Oakland's ace, Tim Hudson, and we beat him again, just like we did in Game 1. I had a double and an RBI in the second inning, when we scored seven runs and took control of the game. Not many people gave us much of a chance in Game 5—we had to go back to Oakland for that one—but we scored three runs in the ninth to take a 5–1 lead and held on for a 5–4 win. I had a double and an RBI in that rally, too, and it meant that we were going back to Minnesota to play in the American League Championship Series.

Can you believe that?

One minute, it seemed like people in baseball were talking about eliminating the Twins, about *contraction*. The next, we're playing for the league title.

When we beat the Anaheim Angels in Game 1, everybody finally started to take us seriously. But then the Angels started to hit and we just couldn't stop them, and there was nothing we could really do. The Angels were hot, bro. They got into the playoffs as the wild card team behind Oakland, but they won 99 games that year. They were a good team. The Angels beat us in the next four games—6–3, 2–1, 7–1, and 13–5—and they got 45 hits, including 8 homers. They were killin'. I had a pretty good series, going 5 for 16, a .313 average, with one double. But the Angels were so hot that nobody could get them out. Before beating us, Anaheim beat the Yankees and scored thirty-one runs in four games; after beating us, they hit .310 against the San Francisco Giants and won the World Series.

Me? I felt like things were really starting to come together.

I had the best year of my career, a season I dedicated to my mother. My twenty-seventh birthday was still about a month away. I was starting to make good money playing in the big leagues and I was starting to build my confidence, and I was playing for a team that went to the American League Championship Series.

I really thought that things were looking up.

ABOUT TWO MONTHS LATER, MY CAREER IN MINNESOTA ENDED. THE Twins released me. My year ended bad and started worse. I lost my mom. I lost my job. And even though I had a lot of fun in Minnesota—I still miss all the boys I played with—I left the organization with a bad taste in my mouth, with a lot of bad feelings.

Looking back, the years in Minnesota made me stronger, right to the end. It was just like my father told me that year in spring training. It was just like my mom told me all the time. You are going to go through some things in life, no matter who you are, and some of my hardest lessons came in 2002. Dudes like me play baseball for a living and it's important to us, but it's important to remember the other things, too. What we do is a game. The really important things are your family, your parents and your kids, what they teach you and what you teach them. My parents taught me a lot. They taught me to be patient and to fight, and they taught me how to deal with the hard times. My mom and pop were both good at that. My pop still is.

Since the end of that year, I made myself some promises. I told myself I was never going to take my family for granted again and I told myself I would never take the other things too seriously. If I did my best, I knew that would be good enough. I knew I was capable of great things. I knew that I could succeed. And I knew that I owed a lot to my mom and my pop because they were always there for me, no matter what, especially when things were going bad and even after my mom died.

Sometimes, when I think about it, it's really unbelievable, bro.

I mean, my mom's been gone for a little while now.

But in a lot of ways, it's like she's still here.

It's like she's still teaching me things.

It's like I can still hear her voice.

STEPPING OUT OF THE BOX:
TORII HUNTER

In baseball, as in life, friendships often are forged in the early years.

David Ortiz and Torii Hunter first met in the Instructional League during the fall of 1996, shortly after Ortiz was identified as the player to be named in a July trade that sent Minnesota third baseman Dave Hollins to the Seattle Mariners. Hunter had been the property of the Minnesota Twins for more than three years by that point, the result of being selected as the twentieth overall selection in the first round of the 1993 amateur draft. A star athlete in four sports at Pine Bluff High School in Pine Bluff, Arkansas—a city of roughly 55,000 people that is approximately a thirty-minute drive from Little Rock— Hunter was the kind of athlete and prospect that baseball teams built their future around. Hunter played basketball, football, baseball, and track during high school. And he was part of a deep 1993 draft class that included, among others, future major-league players Alex Rodriguez, Trot Nixon, Billy Wagner, Derrek Lee, and Jason Varitek, the latter of whom was an All-American catcher at Georgia Tech University and whom the Twins also selected at number twenty-one, the pick immediately following the one with which they selected Hunter.

The point?

From the very beginning, Torii Hunter was a golden child, all but destined to play in the major leagues.

By late 1996, the then-twenty-one-year-old Hunter had reached New Britain, the Twins' Double-A affiliate in the Eastern League. Hunter had begun that season at Class A Fort Myers of the Florida State League and had been promoted slightly more than a month into the season, and he was participating in the Instructional League, where clubs frequently sent young players who were still developing. It was there that Hunter first encountered a big, left-handed-hitting slugger whom the Twins had just acquired by trade.

"Back then, he was David Arias," cracked Hunter, noting that Ortiz used his mother's original surname early in his career. "When we were in the Instructional League, I remember that he had a foot problem. I really didn't know him yet. But his feet kept getting blisters on them and we were all trying to figure out the problem—I mean *everybody*. I went to his locker and looked at his shoes. The guy's like six foot three or six foot four and he was wearing shoes that looked like they were for a midget. He was wearing a size 9. I said, 'Dude, your shoes are too small. You're a size 10 or 11 or 12.' He said, 'Hey, maybe you're right.' So we gave him bigger shoes and after that he was fine."

So began what may be one of the best and continuing friendships in baseball, with the proverbial mouse pulling a thorn from the foot of an elephant.

Now more than ever, of course, baseball is fertile ground for such friendships. By the middle of the 1990s, the game was opening up doors in all corners of the world. It was in 1995 that a Los Angeles Dodgers right-hander named Hideo Nomo went 13–6 with a 2.54 ERA and 236 strikeouts in 191⅓ innings, winning the National League Rookie of the Year Award ahead of an All-American third baseman for the Atlanta Braves, Larry "Chipper" Jones. Nomo came to the United States as a twenty-six-year-old after previously having played his entire professional career in Japan, and his ascension proved a harbinger. In subsequent years, as major-league baseball continued to expand and the need for talent grew, the search for major-league talent extended to new corners of the globe. By the early stages of the twenty-first century, it was not unusual to walk into a major-league clubhouse and encounter players from countries like Japan, Korea, Australia, and Canada. More than ever, America's national pastime was becoming a melting pot for all walks of life—provided that the players had one thing in common.

Baseball.

In the case of Hunter and Ortiz, there was so much more to share. Hunter was at Double A again in 1997 when Ortiz made a meteoric, one-year rise through the Minnesota system that took him from A ball to the major leagues in one season, and maybe it was only fitting that both players made their major-league debuts later that same year.

From 1997 through 2002, as they established their place in the major leagues, David Ortiz and Torii Hunter played at least part of every season together.

"Both of us kind of have the same personality, kind of like cracking jokes and keeping everybody laughing," Hunter said following a 2006 season in which he batted .278 with 31 home runs and 98 RBIs while winning his sixth consecutive American League Gold Glove Award in the outfield. "With David, he had that Spanglish that was hilarious. Just hearing him, the way he said things, he would crack you up. He had some great stories from back in the Dominican and just the way he explained it would crack you up.

"He grew on me and I grew on him," Hunter said.

He added, "If you hear something bad about David Ortiz, it's a lie."

FOR MOST MAJOR-LEAGUE PLAYERS, THE MINOR LEAGUES ARE A LABOR of love. Players fix their sights so squarely on the destination that many do not recognize the difficulties of the journey until well after the fact. They simply do not know any better. Even now, the large majority of minor-league players are paid, say, in the neighborhood of $2,000 to $3,000 per month, and that generally has been true regardless of where a player was signed or drafted. Only recently, following the 2006 season, did the major-league players union bargain for a minimum salary in excess of $30,000 annually for those minor-league players fortunate enough to be on an organization's select list of players known as the "forty-man" roster. Still, the indisputable reality is that most minor leaguers never make it to the forty-man.

Consequently, life in the minor leagues is perhaps best viewed as the ballplayer's answer to the college years, albeit without dining halls and political science. Baseball is the curriculum. Like college students, most players make relatively little money and frequently have to take on roommates (or, more specifically, teammates) to find affordable housing. And while there is always time for socializing—baseball players are reared to be nocturnal from a very young age—the demands of the schedule frequently require players to teach themselves discipline.

In an ideal world, after all, the minor leagues would be nothing more than a stepping-stone.

For *any* player.

"Now that I'm older, I enjoyed the experience," said Hunter, reflecting on his time in the minors. "You know how, when you leave high school, you feel like you want to go back? You kind of miss it, but you kind of don't. It was the same way. It was a hard experience, looking back, but at the same time, we didn't know any better. We had fun.

"We weren't making much money," Hunter continued. "Back then, we were making $950 or $1,000 a month, and we'd only get like $15 a day (in meal money), so you couldn't eat out. Me and David and Jacque Jones, we'd go to the grocery store and buy sandwich meat and put it on ice [in their apartment or hotel]. We'd make sandwiches and that's what we'd eat for the week.

"Chicken fried rice, Chinese food—that stuff was like a delicacy," Hunter cracked. "When we had extra money, we got chicken fried rice."

In some ways, from post to post, baseball has changed over the years; in others, it has not. While there are tremendous differences between life in the minor leagues and life in the majors, the game's skeletal system is unaltered. Whether in the small towns and cities that characterize the minor leagues or the major-league hubs from Boston to Minneapolis, the routine is remarkably familiar. For a night game, players arrive at the ballpark several hours before the scheduled first pitch. They might have a late lunch or take a nap, shower or get in the whirlpool. Maybe they will watch a video. Maybe they will play cards. Maybe they will analyze video of themselves or of the opposing team's starting pitcher. Maybe they will talk on the phone, play video games, or simply do nothing at all.

Whatever the routine, players typically adhere to it religiously, particularly if things are going well, sometimes if they are not. It all depends on their respective personalities. The clubhouse becomes their sanctuary—like a common area in a dorm—and players frequently congregate there to pass the time. It is during those hours that teammates needle one another, joke with one another, form the bonds that make them a team over the course of six to eight months during which there is a game virtually every day and there is almost no time off.

And then, roughly two and a half hours before the scheduled first pitch, the routine becomes more structured. Players are on the field, in uniform, stretching together and preparing for the game ahead. They take batting and fielding practice for slightly more than an hour, then return to the clubhouse again. They pass the time for another forty-five minutes to an hour, then return to the dugout or field. Some like to sit and wait. Others like to jog and stretch. Some sign autographs. The scheduled starting time is now rapidly approaching and there is the proverbial calm before the storm.

And then the game starts.

After the game? That routine, too, is generally familiar. Players shower, get dressed, speak with the media, and depart. Some go home, others go out, others work or linger. Some do a combination of them. Food is provided before and after games in buffet-style serving pans—players typically call this "the spread"—and many players will have something to eat. Each year, players contribute "dues" to ensure that food is always available, and the money usually is collected by a clubhouse or equipment manager, occasionally a player. (The teams do not provide this.) The one seeming constant is that no one is quite ready to sleep because they all need time to unwind, decompress, and relax before beginning the same routine again.

So, almost to a man, players go to bed late and wake up late, then follow the same general routine, even if the particulars frequently vary.

And that is true in the minor leagues as much as it is in the major leagues.

"In the major leagues, you eat steak, lobster, mashed potatoes," a chuckling Hunter said when asked about the differences between the majors and minors. "But the game spread in the minor leagues, it was Chinese food."

In the minor leagues, for whatever reason, a funny thing happens: Players can grow close to one another. For all of the competition that can exist between teammates in the minor leagues—after all, they are all trying to make it to the major leagues—a common bond overrides all others: the struggle to get there. Players arrive in the minor leagues from all corners of the United States—and, of course, beyond—and there are free-agent signees (like Ortiz) and draft picks (like Hunter), from all walks of life. Still, not a single one of them is guaranteed *anything,* though the players feel (and believe) that there are wrinkles in the system that afford some players more opportunity than others.

As a first-round pick, Hunter is one of the players who benefited from those inequities, though he is nonetheless critical of them. He believes that his place as the twentieth overall selection in the draft earned him more patience from the organization, more attention from his coaches. He believes that someone like Ortiz received far less nurturing than he did, though he recognizes, too, that such behavior will never change.

"As a first-rounder, they kind of stay on you and pamper

you and pump you up," Hunter said. "With David, they didn't do that. They stick with the guys who have all the potential."

Added Hunter: "David Ortiz was the Chrysler [in the minor leagues]. There was not much respect for this guy, but he proved to everybody [later] that he was a Mercedes."

Despite all of that, despite all of the elements that could drive players apart, teammates frequently found ways to unite. Hunter recalls spending as many as thirteen hours on a bus, round trip, and playing a game the same day. "It was tough," he said. That reality only highlights another great difference between the minor leagues and major leagues. For all of the luxuries that major leaguers typically are afforded—spacious seating on flights and individual hotel rooms, among them—minor-league players often have countless hours to talk, to truly get to know one another, to feel as much joy for a friend who makes it to the major leagues as they might for themselves.

The failures hurt just as much, too.

"Guys didn't get traded—they got released," Hunter said. "That was a tough thing. You were with those guys for seven or eight months [a year]."

And then they'd be gone, often never to be heard from again.

UNTIL DECEMBER 2002, WHEN THE MINNESOTA TWINS EFFECTIVELY released David Ortiz from the major-league team, Hunter and Ortiz remained together. By the time Ortiz departed, their friendship had grown so strong that his departure had no effect on it. Hunter still remembers being in the minor leagues, living next door to Ortiz in adjoining rooms at a Hawthorne Inn in 1997, and seeing Ortiz emerge as a team leader and unifying force.

"It started in the minor leagues," Hunter said. "David likes to cook. Tiffany"—who was then Ortiz's girlfriend—"would fly into town and he'd have a cookout, but he wouldn't invite just me and Jacque. He'd invite everyone. He'd buy the meat and the vegetables and everything, and he'd pay for it all. In the minor leagues, it was tough because you didn't have the money. But he'd always have these [events] to keep everybody together. That's what I remember about David Ortiz. He was our leader. I respected that. That's when I realized he's great, he's cool, he's a people person."

For Ortiz, that approach continued into the major leagues, where he was similarly regarded as a clubhouse leader on a Minnesota team that was maturing and improving together. Ortiz and Hunter were just two of the personalities who colored the struggling Twins through their difficult, transitional, teenage years. The Twins were growing. They were learning. In that way, under the hand of a demanding, veteran manager, Tom Kelly, they were very much like a minor-league team, a collection of players trying to establish their place in the major leagues and hoping to make a name for themselves.

To cope, the Twins did what most teams do: They tried to laugh as hard as they played. The Minnesota clubhouse, dominated by youth, became a haven for practical jokes and pranks. At the center of it were Ortiz, Hunter, and Koskie, the latter of whom made Ortiz his personal and favorite target.

For Ortiz, the chances to get back at Koskie were plentiful. As a designated hitter, Ortiz spent his time between at-bats on the bench or in the clubhouse while his teammates were on the field. His behavior frequently went unnoticed. According to Hunter, the Twins would be on the field, lined up behind their pitcher or struggling through a long inning, and Ortiz would be in the clubhouse, wreaking havoc on their clothes and belongings. The behavior continued even after Ortiz left the Twins, when the Red Sox would travel to Minneapolis and the Twins would take their positions in the field at the Metrodome, a landscape Ortiz knew all too well.

And so Ortiz would sneak out the back of the visiting clubhouse and down a hallway that led him to the sanctuary of the Twins, where he would continue his menacing antics. In 2003, while Koskie was on the field, he once put juice and peanut butter—"Anything he could find," said Hunter—into the only pair of shoes that Koskie had brought to the game.

With the Twins, everything was fair game.

"He used to get our socks and cut the toes off," Hunter said. "Because he was the DH, he had too much time on his hands. We'd put on our socks and our feet would go through, and we'd be, like, 'Hey, what happened?'"

"Once, he put Koskie's clothes in the freezer," Hunter laughed, recalling a time when Ortiz still played with Minnesota. "When Koskie came back, his clothes were frozen stiff."

In the spring of 2003, Ortiz's first season with the Red Sox, his bonds with Minnesota were still strong. Ortiz knew his Twins teammates better than his Red Sox mates when the season began, and the Twins still were showing an unwillingness to accept Ortiz's departure at all. Because they both trained in Fort Myers, Florida, the Red Sox and Twins could face one another as many as six or eight times in an approximate thirty-game spring schedule, a comfort that was both a luxury and a curse. Because the teams were so close, after all, it made more sense to play one another than it did to make seemingly endless drives on the long, flat highways of Florida. But by the end of spring, when the routine had long grown wearisome, the thought of another game between the Red Sox and Twins became an unbearable thought for all involved parties.

Early in the spring of 2003, the teams had not yet reached that point when the Red Sox traveled to Hammond Stadium for the first time. Ortiz was among those Red Sox players who made the trip and who was expected to play against the Twins, and his former teammates took note. Ortiz remained in the lineup for roughly half the game, then returned to his locker in the visiting clubhouse beneath the first-base grandstands to find that his clothes had been stolen.

In their place hung a bright orange jumpsuit, the assigned attire for work-release prisoners at the county jail.

"That was me," recalled a laughing Hunter, taking credit for the prank. "He put it on and he walked out into the stadium, and the fans saw him. It was hilarious. He was signing autographs and he was cracking up. He was good with it. He had fun with it."

The Twins always did.

WITH YOUTH, OF COURSE, COMES IDEALISM. THE MOST COMMON misconception among young players is that they will remain together forever, that they will play forever, that they all eventually will succeed. The alternatives never really occur to them. Players can talk about retiring or being traded or being released, but reality never truly dawns until crystallization.

And then the dream shatters.

For Hunter, one of the hardest lessons came in December 2002, following Minnesota's first postseason appearance in eleven years and during a time of general optimism in the Twins organization. The teenagers had grown up and become men. They had won. And there was every reason to believe that Minnesota would continue to improve in coming years and that the Twins would be a factor, together, in major-league baseball.

That was when Minnesota general manager Terry Ryan

spoke with Ortiz and, later, Hunter and told each that the Twins had to choose between Ortiz and Matt LeCroy.

LeCroy was staying.

"That was tough for me, to see how he was released," Hunter said. "I thought he was the best hitter on our team. I called Terry Ryan and I said, 'Hey, what's going on?' I told him David Ortiz was our best hitter and he said, 'No, Matt Lecroy is our best hitter.' "

Added Hunter: "I never would have released a guy like that."

By that point, Hunter was familiar with Ortiz's struggles in the Minnesota organization, with the strained relationship between Ortiz and manager Tom Kelly, with his injuries and frustration over an assortment of matters. Like Ortiz, Hunter had failed to hit with the expected power during the earliest parts of his career. Like Ortiz, he was being advised to hit the ball to the opposite field, to forgo his natural strengths, to take something that had come so naturally to him—baseball and, in particular, hitting—and making it forced, methodical, mechanical.

Like Ortiz, too, Hunter eventually rebelled and began doing things his way, launching a career that made him one of the most complete and multitalented players in baseball.

"At the time, with Tom Kelly being the manager, his philosophy was to shoot the ball the other way with a compact swing," Hunter said. "David had a big swing, as you know, but Tom Kelly hated that. David was the only guy in our lineup who had that kind of [raw] power. It kind of limited his game. His game was to swing hard and go deep, which is what he does now.

"In 2001, I told myself, 'Forget that—I'm done with the Twins' way of hitting the ball,' " Hunter said. "I just used my God-given ability. That's what David needed to do and that's what Boston gave him. They let him use his God-given ability, and look what's happened now. Jimmie Foxx's record is broken."

By "now," Hunter was referring to the final days of the 2006 season, when Ortiz broke the Red Sox record for home runs in a single season, eclipsing the mark of fifty formerly held by Hall of Fame slugger Jimmie Foxx. It was a record that had stood since 1938. The Red Sox were known for a long line of accomplished hitters during their history, from Ted Williams to Carl Yastrzemski to Jim Rice. Williams remains the last player in history to hit .400 or better in a season (.406 in 1941); Yastrzemski remains the last major-league player to win the Triple Crown, leading his league in batting average, home runs, and RBIs during the same season (1967); Rice remains the last Red Sox player to eclipse 400 total bases in a season, something he accomplished during the 1978 season (406 total bases) during which he won the American League Most Valuable Player Award.

Yet none of them ever accomplished what Ortiz did on the nights of September 20 and 21, 2006, when he went 5 for 6 over a pair of games with home runs number 50, 51, and 52 against a Minnesota Twins team that had none other than Torii Hunter playing center field.

"If you looked at me out there, I was clapping," Hunter said.

Today, roughly once a year during the off-season, Ortiz and Hunter are among a group of players that try to meet in Las Vegas for a charity poker tournament sponsored by Hunter. Most of the celebrity attendees, like relief pitcher Eddie Guardado, have been members of the Twins organization at one point or another. And during the baseball season, though their paths rarely cross, Ortiz and Hunter remain in frequent contact during an age when friends playing thousands of miles of apart can keep tabs on one another, thanks to cell phones, text messaging, e-mail, and all-sports cable television networks that show highlights twenty-four hours a day.

"We talk all the time," Hunter said. "He might see me have a good game or hit a home run, and he might see me strike out. He'll call up and leave me a voice mail like, 'Hey, good game,' or 'You know what? You suck.' "

After all, what are friends for?

HELLO,
BOSTON

After the 2002 season ended, I knew there was a chance I was not going back to Minnesota. I wanted to stay with the Twins because all my boys were there, but I was eligible for arbitration and my salary was going up. When that happens, when you play for a small-market team like the Twins, you always know there is a chance you aren't coming back.

But I never thought it would happen the way it did.

I was *released.*

Seriously, bro. I thought I might get traded or something, but I never thought about getting released. It just didn't seem like the kind of thing that could happen. I was coming off a pretty good year and I was young, and I thought there would be some team out there that would want to trade for a big dude like me. If Minnesota couldn't keep me, couldn't pay me, I thought there would be another team who would. I thought maybe they would send the Twins a prospect or something, and that maybe that's how it would work. But I still thought the best chance was that I would go back to Minnesota, back with Torii Hunter and Corey Koskie and all of the dudes that I played with in the minors.

But this game—it's crazy sometimes, bro. It doesn't make a lot of sense. Maybe a team wants to trade for you, but maybe they don't want to give anything up. Trades can get complicated. With me, I guess the reason I didn't get traded is because the other teams all knew that Minnesota might have to release me, so why would they trade something when they can get you for nothing? I didn't understand it at the time, but I think that's how it worked. So a guy like me, who is still trying to get the chance to play every day, ends up getting released instead of traded. And once that happens, teams don't have to pay you much because they know you're looking for a job.

Still, I knew there was the chance. After the season ended, the Twins called my agents—Fernando Cuza and Diego Bentz—and told them there was a possibility they would have to do something. Then the middle of December came and Minnesota's assistant general manager, Bill Smith, told Diego to be ready for the chance that I could be released. My agents called me after that and gave me the news, and then I heard from Terry Ryan, the Twins general manager. What are you supposed to say to a call like that, bro? Like I've said a million times, I felt like the Twins never really gave me the chance. I don't feel like they ever helped my confidence. I had some injuries there, too—a lot of things went wrong—and the way it ended, it didn't leave me with a good feeling.

In some ways, I was happy to leave Minnesota.

Not long after that, I was out to dinner at a restaurant in

the Dominican named Vesuvio when I ran into Pedro Martinez and his cousin, Franklin Paulino. You know most of this story already. I told Franklin that I'd been released from the Twins, so he brought me to the back of the restaurant, where Pedro was sitting. We started to talk. Pedro made a call to Jack McCormick, the Red Sox traveling secretary, and I think Jack called Theo Epstein. It didn't take too long for Epstein to call my agent, Fernando Cuza, and before I knew it we had a deal. The Red Sox were looking for a first baseman and they had some other guys in camp, but I was pretty sure I could do the job. I just wanted the chance. The Red Sox gave me a deal for $1.25 million and I signed. A month later I was back in Fort Myers, where I went to spring training with the Twins every year, but I was there with the Red Sox instead.

It was a little strange, bro.

Before I go on, let me tell you something about Pedro: He was the best. I've told people that Pedro has been like a father to me, and I mean it. He has a very good heart. He always tries to help people. He always built my confidence, helped me out, told me I could be a good player. I can never repay him for any of that. All I can try to do is the same for someone else. To the people in the Dominican, Pedro is a hero. When he got to the big leagues from Manoguayabo, everybody saw him as the younger brother of Ramon Martinez, who was pitching for the Los Angeles Dodgers at the time. By the time Pedro finished, he wasn't just Ramon's brother anymore. Ramon and Pedro both are two of the most respected and well-known people in the Dominican, but I know Pedro better than I know Ramon. I played with him. And I can never thank him enough for helping me out when I needed it.

What if Pedro hadn't made that phone call, bro?

What if I had signed somewhere else?

I think I still would have become a good player, but what

if someone didn't give me the chance? What if I didn't get the chance to play in Boston, where people are as crazy about baseball as they are in the Dominican?

Here's another thing about Pedro: He is a very generous person. I think I am, too. I think most people from the Dominican are, but they're just not in a position to help. Pedro has been pitching in the big leagues for fifteen years and he has won three Cy Young Awards, and he's made a lot of money along the way. But you know what? He never forgot where he came from. He never forgot the people of the Dominican. I know that Pedro once paid to build a church in Manoguayabo, that he has paid to help build roads and houses, even a school. He helped set an example for people like me and Vladimir Guerrero, who plays for the Los Angeles Angels. He set an example for everyone. I believe that Dominicans are some of the nicest people in the world, some of the most generous with some of the biggest hearts. We believe in helping each other and helping other people because that is what everyone should do.

I'll give you an example: In 2005, Vladi and I gave $50,000 each to help the Hurricane Katrina relief fund in New Orleans because we know the damage that a hurricane can do. In the Caribbean, in our country, storms like that happen all the time. I remember saying that America always seemed to help the Dominican Republic when we needed it, so Vladi and I felt like it was a way to give something back. We wanted to do it. In 2006, when I hit my fiftieth home run, I tied a Red Sox record held by Jimmie Foxx for most home runs in a season. Like I said before, we decided to auction off the home run ball for charity and, because I finished with fifty-four homers that year, we did the same with one or two of the other balls, too. We gave some of the money to the Boys and Girls Clubs of America and we gave some to the Plaza de la

Salud Hospital de Niños, the children's hospital in Santo Domingo where a friend of my pop's works. It was a good feeling, bro. It's something we were all proud of.

But like I said, in the Dominican, that's what we believe in.

We believe that we are all people first.

And when I needed help, I got it from Pedro.

Since that time, since I signed with Boston, I've had people ask me how many teams were interested in me. The truth is that I'm not really sure, but I know this: The Red Sox made the best offer and they were the most aggressive. A lot of people from New York have asked me why I didn't sign with the Yankees, and I've heard other people say that George Steinbrenner wanted the Yankees' general manager, Brian Cashman, to bring me to New York. I don't really know what happened between Steinbrenner and Cashman, but I never really came close to going to New York. Like I said, the Red Sox made the best offer. It was late in the off-season and we didn't have a lot of time, and the Yankees had Jason Giambi playing first base, anyway. Nick Johnson was still there, too. I wanted to go somewhere where I had the chance to play every day and Boston looked like a good opportunity. My agent thought so, too. And so when the Red Sox expressed interest, when Theo Epstein talked to my agent, it didn't take long to work out a deal.

I was going to Boston.

I'm glad I did.

But it took a little while for me to feel that way.

WHEN I GOT TO THE RED SOX, I KNEW FOR SURE THAT I WAS GOING to like it. The Red Sox had some crazy dudes, bro. Theo Epstein traded for Kevin Millar right after I signed, so it looked like they had a lot of guys competing for first base. Millar came into camp the first day after driving all night from his home in Texas—he pulled in driving a pickup truck—and he was one funny dude. He made everybody laugh. Theo had traded for Todd Walker, too, so the clubhouse seemed like a good group of guys. Right away, it felt a lot like the way it did in Minnesota, where we had all been together for so long.

Me? I was a little quiet at the beginning, bro. I usually am. Pedro was there and my locker was right next to Manny Ramirez's, so I got to spend some time with Manny. He was a big help. In a lot of ways, like I felt with Pedro, I thought Manny took me under his wing. We would go and hit together, work out together, and I learned a lot of what he thinks about hitting. Anyone would, bro. Manny is one of the greatest hitters of all time. Manny has had his share of problems in Boston, but most people really don't know him. He doesn't like to talk to the media, so I think a lot of people think that maybe he's mean. He's not. He's a happy person, a funny dude, and he works his ass off. I don't know anybody who works as hard on his hitting as Manny does. He was a good influence on me, especially at that time in my career. I was still learning how to hit, and I was just trying to fit in.

That clubhouse made everything easier, bro. It was a great group of guys. Johnny Damon, Jason Varitek, Bill Mueller— we all got along so well. Mueller was new, too—like me and Walker and Millar—and we all wondered when we were going to get playing time. But there were a bunch of good players there and we knew we had a lot of talent, so we were pretty sure we were going to be a good team.

On the field, too, I could tell things were going to be a lot different than they were in Minnesota. In the first spring training game I played for the Red Sox—in my first at-bat—I came up with nobody out and a man on second base. The pitcher threw me a sinker away—a pitch I should either take or try to drive to the opposite field—and I pulled a ground ball to second base (on purpose), just so we could move the runner to third. I thought that's what the Red Sox wanted me to do. That was the way we played in Minnesota—move the runners, hit to the situation—so I assumed that was what the Red Sox wanted. In Minnesota, we were taught that there was one way to play the game—the right way—and so they used to drive that shit into our heads. We had to do it their way or we weren't going to do it at all.

With the Red Sox, after I grounded out, I got back to the dugout and nobody said much. That wasn't a big deal. But when I went to the end of the dugout to put away my helmet, Grady Little [the manager] pulled me aside and told me: Swing away. Grady told me that the Red Sox wanted me to bring runners in, to drive the ball, because that's why they brought me there. I couldn't believe it, bro. I was so happy. Here I was doing what I thought the manager wanted me to do—make an out on purpose so we could move the runner— and the manager is telling me to take a hack up there, to let it go. Can you believe that shit? I felt like I just got out of jail, bro. I felt like I could hit the way I wanted to hit.

The Red Sox—they played the game in a completely opposite way than the Twins did. It was totally different. In Minnesota, we used to bunt, hit-and-run, do all of that small-ball shit. That's the way the team was built. The Twins didn't have many home run hitters, so they tried to score runs by bunting, stealing bases, things like that. And when they got a big dude like me who could hit home runs, who could drive the ball out of the park, they wanted me to play the same way. It didn't make sense to me. I mean, they didn't have much power, but they wanted one of their only power hitters to move runners over. I didn't get it. It wasn't the best way for me to be successful. For me to do that, it wasn't the best for the team, either.

But the Red Sox? They wanted us to hack, bro. Every single one of us. We had a great lineup, probably the best one I've ever been in, and every guy could hit. Walker, Millar, Manny, JD—that's what we called Damon—they all could hit. We had Nomar Garciaparra on that team, Shea Hillenbrand, Varitek, and Trot Nixon. By the end of the season, I don't think there was a pitcher in baseball that wanted to face us.

All in all, bro, I thought I had a pretty good spring. I didn't get a ton of at-bats, but I thought I produced when I was in there. I went 18 for 54—a .333 average—with 3 home runs and 10 RBIs in twenty-two games. I thought I made a pretty good case for myself. And then right before the season started, Grady called me and Bill Mueller into his office, and he told us the news: We were going to start the year on the bench. Jeremy Giambi was going to start the year at first base or as the designated hitter, and Millar was going to either play in the outfield or at first, or DH. Grady said he was going to move people around a lot, but that's the way it was going to start. Hillenbrand was going to play some third and, when Mueller played, some first. The Red Sox wanted to get the hottest bats in there, and so, in some ways, we felt like we were playing for jobs.

Just like in Minnesota, bro.

That's what it felt like.

I went all the way from Minnesota to Boston, but somehow I ended up in the same place.

That was bullshit.

For a while there, I felt like I couldn't say anything. Giambi had a terrible spring and he got off to a bad start, but I was new and I didn't want to say much. Giambi and I had exactly the same number of at-bats during spring training, but he hit only .204 with 2 homers and 3 RBIs. It wasn't even close. I deserved the job. Then the season started and Giambi played even worse. He hit .136 in April and struck out 14 times in 44 at-bats, and I still couldn't figure out why we were all sharing time. I didn't have a great April, but my argument has always been the same. I need to play every day. That's when I hit my best. I was pissed off, too, and I'm sure that didn't help. I talked a lot about it to Manny and Pedro.

As a team, we were winning a lot of games. That was another reason I felt like I couldn't say anything to anyone else. It's one thing to go in and talk to the manager about playing time when the club is losing, but it's another when the team is playing well. In 2003, we got off to a pretty good start. We blew the game on Opening Day in Tampa Bay—we gave up five runs in the bottom of the ninth and lost, 6–4—but we finished the month with an 18–9 record and we were scoring a lot of runs. We were having some problems in our bullpen, but we were killin' at the plate. Like I said, I think we knew in spring training that we were going to be able to hit.

By the time we got into the middle and end of May, I have to admit: I was pretty frustrated, bro. I'd had enough. The team started playing .500 baseball—we'd win one, lose one—and I started swinging the bat pretty well, but Giambi was still getting a lot of at-bats. I called my agents and I told them straight: *If you guys don't get your asses up here tomorrow, you're fired.* I told them to get me out of Boston, to get me traded, to do *something*, because I didn't go to Boston to sit on the bench behind a guy who I knew I was better than. Fernando calmed me down and said he would talk to Theo, and so he came to Boston and they talked about it. Theo told Fernando that he was talking about some trades with some other teams, that things would clear up once he made a deal. He said that should open up some playing time. And he told Fernando, too, that he would trade me somewhere else if the Red Sox couldn't find playing time for me, that he would send me somewhere I could play.

I thank God now that it never came to that.

I bet Red Sox fans feel the same way.

Pretty soon after that—about two weeks, I think—we were getting ready for a series in Toronto when Theo made the trade. We had just lost two games during a three-game series against the Yankees in New York, and I went 2 for 4 with a double in the only game I played. We had an off day before the Toronto series when Theo traded Hillenbrand to the Arizona Diamondbacks for Byung-Hyun Kim, which meant that Mueller was pretty much going to play third base every day. The rest of us still had to compete for some playing time, but things started to get better. I played twice in the Toronto series—I went 4 for 9 with three doubles—but then I sat for two days before I got back in the lineup. I had three more hits a few days later . . . then sat for two days . . . then played again and had three more hits. I was starting to get hot. I wasn't hitting a lot of home runs yet, but I hit a bunch of doubles and was knocking in runs. I think I had 10 RBIs in a week. But then I would play and sit, play and sit, and I cooled off a little. I got hot again at the end of the month and finished June with 74 at-bats, more than I had in either April (52) or May (51). I hit .324 for the month with 2 homers, 10 doubles, and 17 RBIs, and after that I started playing pretty much every day.

The Red Sox couldn't take me out of the lineup if they wanted to.

By then, bro, we were still going up and down as a team. We would win two, lose one, win one, lose two. That's just how it was going. But we started to get hot at the end of the month, and we had a game on June 27 that I don't think anyone will ever forget. It was unbelievable, bro. We were playing at home against the Florida Marlins and we won 25–8. We scored 14 runs in the first inning and we were up 10–0 before we made an out. I've never seen anything like it. Everybody hit. JD doubled to start the game and it was like nobody wanted to make an out. Walker singled. Nomar doubled. Manny homered. I doubled. Millar singled. Nixon singled. Mueller walked. Varitek singled. JD tripled. Walker singled.

When Nomar finally popped up for the first out, the crowd at Fenway went crazy. We scored four more runs in the inning and sent nineteen men to the plate—I walked in my other at-bat—and the inning ended only when Bill Mueller got thrown out at the plate on JD's single. Can you believe that? We played one inning and JD was 3 for 3 with a single, double, and triple. We were ahead, 14–1. We finished the night with twenty-eight hits. We scored two more runs in the second, one in the third, two in the fourth, one in the fifth, one in the seventh, and four in the eighth. We scored in every inning but the sixth, and we set more records than I can remember.

The next night, even though we lost, we scored nine more runs.

And the night after that, we went crazy again and won, 11–7.

By then, I'm pretty sure nobody wanted to pitch to us. The weather was hot—good weather to hit, even in Boston—and we were settling into a regular lineup. Mueller was playing third. Millar was playing first. I was the designated hitter, and Giambi wasn't playing much, and things were really starting to come together for our offense.

As for me, I was just getting warmed up.

LET ME TELL YOU SOMETHING ABOUT PLAYING IN BOSTON: EVERY-body says it's tough—and it is—but there are a lot of good things about it, too. Every night, the stadium is full. The place is packed. You hear players talk sometimes about how the media and the fans can be tough, and it's true that they expect a lot from you. I never looked at that as being too much of a problem because I expect a lot from myself.

In Boston, if you do your job, the rest pretty much takes care of itself.

Like I've told you before, the baseball season is long. It wears you down. That's the way the game is designed. You start spring training in February and you basically play every day for eight months, and by the end of the year you're tired. You need the three or four months to recover. That's especially true if you make the playoffs, and it doesn't include winter ball, Instructional League, things like that. Sometimes you can feel like you're playing twelve months a year and that you never get a break.

In a lot of ways, if you ask me, playing in Boston makes it easier to deal with that instead of making it tougher.

Let me tell you what I mean. When you play for a team like the Red Sox, at a place like Fenway Park, you don't have a choice: you have to stay focused. The team and the fans demand it. There are a lot of times during the year when you show up at the ballpark and you're tired, when your legs are heavy and you feel like you never should have gotten out of bed. We all have those days, bro. Ballplayers, too. Sometimes, we might have a night game in Detroit and then a day game in Texas, and maybe we didn't get much sleep on the plane. Maybe we got into the hotel at four or five o'clock in the morning. Maybe we had flight delays and got there even later, and maybe a cold or the flu or a virus. It happens to us, too. I think sometimes that people see us play the games and think it's all easy, that it's all fun. It's not. Baseball is our job, bro. It's how we earn a living. And sometimes, when you travel from city to city without any breaks, it can wear you down.

Again, don't get me wrong. I like the game, love to play, love what I do. Most of us do. But there are times when it *is* hard, when it really tests you, and those are the days or nights you show up at the ballpark and don't feel like playing against anybody.

You just want to rest, bro.

You want to sleep.

You need a break.

You know what I've figured out? In Boston, the days like that are easier to deal with. I'm serious. For all of the things people say about playing in Boston—the intensity and how crazy the fans are—it can actually be easier to play there. When you show up at the ballpark every day, you can feel the energy from the minute you walk in the ballpark. People are excited about the game. At Fenway, for a night game, there are fans on the street corner outside of the players' parking lot starting pretty early in the day. The people who work at the stadium get excited about every game, and you can feel that when you walk past them. And then you go through your routine—go to your locker, get dressed, maybe have something to eat or even take a nap—and you put your uniform on, go out to the field, begin stretching, and take batting practice.

And while you're out there, the stadium starts to fill up.

People start calling your name.

And then, all of a sudden, it's seven o'clock and you're ready to go.

You're not tired anymore, bro.

You're ready to play.

When I was in Minnesota, it wasn't like that, bro. It wasn't anything close. There are people in Minnesota who care about baseball, who love the Twins, but it's nothing like Boston. Most places aren't. The people in Boston are as crazy about baseball as the people in the Dominican, which I think is part of the reason why people like me enjoy it so much. I know that when Pedro got traded from Montreal to Boston, he didn't really know what it was like to play at Fenway. He just hadn't experienced it. Pedro had one year left on his contract at the time and he said he wasn't sure if he was going to re-sign with the Red Sox because he wanted to play somewhere like Cleveland, where they had a packed house every night. At the time, the Indians were selling out every game and the Red Sox were coming off a bad year, so Pedro didn't know too much about the Red Sox. He ended up signing a six-year con-tract, I think, and then he learned what I did: When it comes to baseball, places like Cleveland *want* to be like Boston, bro. That's what they're shooting for. I came to the Red Sox five years after Pedro did, and I think we've sold out just about every game since I've been there. I'm serious. By the end of the 2006 season, the Red Sox had sold out over 300 games in a row—it was 307, I think—and that's almost four full years without having an open seat in the house. *Four years.*

That's about how long I've been there!

In Boston, it all goes together—the team, the ballpark, everything. The Red Sox don't have as much money as a team like the Yankees, but we have a bigger payroll than just about everybody else. That helps a lot, too. When you play for a team like the Red Sox, you know you're going to have a good team every year, that you're going to have a chance. If some things go right—if you stay healthy and avoid injuries—you're going to be there at the end. That makes playing easier, too. A lot of people ask about the pressure of playing in big games, of how hard it can be in August and September and October, but I never really looked at it that way. At least you're in it, right? The hard games are the ones when your team is fifteen or twenty games out of first place with two months to go, when you have no chance at making the play-offs, when you're playing games that really don't mean any-thing. My first few years in Minnesota, we had a lot of those games, bro. There were no people in the stands and there was nothing to play for, and you still had to show up every night and be focused, get motivated, play hard.

Those were the hard games.

But in a place like Boston, at Fenway, the atmosphere is so different. *Everything* is different. When I was with the Twins, we'd show up at the ballpark half the time and we *knew* we were going to lose. I don't know if it's because we were young, or we didn't have as much talent as a lot of teams, or what. I'm really not sure. But one of the bad things about losing is that, after a while, you start to expect it. You start to accept it, too. Your whole mentality changes, and all of a sudden you start going into games with a bad attitude, thinking negative things. It's not that you don't want to work or try, but you just don't have the same confidence, I think that's why it's so important for the older guys to be positive around the young guys, to keep telling them that they're good enough, even when they're struggling. You don't want to get into bad habits. It can weigh you down. You start thinking like a loser instead of like a winner, and that's not good for anybody.

When I was with the Twins, I don't think we knew better. We were all so young. We'd go into a series against a team and look at the pitching matchups, and we'd know right away which games we were going to get our asses kicked in. We might go up against a team like the Red Sox, after Pedro got there, and we'd just *know* we couldn't beat him. Guys would joke with each other—like, "Hey, we better get our hits tonight, bro, because we're not getting any tomorrow"—and guys would laugh. But it was a bad way to go into games because then, if things started going bad, the fight would already be over. And let me tell you, bro, the pitcher knows it, too. He can sense it. He can look in and know which guys and teams are going to fight him, and he knows which ones aren't.

But when you're losing a lot of games, it's hard to get out of that habit.

With the Red Sox, from my first year there, it was totally different. I don't know if it was because we had veteran guys or more confident guys, better players or what. Maybe it was a little bit of everything. But any time we faced a team, we didn't look at it like we were going to have a fight on our hands. We looked at it like *they* were. We had a great lineup, bro. We had a lot of good players, tough guys who worked hard and believed they could beat anybody. It made a big difference. We'd be getting ready for a big series against the Yankees or something, and a guy like Millar would be walking around the clubhouse, talking out loud, keeping everybody loose. And then he would say something like this—"The Yankees better watch out this week because they have to pitch to the Sox!"—and we'd all start cracking up. But we believed it, bro. We really did. We had this attitude like we were going to take our hacks up there, beat the other guy so badly that he didn't want to stay in the game, keep fighting and swinging until we won.

And when that happens, then *you* can see it in *his* eyes.

In Boston, for me, that's what it was like at the beginning.

We felt like we were some bad dudes, bro.

Every night we took the field, we felt like we were going to take names and kick some ass.

What's so bad about that?

IN 2003, ABOUT HALFWAY THROUGH THE SEASON, I HAD ONLY THREE or four home runs. Guys like Manny and Millar were giving me shit, calling me Juan Pierre, a little dude who played for the Florida Marlins and who, even now, three years later, has twelve home runs in his career. Pierre is the kind of guy who hits one or two homers a year, at most, and steals a lot of bases. He's a good hitter, a good player, but the style of his game is completely different than mine. And at that time, I think, Pierre had only three or four homers in his career.

I had four for the season, so Millar and the rest of the guys started busting my balls.

In our clubhouse, in most clubhouses, that's how it is. The season is so long, the game can be so tough, that you have to laugh about stuff. Home runs come in bunches sometimes, but usually, by the end of the season, you're going to be where you're supposed to be. You might go two weeks without a home run and then hit four in three days, and at the end of the year you'll have thirty or forty. Every player gets hot or goes into slumps, so you try to be as consistent as you can. But that's hard to do when you're not playing every day because you can never really get comfortable, get into a rhythm, get relaxed. Hitting is like anything else; the more you do it, the better you get. Your swing becomes more natural and your body takes over—not your mind—and that's usually when you start playing your best.

In those times when you struggle—and we all have them—your teammates help you laugh about it. So we joke with one another and make fun of each other because you have to. I remember once, in 2004, we were playing the Los Angeles Dodgers in a game at Fenway. We had a 1–0 lead going into the top of the ninth inning and the fans were really into the game. It felt like a playoff game. Keith Foulke came in to close out the game for us and got the first two guys out, then gave up a single to Alex Cora. (Cora and I became teammates in 2005, when he got traded to Boston from Cleveland.) Then Olmedo Saenz came up and hit a pop fly to left field that looked like an easy out, and we all couldn't believe what happened next.

Manny dropped the ball.

Because there were two outs, Cora was running hard all the way; he was a good player like that. He always knew the situation, played hard, knew the game. So when Manny dropped the ball, Cora was already on the way home and the Dodgers tied the game, 1–1, and now we had to fight. Saenz ran hard, too, and he was on second base, so a single would have scored him and given the Dodgers a 2–1 lead. The Dodgers sent in a pinch runner—it was Jayson Werth—but Foulke got the last guy out to keep the game tied, and we had a chance to win the game in the bottom of the ninth.

Fenway got pretty quiet when Manny made the error, but let me tell you: It didn't stay like that for long. Manny came back to the dugout and put down his glove, and nobody said much at first. Then Manny started walking along the dugout and started talking out loud, and I'll never forget what he said.

None of us.

"Well, there goes my Gold Glove."

We all starting laughing, bro.

It was hilarious.

When you're on a team, that's the kind of stuff that happens. You're all in it together. Manny gets a lot of shit about his defense when he plays, and he's not as bad as everybody thinks. But he's probably never going to win a Gold Glove, either, so guys like Millar would bust his balls whenever something crazy happened in the outfield. And with Manny, there was always something crazy. But when you play next to a guy like that, you learn to take the good with the bad. We're all people, bro. Nobody's perfect. So the best way to deal with it is to joke about it, laugh about it, because there's really nothing else you can do. Manny wasn't trying to drop that ball, but it happened. What can you do? So you just come back to the dugout and put your glove down, laugh about it, and move on. The more you worry about it, the worse it gets.

In Boston, with that team, we were always good at that.

After Manny's error, we came right back in the bottom of the ninth. JD led off with a walk and Mark Bellhorn doubled—he joined our team in 2004—and then I came up. Manny was on deck, so the Dodgers decided to pitch to me, even with first base open. I singled to right field and JD scored to give us a 2–1 win, and it was like the top of the ninth never happened. We didn't even make an out, bro. We just came right back and won the game.

That's what good teams do.

And in Boston, that's what we did.

So in 2003, halfway through the year, my teammates were riding me pretty hard. But I knew the home runs would come. On July 3, in a game we lost at Tampa Bay, I hit my fifth home run of the year. We went to New York the next day, the Fourth of July, and I hit two more in a 10–2 win over the Yankees. On July 5, another game we won 10–2, I hit another two homers. I was killin'. In three games, I had six RBIs and six hits—five of them home runs. The other hit was a double. All of a sudden, I was up to nine home runs, and nobody in the clubhouse was calling me Juan Pierre anymore. I'm pretty sure Juan Pierre has never hit five homers in three games.

We lost the last two games of the Yankees series—New York shut us down—but people were starting to notice me. I was starting to play every day and I was producing, and I was starting to get more confidence. In the second game of the series, when I hit two homers for the second game in a row, the Yankees starting pitcher was Roger Clemens, who might be the best pitcher of all time. I have a lot of respect for him. After the game, I guess the reporters in New York asked Clemens about me, about a home run I hit off him, and Clemens said something about my "plate coverage," about how he would have to make adjustments against me. I'm not sure what he meant. But some of the reporters thought Clemens might try to pitch me inside the next time, maybe knock me down, because I guess that's what he did against Mike Piazza once.

When they asked me about it, here's what I told them:

"If he makes adjustments, then I'll make mine. But if you want people to respect you for what you do in this game, you've got to respect other people, too. That's the way it goes. I respect him because I think he's one of the greatest in the game, but I think I deserve respect, too. I'm a man, just like him."

As far as I was concerned, it was over. There was really nothing more to say. I've faced Clemens other times since then and I've never had any problems, and I still think he's one of the best ever. The guy's numbers speak for themselves, bro. He's won over 300 games and had over 4,000 strikeouts. If a guy like Clemens thought that he had to make adjustments to get me out, then I think that's a compliment. But I have to believe that I'm as good as he is, that he has to get *me* out, or I'm never going to get another hit against him.

That's just how the game works.

After we left New York, we started hitting again and we started winning again. We swept Toronto and won two out of three in Detroit, then went into the All-Star break. My average was up to .299 and I had 10 home runs. We lost the first two games after the break and then won five more in a row, and we beat Detroit, 14–5, and Tampa Bay, 10–4. I had cooled off a little, but as a team, we were killin'.

By the time the Yankees came into Fenway at the end of July, I was struggling a little. My average was down to .285 and I think I was something like 5 for 29. It was just one of those times where I was in a little bit of a slump. Mike

Mussina was pitching the middle game of the series for the Yankees and he always gave me trouble, so Grady gave me the night off. Giambi started that night as the designated hitter and Grady told me that maybe I would pinch-hit if we got the chance. Mussina had faced us in New York the last time we were there—two days after I hit the two homers against Clemens—he totally shut us down. I think we got like three hits. I went 0 for 3 with a strikeout, but Mussina was tough on everybody that night. He could be like that. The dude throws a lot pitches—fastballs, curveballs, changeups—and he's got great control. He can throw them all for strikes and can put the ball wherever he wants. And when he's on, he can be really tough to hit.

In Boston, we got on Mussina quick. Nomar hit a two-run homer and Manny hit another, and we had a 4–0 lead. It looked like it was going to be an easy one. But the Yankees came back and tied the game—they had a great lineup, too, bro—and it was 4–4 going into the bottom of the ninth. I remember that we had a man on second [Giambi] with two outs when the Yankees intentionally walked JD with Damian Jackson on deck. Armando Benitez was pitching. Once the Yankees walked Damon, Grady told me that I was going to hit for Jackson, so I still got a big at-bat even though I didn't start the game.

Against Armando—he's a Dominican, bro—I hit one off the wall to score Giambi and win the game, 5–4.

That was my first walk-off hit as a member of the Red Sox.

The next night, we played the Yankees again on ESPN—it was a Sunday night game—and this time it was the Yankees who jumped on us. We were down 3–0 going into the bottom of the seventh and we hadn't done too much against the Yankees starting pitcher, Jeff Weaver. But like I've said before, none of that stuff really mattered to us. We knew we could hit. We always believed we could win. We could be down by five runs and a guy could be throwing a no-hitter against us going into the ninth inning, but we always thought we could score six and win. That's just the way it was with that team. We had a lot of confidence.

In the seventh, we rallied against Weaver. With one out, we put a couple of guys on and Varitek hit a three-run homer against Chris Hammond to tie the game. We weren't done yet. JD hit another homer to give us a 4–3 lead and we had two outs and a man on second when Manny came up. The Yankees didn't want to pitch to him, so they brought in a lefty [Jesse Orosco] and walked Manny to get to me. I hit a triple into the right-field corner—you should have seen a big dude like me running around the bases, bro—and we took a 6–3 lead. We won, 6–4. I had never faced Orosco before, but I was starting to become a big part of the team, and so Grady let me hit.

How's that for a change, bro?

Early in the year, the Red Sox didn't want to play me every day.

Now, late in the year and against the Yankees, they were asking me to pinch-hit on some nights, then leaving me in to hit in the late innings against the lefty out of the bullpen.

Things had changed.

After the game, I remember people asking about our offense, about my ability to hit in the clutch, and it was like, all of a sudden, everybody was seeing me do the things that I always thought I could do.

I just needed the *chance*.

"Nothing surprises me about David. I'm not going to get excited about David because I've seen him do that so many times," Manny said when someone asked him about it. "I'm used to seeing him do that because he's a good clutch hitter."

After the Yankees left town, we played .500 ball for about a month, but we were in the race. We had a good chance to go to the playoffs. Theo made a couple of moves to help us out, getting us a little more starting pitching and some bullpen help. At the beginning of September, we won five in a row and eight out of ten, and from that point on I didn't think anyone would catch us. We went into the final week of the season ready to clinch the American League wild card spot—the Yankees were leading the division—and nothing was going to happen. I was having a big second half—I was killin', bro—and people were actually starting to mention me as a candidate for the Most Valuable Player Award.

Can you believe that, bro?

Less than a year earlier, I got released by the Twins. Then I came to Boston and sat on the bench for two months.

And now people were talking about me as the MVP.

I didn't win the award and I didn't expect to—I ended up finishing fifth, pretty good for a guy who didn't have a job at the beginning of January—but at the time it didn't seem to matter. We were rolling. On September 23, we played a game at home against the Baltimore Orioles and we were losing for most of the night. We were down 5–2 going into the bottom of the ninth and it looked like we were going to lose. We had a man on third with two outs when Nomar walked. Then Walker came up and hit one out of the ballpark to tie the game at five, and the place went crazy. We stopped the Orioles from scoring in the top of the tenth and I led off the bottom of the inning with a homer against a right-handed pitcher named Kurt Ainsworth, and there we were again, walking off the field, winning a game everybody thought we would lose.

Everybody but us.

That was my first walk-off homer as a member of the Red Sox, bro, and by then, even the fans started to feel what we felt. It was like they knew we were never out of a game, that we would always come back and win. And a lot of times, we did. At the end of the 2003 season, we led the major leagues in runs scored, and we set a major-league record for slugging percentage, breaking the record held by the 1927 Yankees, one of the greatest offensive teams of all time. We scored almost 1,000 runs. We ended up winning 95 games and, in 40 of them, we came from behind. In 23 of those, we scored the winning run in our final time at-bat as a team. In 8 of those, we won on the last pitch of the game.

It was unbelievable, bro.

Sometimes, it was like we just wouldn't lose.

And the fans were a big part of that.

"Right now we are worried about winning games, to give this city, to the great fans down here, the opportunity to see a championship. They deserve it," I remember telling reporters after I hit the homer against Ainsworth. "We were down by three runs and they were still out there giving us support. That's the reason we won that kind of game. They deserve for this ball club to give them a championship."

Three days later, against the Orioles again, we won 14–3 and clinched a playoff spot. Varitek, Nomar, and Bill Mueller all hit home runs and Fenway went crazy. After the game, Millar and Walker and some of the other guys were running around outside the ballpark, on the street, going to bars in their uniform and partying with fans. That's what that whole season felt like, bro—one big party. And we felt like no matter how how far we got behind, no matter who we played, that we would come back and win, that we could beat anybody, that everybody was afraid of us.

That's what confidence can do for you, bro.

That's what it did for the team and that's what it did for me.

BIG PAPI

BY NOW, YOU PROBABLY KNOW WHAT HAPPENED IN THE PLAYOFFS,
but let me tell you a few things: I learned a lot from the playoffs that year. I had been to the playoffs the year before, with
the Twins, but this was different. Everything was different.
With the Red Sox, we opened the Division Series against the
Oakland A's and I really struggled in the first few games. The
A's had a great pitching staff and they were really shutting us
down. We had to hit to win because that was the way we
played all year. Our pitching was pretty good that season, but
we were an offensive team.

We lost the first two games in Oakland, and when we
came back to Boston for Game 3, I didn't have a hit yet. We
had scored only six runs as a team. The Division Series is best
of five, so if we lost another game we were out and our season
was over. All of our work would have been for nothing. We
struggled to score again in Game 3, but we got good pitching
and we were tied, 1–1, going into extra innings. Then Trot
Nixon hit a two-run homer against Rich Harden in the bottom of the eleventh inning to give us a 3–1 win, and it was
like we were alive again. We knew we could come back and
win the series now. Our fans knew it. And deep down, I bet
you the A's knew it, too.

It's funny, though. A lot of people don't remember it now
because of what started happening in 2004, but I really struggled in the Oakland series. I didn't have a hit in Game 3, either, and I went without a hit for most of Game 4. I was 0 for
16 with six strikeouts in the series when I came up against
Keith Foulke with two men on and two out in the bottom of
the eighth inning, and our season was on the line. I needed to
produce. Foulke had a great changeup and he used it all the
time against lefties, but you had to guard against his fastball,

too. If you weren't looking for it, he could sneak it by you. I had two strikes on me when Foulke threw a fastball I could handle, and I smoked one to deep right field that ended up being a double. Nomar and Manny scored and we had a 5–4 lead, and we closed out the game in the top of the ninth to tie the series at two games each and go back to Oakland.

That was my first hit of the series.

And the monkey was off my back.

We won Game 5 by a 4–3 score—Derek Lowe threw a nasty pitch to strike out Terrence Long for the final out *with the bases loaded*—and that meant we were going to the American League Championship Series to face the Yankees. Boston was going crazy. The Yankees played Minnesota in the first round of the playoffs, and because I had played for the Twins, everybody was asking me who I wanted to win. I told them all that I was rooting for Minnesota—and I was—because I wanted all of my old boys to do well—Torii and Koskie and all of those guys. But the Yankees won the series in four games, which we already knew by the time we played Game 5 in Oakland, and the truth is that we didn't really care who was playing for the American League Championship as long as they were playing against us.

The Yankees series was unbelievable. We played New York nineteen times during the regular season and they won ten games, we won nine. It felt like they were all close. The playoffs felt the same way. We won Game 1, the Yankees won Game 2. They won Game 3, we won Game 4, and they won Game 5. That meant that we had to go back to New York, down 3–2 in the series, for Games 6 and 7. And even though we had come back all year, even though we kept winning when everybody thought we would lose, not many people gave us a chance.

We came from behind to beat the Yankees in Game 6—we

scored five runs in the last three innings and won, 9–6—and that made it easy for everybody. Game 7. One game. Winner take all. It doesn't get any better than that, bro. The way our pitching set up, we had Pedro ready to go for our biggest game of the year, so we liked our chances. I'm sure the Yankees liked theirs, too. The Yankees were a lot like we were—they thought they could win any game at any time—and they weren't afraid of Pedro. They'd had some success against him. We all went into that game knowing that it wasn't going to be easy, thinking that it would be a fight.

And it was.

We had a 5–2 lead going into the eighth inning when Grady sent Pedro back out to pitch, and I guess a lot of people were surprised by that. A lot of times during the year, Pedro would pitch seven and then we would go to the bullpen, even though our bullpen was having some problems. It was a way to take care of Pedro, too. But our bullpen was pitching great during the postseason—Mike Timlin and Scott Williamson were lights-out—and so a lot of people thought Grady would go to the bullpen. He didn't. He sent Pedro back out to the mound and the Yankees ended up scoring three runs to tie the game at five, and all of a sudden we were in a fight again. We lost the game in the bottom of the eleventh inning when Aaron Boone hit a home run against Tim Wakefield, and that was it.

The Yankees were going to the World Series.

Our season was over.

We were devastated.

Right until the end, bro, I thought we were going to win. We all did. I think we all felt especially bad for Wakefield because he had a great series and won two games. We wouldn't have been there without him. If we had won, he probably would have been the series MVP. Some guys were crying in the clubhouse and we were all stunned, really, because we thought we were as good as the Yankees. We thought we were better. Until Boone's home run, in seven full games, we had scored exactly the same number of runs that they did. I think it was 29–29. Can you believe that? We played seven games, won three games each, and we tied going into the extra innings of Game 7. We had scored the same number of runs. We were just two even teams—two good teams—but they ended up on top.

It was a tough thing to live with.

Not too long after that, Grady got fired. I was a little surprised by that. A lot of people thought he should have taken Pedro out of the game after the seventh inning—including Theo and our owners, I guess—but I didn't feel that way. It was a tough call, bro. Pedro was our ace. If you ask me, you want your best guy on the mound for a game like that, and Pedro was our best. I didn't really talk too much about that decision at the time—and I haven't really talked about it since—but that's just the way I feel. If we're winning a game like that and we need to close it out, I want the ball in Pedro's hands. It has nothing to do with our bullpen. Like I said, our bullpen was doing a great job at that time, but I think Grady went the right way. I really do. I think he made the right decision.

After beating us, the Yankees lost to the Florida Marlins in the World Series. It only took six games and the Marlins beat the Yankees in New York, in Game 6, just like we did. A lot of people were surprised that the Marlins won the series, but I think we had something to do with it. I think we really took a lot out of the Yankees, made them fight, and I don't think they had too much left by the time they had to play Florida in the World Series.

For us, that didn't make the ending any easier. We wanted

to win it, bro. We knew the Red Sox hadn't won the World Series in a long time. But we had a good team with lots of good players—guys who liked each other—and we knew we'd be back. We knew we'd come back even stronger. Losing is hard sometimes, but it can make you come back even harder. It can make you stronger. It can make you want something even more, like it did for me when I was Minnesota, when I wanted the chance to prove to everybody that I could play every day and that I could produce.

In 2003, I felt like I showed people that.

I finished the year with a .288 average and 31 homers with 101 RBIs. After July 1, when I pretty much started playing every day, I hit more homers than anybody in the league but Alex Rodriguez, who also hit 27. After struggling in the playoff series against Oakland, I hit .269 with 2 homers and 6 RBIs in the series against the Yankees.

I was getting better, bro.

I was more motivated than ever.

We all were.

We wanted to come back in 2004 and finish the job.

SEÑOR
OCTUBRE

For us, the Red Sox 2004 season began the day the 2003 season ended. After Grady got fired, our owners and our general manager went right to work to make us a better team. Theo Epstein hired Terry Francona as our manager, and the truth is that I didn't know too much about him. But right around the same time that we hired Francona—everyone calls him Tito because that was his dad's name—Theo traded for Curt Schilling and then signed Keith Foulke to be our closer. Foulke was the same guy I doubled off to win Game 4 of the Division Series against Oakland, but he was a good pitcher. So was Schilling. Two months after the season, two months before spring training 2004, we were already a better team.

We were ready to go, bro.

We couldn't wait to get started again.

There were a lot of other things that almost happened

that winter, and I'm glad they never did. Manny Ramirez liked parts of playing in Boston and didn't like others, and the team was thinking about trading him. They even put him on waivers. Nomar Garciaparra had just one more year on his contract and the team hadn't been able to re-sign him, and Pedro's contract was going to be up at the end of 2004, too. It seemed like everybody's contract was going to be up. Jason Varitek could be a free agent at the end of the year and so could Derek Lowe, and so Theo Epstein and John Henry, our owner, and Larry Lucchino, the team president, looked at a lot of ways to make us better. And by late January, less than a month before spring training, it looked like Manny and Nomar weren't going to be back.

It looked like the Red Sox were going to trade both of them and that we were going to end up with a couple of new players.

One of them would have been Alex Rodriguez.

Before I go on, let me explain something: As a player, you don't have much control sometimes. I learned that when I was with Minnesota. Before the Twins released me, I thought I was going to spend the rest of my career there. And as hard as it was for me when I learned that I was leaving, that the Twins didn't want me back, it was hard on those guys, too. We all wanted to stay together, play together, win together. But the people upstairs, in the front office, they're the ones who make the decisions. They pick who stays and who goes. And after you've been in the game awhile, after you get some experience, you learn something real fast.

There is nothing you can do about it.

That winter, before the 2004 season, I was on the other side of things. I got to understand what it felt like for Torii and Koskie and the rest of my boys when the Twins let me go. I started to understand how frustrating it was for them, too.

At the same time, I understood that Theo, John Henry, and Larry Lucchino had jobs to do, so that makes it tough. You're stuck in the middle. You want to play with the same guys and keep the same relationships, but you want to win, too. Sometimes, it's hard to do all of those things at once. And then you have things like free agency and contracts to worry about, and it makes things really complicated. The team has to worry about the short term and the long term, and they can't just go out and sign everybody. As a player, the best thing to do sometimes is to just wait and see what happens, to keep your mouth shut and accept whatever it is that you have to accept.

Either way, our jobs are the same, bro.

We have to produce.

We have to win.

And the rest of the stuff isn't really worth worrying about.

With Manny and Nomar, at least before the season started, it looked like it was going to be a package deal. We were either going to have both of them or neither of them. The Red Sox wanted to trade Manny to the Texas Rangers for A-Rod, but the only way they could do it was to trade Nomar first. Nomar and A-Rod both played shortstop, so we couldn't have them both. At the time, the idea of playing Alex somewhere else—like third base—really hadn't come up, so it looked like there was only one way to make room for him: We had to trade Nomar. So Theo arranged a trade with the Chicago White Sox that would have sent Nomar there and brought Magglio Ordonez to Boston, and that made it easy for us to trade Manny to Texas for A-Rod.

And then it *still* didn't happen.

I guess there were a lot of reasons that A-Rod never came to the Red Sox, that Manny and Nomar stayed, but the biggest one was money. To tell you the truth, I didn't follow it too much. Alex and Manny had two of the biggest contracts in the game, so trading them wasn't as easy as everybody thought. Alex had more years (and more money) left on his contract than Manny did, so the teams had to figure that out, too. Then the union got involved . . . and the commissioner's office . . . and everything got really complicated. All I know is that when it all ended, Manny was still in Boston and Nomar was with us, too, and we still had a damn good team going into the 2004 season.

Alex?

He ended up with the Yankees.

Seriously, bro, can you believe that? After all of that, after a whole winter of talk about Manny and Alex and Nomar and Magglio, the Yankees traded for Alex and sent Alfonso Soriano to Texas. Just like that, it was over. The Yankees had a great shortstop just like we did—they had *Derek Jeter*—but Alex agreed to go there and play third base, just before spring training, so the Yankees made the trade. I think everybody was a little surprised. A-Rod won the American League Most Valuable Player Award in 2003 and he won his second straight Gold Glove Award with the Texas Rangers, so nobody ever thought about him moving to third base. It didn't make any sense. And the Yankees probably wouldn't have thought about it, either, but Aaron Boone hurt his knee during the off-season and all of a sudden the Yankees didn't have anyone to play third.

Is that unbelievable or what?

First Boone beats us with a home run in Game 7 in 2003, then he hurts his knee.

And because of that, the Yankees got A-Rod to play third base.

I'm telling you, bro.

That's why, as a player, you can't spend too much time worrying about that kind of stuff.

By the end of 2006, after Alex's third season in New York, here's the even funnier thing: There were rumors that the Yankees were thinking of trading him. Alex won the Most Valuable Player Award again in 2005—he beat me out in a close vote, and I'll get to that later—but he struggled for part of 2006, mostly with his defense. He made twenty-four errors, I think. The Yankees still hadn't won a World Series during A-Rod's three years in New York, so I guess somehow that became his fault. I'll never understand why people sometimes think the way they do, but that's just part of the game. A guy like A-Rod has been putting up the numbers he has for as long as he has, but people always want more. In 2006, Alex hit .290 with 35 home runs and 121 RBIs, numbers that most guys couldn't put up in two years. But for whatever reason, there were rumors that the Yankees wanted to move him after 2006 the same way we wanted to move Manny after 2003. So as a player you're better off not thinking about it too much.

Still, people sometimes ask me how I think Alex would have done if he came to Boston, and I tell them all the same thing: He would have done fine. If you look at guys like Manny and Alex, they put up the same numbers year after year, no matter where they play. They're some of the best hitters in baseball, bro. At the end of the day, in a place like Boston or New York, all they really care about is if you put up the numbers and if you win. The rest of it doesn't really matter too much. And if you don't win, people are always going to be unhappy and they're always going to want more, but how much more can guys like Manny and Alex really give? I mean, seriously, bro. Take a look at the numbers those guys have put up. Every year, they produce. If you ask me, it's hard to complain too much about players like that.

But in 2004, when Alex went to the Yankees, we really didn't care too much. I'm telling you the truth. We knew we had a good team and we believed we were better than the Yankees. Schilling and Foulke were big additions for us, big improvements for our pitching staff, and we weren't going to have to rely on Pedro as much. Our lineup was still the same, and we were coming off a year where we led the major leagues in runs scored. Nobody could hit like we could. Reporters were asking questions about Manny and Nomar, about whether they would be upset, but I really wasn't too worried about them. Those guys are professionals, bro. They're good players. Once the games start, nothing else matters anymore and everybody gets focused and gets to work. The season moves so fast that you don't have time to worry about anything else.

Want to know how we really felt when A-Rod ended up with the Yankees? Here's what we thought: *We're going to beat their asses, anyway.* I remember reporters asking all about Alex and the Yankees, about how much better New York was. I think a lot of people just stopped paying attention. To get Alex, the Yankees had to trade Soriano, who was a good player, too. He did a lot of the things that A-Rod did. We had added pitching, Schilling and Foulke, and our lineup was *better* than New York's the year before. Everybody was running around talking about how good the Yankees would be now that Alex was in New York, and we knew the Yankees would be good, too.

We just thought we were as good, if not better.

With or without Alex.

"Nobody said it would be easy and George [Steinbrenner] is going to do whatever it takes to stop us," I remember Alan Embree, one of our relief pitchers, telling reporters when they asked him about the A-Rod trade. "I think it's kind of exciting. They're worried about us. They know we have a very good ball club."

Said Doug Mirabelli, our backup catcher: "I think there's definitely respect for the Red Sox there, but I don't know if they'd admit that. They know they've got a fight on their hands every time they play us, regardless of who they've got on their team. Look, A-Rod would help any team, but, still, on paper, the Red Sox are right where they need to be."

We all felt that way, bro.

Deep down, we knew.

We felt like the Yankees were the ones chasing *us*.

No matter who played third base for them.

WE GOT OFF TO A FAST START. WE KNEW WE WOULD. WE PLAYED the Yankees for the first time about two weeks into the season, and we took three out of four during a series at Fenway Park. A-Rod got booed. Schilling pitched the second game of the series and beat Mike Mussina, 5–2, and then we went to Toronto and took two out of three from the Blue Jays. That's when we started rolling. We went into New York for the first time since Game 7 and we swept a three-game series, and Pedro won the last game by a 2–0 score over Javier Vazquez, who joined the Yankees in an off-season trade with Montreal. (He was their Schilling.) Then we went to Tampa Bay and won three more in a row, and we were 15–6 after the first month of the season.

But like I've said a bunch of times already, the baseball season is long. A lot happens and a lot changes. That's part of the reason it's so important to stay even, to not get too high or too low. After all of the stuff that happened over the winter with Manny and Nomar, we ended up opening the season without Nomar, anyway. He hurt one of his ankles during spring training, and it took a while for him to get better. When we left spring training, we thought he might miss a couple of weeks, maybe a month. He ended up not coming back until almost the middle of June. And early on, even though we were winning, we felt like we weren't playing our best yet. We weren't really hitting like we thought we could, and like I said, we didn't have Nomar. We had every reason to think we were going to get better. We were 15–6 and it only looked like things could improve.

They didn't.

If you ask me to explain why we played .500 baseball for the next three months—and it was actually a little longer—I don't think I could tell you, bro. That's just the way baseball works sometimes. The season is so long and there are so many pieces to the game—pitching, hitting, defense—that it doesn't take much to mess things up for a little while. You might pitch and you might hit one day, but you might also make an error that will cost you the game. The next day it'll be something different. And unless you're doing almost everything rght, unless you pitch, hit, *and* play defense, there is always the chance that you are going to lose.

That's just the way baseball works, bro.

You can go 0 for 4 and hit four line drives right at people.

The next day, you hit four bloopers and get four hits.

But in the end, you usually end up where you should be.

For us, the other good thing was that we had a lot of veteran guys, a lot of players who had experience and who didn't panic. We had just gone through it in 2003. Our front office made some changes after the season—besides Schilling and Foulke joining us, Mark Bellhorn and Pokey Reese came in to replace Todd Walker at second base—but the new guys were all veterans, too. They'd been through it all before. Foulke had been in the playoffs with Oakland, and Schilling beat the Yankees in the World Series with the Arizona Diamondbacks in 2001, so we knew how to deal with the season and the pressure. That was an important thing in a place like Boston, because the media there can be tough. Once you start losing a few games—and every team does—people start asking you what's wrong. And if you're not strong enough to deal with it, if you don't have the experience, it can make winning really difficult.

It can make it almost impossible.

But in 2004, with that team, we didn't worry too much. We *knew* we were good. We always felt like we were just about to start a winning streak. We had a loose clubhouse and guys who liked to make people laugh—Kevin Millar and JD and even Manny—and we believed in ourselves. We gave each other confidence. And I know I've probably said this a million times already, but I really think that the biggest thing between winning and losing sometimes is that you have to have confidence.

Still, by the time we got to the All-Star break, we were all a little frustrated. We weren't playing like we knew we could. At the end of April, we were 15–6 and the Yankees were 11–11 when we left New York, and we knew we were the better team. The standings don't mean anything at that time of year, but we were 4½ games in front; by the time the All-Star Game came around, we were 7 games *behind*. After we left New York, we played fifty-five games before the All-Star break and we went 33–32, and I can't really explain to you why we weren't better. We just weren't. The Yankees went 44–20 over the same stretch of time, so they picked up 11½ games on us in the standings in a little more than two months. *Eleven and a half games.* We only played them head-to-head three times during that stretch, but they swept a series from us in New York—that was payback for April—and they won the last game, 5–4, in thirteen innings. Nomar had been back for just a few weeks by that point, but he didn't play that night because the team was still being careful with his injury. Reporters started asking a lot of questions about why he didn't play, and it only looked worse when Jeter made a great, diving catch in the stands against Trot Nixon to kill our rally in the top of the twelfth.

Still, people were missing the point.

It was July.

We had a long way to go.

We just had to get our shit together.

THEN I SNAPPED. I'M NOT GOING TO LIE TO YOU, BRO: I JUST LOST IT.
I got so mad that I didn't know what I was doing anymore.

But at least I learned a lesson.

Up to that point—it was July 16—I was having another good season. When I got to spring training that year, people were asking if I could have another year like I did in 2003, if my first year in Boston was a fluke. I thought I could do *better*. I didn't play much for the first couple of months in 2003, and my numbers in the second half were as good as anybody's. I got off to a good start again in 2004—I hit .301 with 5 home runs and 17 RBIs in April—and nobody was asking too many questions after that. The Red Sox signed me to a two-year contract extension a little while into the season, so I knew I was going to be in Boston for a while.

At the All-Star break, I was hitting .304 with 23 home runs and 78 RBIs, numbers that weren't far off from the numbers I put up in 2003. We were only *halfway through the season*. I was killin'.

After the break, we opened the second half with an 8–1 loss at Anaheim. The next night, we were playing the Angels again and Pedro was pitching, and we had a 3–2 lead when I came to the plate to lead off the seventh. A lot of us were getting frustrated with the umpiring that night, including Pedro, but that's going to happen over the course of a season. The umpires make mistakes, too, and they have hard jobs. They have a lot of people to please and the fans are on them all the time, and I'm not sure I'd ever want to do what they do. But as players, we take what we do seriously. We want to win. We spend a lot of time preparing for the season and we take pride in our performance, and we get frustrated when things don't right.

And no matter what we do—any of us—we all want things to go right.

Up to that point in the game, I was 1 for 2 with a walk against Kelvin Escobar, the Anaheim starter. Angels manager Mike Scioscia brought in right-hander Scot Shields to start the seventh, and Shields struck me out on a 3–2 pitch that I thought was inside. I turned to the home plate umpire, who I didn't even know, and I told him I didn't like the call. And before I knew it, before I knew what was going on, I'd been thrown out of the game and I was throwing bats from our dugout out onto the field. One minute I'm standing in the batter's box waiting to hit. The next minute I'm looking at a five-game suspension with our team fighting to make the playoffs.

Before I go on, let me say something, bro: I made a mistake. I told the reporters that when they asked me that night. I haven't really had any problems with umpires since that game, and I try to keep my mouth shut now. Arguing does you no good. No matter what you say, no matter what you do, the umpire is not going to change his mind. Usually, if you complain, it just makes things worse. You start to get a reputation that you complain, that you talk too much, and then you don't get calls when you need them. Over the season, there are lots of pitches that are close, that could go either way, that an umpire could call a ball or a strike. You want as many of those pitches as you can get. For a guy like me, part of the key to being a good hitter is to swing at good pitches. I guess that's true of any hitter. And if the strike zone gets bigger, if you have to start chasing pitches that you really can't hit, you can't do your job right. And then maybe you start trying too hard, maybe you get into bad habits, and you've completely lost focus with what you're trying to do.

If you look at the stats since I've played in Boston, my walks have gone up every year. I went from 58 walks during my first year in Boston to 75 (in 2004), to 102, and then to 119 (last year). In 2006, no hitter in baseball had more walks than me. I've learned discipline and not to chase pitches. I've learned to keep my mouth shut and accept what the umpires say, and that's been the best thing for everybody—for me, for the Red Sox, for the umpires.

Looking back, on the night I was ejected, maybe we were all a little mad about how the season was going, about how we got off to such a good start and then played .500 for two months, about a lot of things. But I know that I was so mad I couldn't see straight, think straight, act right. I think that's why I ended up throwing bats on the field—and I think that's what really cost me. Lots of guys get thrown out of games every year. Not that many throw bats on the field.

I ended up getting suspended for that, and I really could have hurt our team.

I'm lucky I didn't.

Generally speaking, I'm not one of those guys that just complain all the time. Really, I'm not. The umpires make the right calls almost all of the time, and I usually try to tell them when I think they got something right. Because I'm a designated hitter, I'm in the clubhouse during the game sometimes, and I can see replays on television. A lot of guys can't do that. A guy might get called out on strikes and then go out to the field, and he'll try to come in later to see a pitch on video, just to see if the call was good. Sometimes, I get to see calls right away. And if there's a call that close, if there's a call that the umpire made *right,* I try to say something to him the next time I come to the plate, even if it had nothing to do with me.

They have tough jobs, bro.

They need to have confidence, too. The game gets emotional for them, just like it does for us, and it can be hard for everybody to think straight when that happens.

Since 2004, I've only been thrown out of a game one more time. That came in 2005, and that's when I realized *it was against the same team.* The Anaheim's catcher during those two years was Bengie Molina, who is probably one of the best receivers in the game. He really knows how to catch. Bengie is from Puerto Rico and he's great at *framing* the ball, which means he can make a ball look like a strike just by the way he holds his glove. He's one of the best. With umpires, a catcher can make a difference. If a catcher has to move his glove all the time—and if he has to move it fast—even a good pitch can look like a ball. It just looks like the pitcher missed the target. But if a catcher is really good at receiving the ball, at *framing* it, he won't move his glove much at all. He'll set up on the corners of the plate and he'll stay there, and even if a pitch is an inch or two outside (or inside), he can fool the umpire into thinking it's a strike.

Bengie was always good at that. He was good at other things, too—like talking. He was always finding a way to mess with you. Bengie is a good guy and I like him a lot, so sometimes we'd get together for lunch or breakfast before the games at night. And then we'd get to the ballpark and Bengie would know who was umpiring, and he'd start joking with me that I'd better protect the plate, that he was out to dinner with the umpire the night before, that he bought the drinks, and that the umpire was in his pocket. And then you'd get up to the plate and Bengie would start framing pitches, start getting calls, and you'd start laughing because maybe he really *did* take those guys out to dinner and maybe you really had no chance.

Of course, he was joking.

But still, I've been thrown out of games twice.

Bengie was behind the plate both times.

I mean, he had to have *something* to do with it, didn't he?

Then again, what are friends for?

I WASN'T THE ONLY ONE WHO SNAPPED, BRO. ABOUT A WEEK LATER, we all did.

But this one had nothing to do with the umpires.

We were still playing .500 ball when the Yankees came into town at the end of July and we knew we had to start playing better. It was starting to get late. We lost the first game of the series, 8–7, and it looked like the second game was going to get rained out. Our front office people were meeting with Tito before the game, and Varitek walked in there and told them we wanted to play. So they got the field ready and we finally got out onto the field, and then we fell behind 2–0 before we got to the third inning.

Three batters later, the Yankees were up 3–0. First Bernie Williams doubled and Derek Jeter singled him to third, and then Gary Sheffield grounded into a double play that gave the Yankees their third run. We looked like were in trouble. Then Alex Rodriguez was hit by a pitch from our starter, Bronson Arroyo, and I guess Alex thought that Bronson did it on purpose. I don't know why. But before we knew what was going on, Varitek stood up and said something to Alex, and Alex yelled back. They started swearing at each other, and Jason grabbed Alex by the legs and pushed him to the ground, and all of a sudden we were in a brawl. The Yankees pitcher that day was a guy named Tanyon Sturtze, and I remember him running over and grabbing Gabe Kapler in a headlock. The fight was out of control. I grabbed Sturtze from behind and we all tried to calm everybody down, and I had to be careful because I was still waiting to hear about my suspension from Anaheim.

How about that, bro?

I was already looking at one suspension, and I didn't need another.

After the fight, for whatever reason, we started playing better. I don't know if the Yankees woke us up or not, but we started to hit. We went ahead of the Yankees, 4–3, but then they got six runs in the sixth and went ahead, 9–4. We got four runs in the bottom half and made it 9–8. But then the game slowed down and the Yankees got one run in the seventh, and they had a 10–8 lead going into the bottom of the ninth, with Mariano Rivera coming into the game. Rivera is probably the best closer in baseball, and he can be really dominating. He's a big reason why the Yankees won the World Series four times in five years from 1996 to 2000. When he came in, it usually meant the game was over.

A lot of people probably thought this game was over, too. It wasn't.

After Nomar led off the ninth with a double, he moved to third on a flyout by Trot Nixon. Kevin Millar came up and singled to right to make it 10–9, and then Bill Mueller hit a two-run home run to right field that gave us an 11–10 win that felt like it came in the World Series.

You have to understand, bro. With the Yankees, almost all

of the the games felt that way. We were both good teams, and we had gone to Game 7 in October 2003, and we both knew how much all those games meant. We swept the Yankees in April and they swept us in June, and they had won four straight against us until Billy Mueller beat Rivera. We beat the Yankees on the next night, too, and all of a sudden it felt like we were starting to get our shit together again, like we starting to get our confidence back and like we were going to catch them.

A lot of people asked about the fight after the game, about whether maybe the Yankees actually woke us up. It really wasn't like that. I mean, we had been playing .500 ball for a long time and we needed something to get going, but we've always had nothing but respect for the Yankees since I've been a member of the Red Sox. I think they feel the same way about us. We played the Yankees hard and they played us just as tough, but not much went on that was dirty or cheap. I think it was just two good teams playing each other eighteen or nineteen times a year—and that didn't include the playoffs—and there was just so much history between the teams that the intensity was high.

Seriously, bro.

I know there were a lot more fights in the stands during those games than there were on the field.

After New York left, we took two out of three in Baltimore and then went to Minnesota, and that's when it happened. Theo made a big trade. We'd been having problems with our defense all year and Theo wanted to fix it, so he sent Nomar to the Chicago Cubs in a three-team deal. We ended up with Orlando Cabrera at shortstop and Doug Mientkiewicz at first base—Mientkiewicz was one of my Minnesota boys—and Theo made another trade that got us outfielder Dave Roberts from the Dodgers. We still had two months of the season to

This is from my days with the Rock Cats, the Minnesota Twins AA minor-league team. I learned early that there was a lot more to making it to the big leagues than I thought. *(Courtesy of David Ortiz)*

Mo Vaughn and I when I was with the Twins. Mo was beloved by the fans, and that's something I had always hoped would happen to me. *(Courtesy of David Ortiz)*

My dad has always supported me. Without my family, I'm not sure where I would be or what I would be doing. *(Courtesy of David Ortiz)*

This is me pouring champagne on Manny after we clinched a playoff spot with a win at Tampa Bay in September 2004. *(Courtesy of Associated Press/Chris O'Meara)*

With our season on the line, I hit a two-run homer in the twelfth inning of Game 4 of the 2004 ALCS to give us a 6–4 win over the Yankees. This is what being a team is all about. *(Courtesy of Boston Herald/David Goldman)*

Here I am celebrating a game-winning single in the fourteenth inning of Game 5 of the 2004 ALCS vs. the Yankees. This one ended a game that lasted 5 hours, 49 minutes, and sent the series back to New York for Game 6. *(Courtesy of* Boston Herald/*Michael Seamans)*

A lot of people remember my game-winning hits in the 2004 season, but some might forget that I also homered in the first inning of Game 7 of the 2004 ALCS. This swing gave us a 2–0 lead in a game we eventually won, 10–3. *(Courtesy of* Boston Herald/*David Goldman)*

Pedro Martinez helped bring me to Boston and was an important part to us winning the World Series. This is me and Pedro hugging at Yankee Stadium after Game 7 of the 2004 ALCS, when we became the first team in history to win a seven-game series after falling behind three games to none. *(Courtesy of* Boston Herald/*Matt Stone)*

After we beat the Yankees in the 2004 ALCS, we felt like we were unstoppable. This is me and shortstop Orlando Cabrera celebrating after we beat the St. Louis Cardinals, 6–2, in Game 2 of the World Series. *(Courtesy of* Boston Herald/*David Goldman)*

When we swept the Cardinals to win the World Series, we became the first Red Sox team since 1918 to win a world championship. This is me celebrating our victory with our manager, Terry Francona, who I've really enjoyed playing for. *(Courtesy of* Boston Herald/*Matthew West)*

April 11, 2005, wasn't just the date of our home opener at Fenway Park—it was also the day we got our 2004 championship rings. Winning the World Series meant a lot to all of us, and watching the championship flag go up meant just as much. *(Courtesy of* Boston Herald/*Matthew West)*

From 2003 to 2005, Kevin Millar was an important part of our clubhouse—and a good friend. On this night, Millar bleached his hair blond to try and get out of a slump. In the background are Ino Guerrero, who helps our coaching staff, and Ron Jackson (our hitting coach through 2006). *(Courtesy of* Boston Herald/*Stuart Cahill)*

This walk-off homer came against the Los Angeles Angels of Anaheim on September 6, 2005, and gave us an important 3–2 win. Notice how I threw my helmet off. *(Courtesy of* Boston Herald/*Matthew West)*

When you play for a team like the Red Sox, there's a lot of history that comes with the uniform. This is me and Johnny Pesky, who has been with the organization for over sixty years. *(Courtesy of* Boston Herald/*Matt Stone)*

Manny Ramirez can really make you laugh—and sometimes he doesn't even know he's doing it. (*Courtesy of* Boston Herald/*Matthew West*)

This picture was taken on August 16, 2006, just after I connected for a home run against the Detroit Tigers; it was my forty-second home run of the season. We won the game, 6–4. (*Courtesy of* Boston Herald/*Matt Stone*)

The fans at Fenway Park are one of the best things about playing for the Red Sox—they're always into the game. Here, the fans sitting near our dugout are congratulating me after my home run against the Tigers. *(Courtesy of* Boston Herald/*Matt Stone)*

On September 21, 2006—and against my former team, the Minnesota Twins—I set the Red Sox record for home runs in a season with my fifty-first and fifty-second of the year, breaking a record held by Hall of Famer Jimmie Foxx. Thanks to the fans at Fenway Park, I'll never forget that night. *(Courtesy of* Boston Herald/*Matt Stone)*

On the night I broke Foxx's team record, I got to meet the fans who caught the homers—a 29-year-old man named Joel McGrath (on my right) and 10-year-old boy named Tommy Valeriani (on my left). Tommy was at the game with his pop. *(Courtesy of* Boston Herald/*Matt Stone)*

go and we had three new players, and we had to figure out where they were going to fit in and how it was going to work.

I have to tell you the truth: I was surprised about Nomar. He was a good player, bro, and he'd been with the Red Sox his whole career. He's one of those guys that you just didn't think could be traded. The trading deadline comes on July 31 every year, so you always know there is a chance that something could happen. But most of the time, it's nothing big. Maybe you trade some prospects or maybe you move a bench guy, but nobody was expecting that we were going to trade Nomar. Before he got hurt in spring training, he was our number-five hitter, bro. He was our shortstop. The guy had won batting titles and done all kinds of shit, and he was one of the best players in the game. He had good games and bad games after he came back, but that's the way it works when you come back from injuries. I knew that as well as anyone. I always thought he would be fine.

A lot of people asked us a lot of questions after the trade, and some reporters started writing that Nomar was a problem on the team, that nobody liked him. It wasn't really like that. I got to know him a lot better during my second year in Boston and he was always cool with me—he was a good dude—but he wasn't the kind of guy that would go around the room and talk to everybody, crack jokes, keep them loose. He just liked to do his own thing. You have to be who you are. Guys like me and Millar, we like to walk around the room and talk to guys, make people laugh. But Nomar is a different person. He's Nomar and I'm David Ortiz. We can't all be the same. He was raised one way and I was raised another. When you've got twenty-five guys on a ball club, there's no way you can make them all the same, keep them all on the same page all of the time. We're all different, bro. And unless everybody realizes that, you're going to have problems.

With those teams, we were always good about that. Nobody put pressure on anybody, Tito let us do our thing and we had a good time, and some guys liked to keep to themselves more than others. Billy Mueller—he was a quiet guy, too. But because Nomar was a superstar, because he was in Boston so long, it was like people expected more from him. I think it was tough. The guy just wanted to come to the ballpark and play every day, and I think a lot of people blamed him when we didn't play as well as we could have. We played .500 for a long time, bro, before Nomar came back and after. He was on our team in 2003, when we almost won the whole thing. Now it was a year later and he was the same dude, and he was the problem? It didn't make sense to me. I didn't see it that way.

To tell you the truth, we played .500 ball for another two weeks after the trade. By the time we got to the middle of August, we were 10½ games behind the Yankees and nobody gave us a chance to win the division. We were fighting to make the playoffs. From May 1 to August 15, we played 95 games and went 49–46. There was still a long way to go yet, a lot of baseball to play, but we were running out of time and we needed to start playing better or we were going to go home unhappy again.

And then it happened, bro.

We got hot.

It was like we couldn't lose.

From August 16 until the end of the season, we went 34–12 and we almost caught the Yankees. At one point, we went 20–2. We won six straight, lost, won ten more, lost, won another four. We were doing everything right. We got good pitching and we were hitting like crazy, and our defense got a lot better. By the time we went back to New York in the middle of September, we were just 3½ games out and we were the hottest team in baseball. We beat the Yankees in the first game of the series—again we beat Rivera—but they came back and beat us in the last two. The losses meant that it would be almost impossible for us to catch the Yankees and to win the American League East, but after what happened a year earlier, the division didn't mean as much. We knew we were going back to the playoffs. If we played well, we knew we would face the Yankees again. And with the way things had been going, we knew we could beat them.

About ten days after we left New York, we clinched a spot in the playoffs with a 7–3 win at Tampa Bay. We were still playing great, and we knew we were a better team than we were in 2003. We felt like we could beat anybody. Guys sprayed champagne and beer on each other after we clinched the playoff spot, and I guess some people asked Tito if we celebrated too much, if we were happy to just get back into the playoffs. They just didn't understand. We were just having fun, blowing off steam, and we had a crazy clubhouse where guys liked to cut loose. While guys were spraying champagne all over the place, I walked into the bathroom and put on some goggles, and I hooked a hose up to the sink. I walked back into the room and pretended like I was going to spray everyone, and you should have seen 'em all run. They were scared shitless, bro.

But that's the way that team was.

We played hard and we had fun.

And we won.

If people thought we weren't serious enough, they didn't understand. We wanted to win more than they did. After what happened in the Yankees series the year before, we wanted to get back there and beat them. The way the rules work in baseball, there was no chance of us playing the Yankees in the first round because we were in the same division.

So the way things lined up, we were going to play the Angels and the Yankees were going to play against my boys, the Twins. In some ways, we didn't care if the Yankees beat Minnesota or not because we felt like we were going to go to the World Series, no matter what. In other ways, we *wanted* the Yankees to win because we wanted to beat their asses after what happened in 2003.

If people couldn't see that, if they thought we were happy just to go back to the playoffs again, they weren't paying attention to us. I remember Pedro telling one reporter: "I'm expecting to go further and further. I don't want any more of [just] clinching the wild card. I want to go further and I'm pretty sure the whole team feels the same way."

We all did. We all said the same things. After we won ninety-five games in my first year in Boston, we won ninety-eight in 2004. We led the major leagues in runs scored both years. In 2004, we could hit, our defense was better, and we had good pitching. How could we be satisfied with just getting to the playoffs again? How could anybody think that? In some ways, we felt like our season was just starting. We felt that we had a lot of work to do. We felt that nobody was going to beat us.

Looking back, I don't think there was a way we could have lost.

BY THE TIME THE PLAYOFFS STARTED, I WAS READY, BRO. WE ALL were. I went to the playoffs with the Twins in 2002 and with the Red Sox in 2003, so I had the experience I needed. There wasn't any reason to be nervous. I had another good year—I finished with a .301 average, 41 homers and 139 RBIs—and I was ready to prove that I could play in October, too.

The Angels were really no match for us. Bengie could talk

all he wanted, but we had Schilling going in Game 1 and Pedro going in Game 2, and we felt like we were going to kick their asses. I'm sure they felt the same way about us, but we were just a better team. Some people were worried about Pedro's confidence because he didn't pitch well down the stretch, but I wasn't. I knew he'd be ready to go. I think Pedro wanted to pitch Game 1—wouldn't anyone? Tito decided to go with Schilling. I knew that would make Pedro pitch even better. Pedro was always at his best when people started to doubt him, when he had something to prove, and that's why he's one of the best ever. In a big game, I'd take my chances with him anytime.

Because Anaheim won their division, they had home-field advantage—even though we won more games than they did. It didn't matter. We won the first game, 9–3, and we won the second one, 8–3. As a team, I think we had twenty-three hits. We came to Boston for Game 3 and we were beating their asses again, 6–1, when they scored five runs in the seventh inning and tied the game. Vladimir Guerrero hit a grand slam that made the game 6–6, but that was about the only good thing that happened for Anaheim in the series. Vladi had a great September and he basically got the Angels into the playoffs all by himself—he ended up winning the MVP—but he was just one man. We were a whole team. We had a much deeper lineup. The game was still tied at six when I came up with a man on in the bottom of the tenth inning, and the Angels manager, Mike Scioscia, brought in Jarrod Washburn to pitch against me.

Washburn was a left-hander, but he was the kind of guy I could hit to the opposite field if I took the right approach. He threw mostly fastballs and he pitched up in the strike zone, and at Fenway Park, especially, I knew that my best chance was to hit the ball the other way. I had faced him twice in

Game 1—he started that game for them—and I had an RBI single and a walk. Pokey Reese was pinch-running at first base, so I knew we had speed on the bases. And because there were two outs, I knew that all I had to do was to hit the ball hard to the opposite field—maybe get a double—and Pokey could score. He'd be running on contact. Washburn gave me a pitch I could handle—a fastball up—and I drove it to the opposite field, toward left center. The ball ended up clearing the wall for a two-run homer that gave us an 8–6 win, and Fenway was going crazy while I was running around the bases.

At that time, I didn't really know what I started. The walk-off homer against Anaheim was the fourth of my career, the third with the Red Sox, but I hadn't hit one since April. That was very early in the year. Nobody—especially me—had any reason to believe that I would be getting walk-off hits all October or that I would be hitting walk-off homers, too. The playoffs don't usually work like that. The *game* doesn't work like that. At the time, all that really mattered was that we beat the Angels in Game 3, and everybody knew what that meant.

We swept the series, three games to none.

And we were going back to the American League Championship.

In the three games against the Angels, I went 6 for 11 with a home run, two doubles, and five walks. I was killin'. I had four RBIs and I scored four runs, and Manny had a big series, too. He went 5 for 13, with a homer, two doubles, and seven RBIs, and the Angels couldn't get either one of us out. They couldn't get *anybody* out. We were hot. We were hitting, we pitched, we made the plays. The Yankees were still playing against the Twins, and we didn't think it mattered who won. We were playing our best baseball of the year. We were peaking. We felt like we could beat anyone.

When the Yankees beat the Twins in four games, I think

everybody got what they wanted: Boston against New York again. Deep down, I think that's what we wanted. I think that's what the Yankees wanted, too. Because we swept the Angels, we had the chance to line up our pitching again, so we knew we would have Schilling in Game 1 and Pedro in Game 2, just like the Anaheim series. We were ready to go. We had to open the series on the road again—the Yankees had won the division—but that didn't bother us. We knew we could win there. We'd played a lot of games there over the last two years. We weren't intimidated by it anymore. We beat the Yankees in Game 6 at Yankee Stadium in 2003 and we had them beat in Game 7 until some things went against us, but we weren't afraid about playing them in New York.

By now, you know what happened. The Yankees beat us in Game 1, but it was only one game. The worst part for us was that Schilling hurt his ankle—he'd been pitching with a problem all year—but we still felt like we could win. The Yankees were beating us 8–0 in Game 1—that's *8–0*, bro—and we almost came back and won. We scored five runs in the sixth inning and two more in the seventh, and we would have tied the game if we'd caught a break. The Yankees had an 8–6 lead when I hit an RBI triple to left-center, and the ball just missed being a home run. It hit *the top of the wall*. It was 8–7 when Torre brought in Rivera, and then the Yankees scored two more runs and beat us 10–7.

But I think we sent them a message that night.

No matter how far ahead they were, we were going to fight.

The Yankees beat us again in Game 2, and this time we got shut down for the first time in the playoffs. Jon Lieber beat us (and Pedro), 3–1. It was a frustrating night. We were used to scoring against everybody. For Pedro, the start was his first against the Yankees since the end of the regular season, when he pitched a game against them in Boston. We were winning that game in the late innings until the Yankees rallied against Pedro to win—the game didn't really mean anything because we were both going to the playoffs—but Pedro was really frustrated. He wasn't pitching well then, and the Yankees were giving him some trouble. When the reporters asked him about the loss after the game, Pedro said that the Yankees were his "daddy" and that all he could do was tip his hat to them, and the media made a big deal about his comments, in Boston and in New York.

By the time the playoffs came, the fans at Yankee Stadium hadn't forgotten anything. They never do. They got on Pedro from the very beginning, and we all knew it was coming, right up until they started singing. *"Who's . . . your . . . daddy?"* Pedro ended up pitching a really good game, but we just couldn't get him any runs. I think we all wanted to score for him that night more than we've ever wanted to score for anybody. But even with the loss, we still weren't worried. We went back to Boston down two games to none, but we loved playing at home and we were tough to beat there. Our fans gave us a lot of confidence and we really liked to hit in our ballpark.

The way things went, I guess the Yankees did, too.

New York kicked our asses in Game 3, bro. They beat us, 19–8. I think everybody thought we were done. That game was one of the few times all postseason when our pitching failed us, but that's the way the game goes. You just don't have it some nights. The Yankees had a great lineup, too—A-Rod, Gary Sheffield, Hideki Matsui, and Bernie Williams all hurt us in that game—and you couldn't make mistakes against them. They'd make you pay. You had to make good pitches or they were going to beat your ass, and that's what they did to us. We pitched just about everybody we could—even Wakefield pitched in relief, and he was supposed to start Game 4—and everybody thought the series was over. Schilling was hurt. It looked like we didn't have a Game 4 starter. Pedro wasn't going to pitch until Game 5, at the earliest, and the Yankees had just kicked our asses on our home field. After the final out, I remember seeing this woman at Fenway Park in the stands, crying, and that was one of the first times I really saw how much the Red Sox meant to the people of Boston.

That's when I realized, too, that everybody thought we were done.

Everybody but us.

Before I go on, let me tell you again, bro: Baseball is a funny game. Confidence can make all the difference in the world. We knew we had a good team—we won 98 games and swept Anaheim—and we knew we could beat the Yankees. We just had to get rolling. Everybody was a little down when we left the ballpark that night, but we were ready to go when we showed up for Game 4. We felt like we could win. We felt that way every day. Tito decided to give the ball to Derek Lowe, and we had a lot of confidence in him. He was a good pitcher. D-Lowe could beat the Yankees. All we had to do was to start hitting and we'd be fine.

Before the game, we were loose, like always. I remember Millar going around the clubhouse and telling people not to count us out, that we were going to come back and win. That's the kind of team we were. Going back to the start of 2003, we won so many times when it looked like we were going to lose. We had a lot of tough guys, bro. We had a lot of good players. All we needed to do was to get a little momentum, get our confidence back, and we knew we could beat the Yankees. If we won one game, we could win two. If we won two, we could win three, If we could win three, we could win four.

That's just how we felt.

I just didn't know that I would be so important.

IT ALL STARTED IN GAME 4. WE WERE LOSING 2–0 WHEN WE SCORED three runs in the fifth inning, and I knocked in the last two with a single against Orlando Hernandez, who everybody called El Duque. The Yankees got two more runs in the sixth to go ahead, 4–3, and it stayed that way until the bottom of the ninth. Rivera was pitching and he walked Kevin Millar. Dave Roberts ran for Millar and stole second. Then Billy Mueller singled up the middle—his second big hit against Rivera, going back to the homer in July—and Roberts scored to tie the game at four.

I think that's when everybody really started to believe in us again.

A lot of people ask me about all of the clutch hits I had in 2004, but let me tell you: It was a lot more than me. What if Millar didn't walk? What if Roberts didn't steal? What if Billy Mueller didn't get a hit? We would have lost, bro. It would have been over. In baseball, it takes a lot of people to win a game. It's like I said before. You have to pitch, you have to hit, you have to play defense. If you don't do any one of those things right, you can lose the game. We had a lot of people do a lot of things right when we started to play better against the Yankees. It wasn't just me.

I just happened to be in the right place at the right time.

Game 4 was still tied, 4–4, when I came to bat against Paul Quantrill in the bottom of the twelfth. Manny led off with a single and was standing on first base, and I was pretty sure I knew how Quantrill would try to get me out. Quantrill was good pitcher and a tough guy, but he didn't throw hard like

Rivera. One of his best pitches was a sinker or what some guys call a two-seam fastball that usually gets the batter to hit a ground ball. Against left-handed batters like me, Quantrill could start the pitch at my thigh and make it bend back toward the plate—left to right from where he was standing—and that could make it tough for a guy like me to hit. With the pitch coming at you, your instinct is to back away a little, to move off the plate. But the ball would change direction and catch the inside corner, so you had to stay in the batter's box as long as possible and wait for the ball to break.

Remember when I talked about the Oakland series in 2003, when we came back and won the last three games after losing the first two? In the last game of that series, D-Lowe struck out Terrence Long with the same kind of pitch that Quantrill uses. The bases were loaded. We were winning by one. D-Lowe threw the pitch inside—it looked like it might hit the batter—and Long backed off the plate. Then the pitch changed direction and hit the inside corner, and Long didn't know what the hell happened.

Strike three.

Game over.

We win.

With Quantrill, I was pretty sure he would try the same thing. At that stage of the season, my confidence was so high that I was sure I could hit anyone with the right approach, so I was willing to take my chances. I just had to be patient. People ask me a lot now about clutch hitting, about why I'm so good at it, and I usually tell them the same thing: You have to be patient, bro. You can't try to do too much. Whenever I have a big at-bat, I try to simplify things, slow down, think about only positive things. I think about the pitcher I'm facing, how he'll try to get me out and what he's done against me in the past. But it's not like you have that much time. So you stand in the on-deck circle and try to prepare yourself, to keep things simple, and then you go up and hit.

When I finally got to hit against Quantrill, he did exactly what I thought he would. He pitched me inside. Washburn was trying to run the ball away from me when I homered against the Angels, so I knew I had to try to hit to the opposite field. With Quantrill, it was the opposite. I just had to stay back and wait for the ball to break, and then I had to open my hips and try to pull. And when I finally got the pitch I wanted, when I got one I could handle, I did exactly what I wanted to do.

I smoked it, bro.

By the time the ball landed in the Yankees bullpen, a two-run homer, we had a 6–4 win and everybody was going crazy. My teammates all came running out of the dugout and we celebrated at home plate, and I threw my helmet in the air just before I stepped on the plate. Against the Angels, when I homered to win Game 3 of the division series, I left my helmet on and I learned the hard way: It really hurts when people hit you on top of the head. Because you have a helmet on, everybody pounds away at the top of your head, and eventually you can't see. The helmet is pushed down over your eyes. So against the Yankees, when we won Game 4, I threw my helmet away right before I jumped into the pile. Now I see people do it all the time and I have to wonder: Did I start that?

Against the Yankees, we knew we still had a lot of work to do. The Yankees still led the series, three games to one, but Game 4 gave us some of our confidence back. We got some momentum. A lot of reporters wanted to talk to me after the game, and I remember telling them not to give up on us, not to think that it was over yet.

"Things can change," I said. "You never know what can happen from now on. We played a really good game tonight. It was a totally different game than the one we played [in Game 3, when we lost 19–8]."

We were alive, bro.

And we were feeling a little better about ourselves.

In some ways, Game 5 was a lot like Game 4. This time we were losing in the eighth inning, 4–2, when I led off with a home run against Tom Gordon. (Everybody called him Flash.) That made it 4–3. After Millar walked, Trot Nixon singled to center and we had runners on first and third with nobody out. Torre brought in Rivera again—and Rivera did a good job—but Jason Varitek hit a sacrifice fly against him that tied the game at four. We were even again. Rivera got out of the inning and got through the ninth, too, but our bullpen was pitching better now and the Yankees couldn't score against us, either. We played the tenth, eleventh, twelfth, and thirteenth innings without anybody scoring, and we went to the fourteenth with the game still tied at four.

By that time, a lot of guys had pitched. Torre had called in Esteban Loaiza to pitch against us, and Loaiza had good stuff. He shut us down for three innings. In 2003, when he was pitching for the Chicago White Sox, Loaiza won twenty-one games and he was one of the best pitchers in the league. His best pitch was a cut fastball, the same pitch Rivera throws, but nobody's is as good as Rivera's. But Loaiza could throw that pitch to both sides of the plate—and he could throw it for strikes. Against lefties like me, Loaiza could start the pitch off the outside corner, so that it would look like a ball, then bring it back over the plate for a strike. Other times, he could start the pitch in the center of the plate and move it in on your hands—like Rivera did—making you think you had a chance to hit it. And then, after you had started your swing, the ball would move in on you, tie you up, and you would end up hitting a weak grounder to second base or worse.

Compared to Quantrill, Loaiza was completely different. His ball usually moved in the opposite direction. I had to take a completely different strategy. We had runners at first and second base with two outs when I came up against him, and I knew I was in for a fight. I can't remember every pitch of the at-bat against Loaiza, but most of them (or all of them) were cutters. He moved them in and out, up and down, and I did all I could do to just keep the at-bat alive. I fouled a bunch of pitches off. I got to the tenth pitch of the at-bat—another cutter—and I was able to get enough good wood on it to muscle the ball into center field, just in front of Bernie Williams. JD was on second and he was running on contact, and he crossed the plate to give us a 5–4 win and make Fenway go crazy again.

I couldn't believe it, bro.

On two straight nights, against the Yankees in the American League Championship Series, I had two walk-off hits. My phone was ringing off the hook. The chances of anybody getting two walk-off hits like that, in about twenty-four hours, are probably about the same as a team coming back to win four straight after losing the first three games of a seven-game series.

But we were halfway there now, bro.

The series was now three games to two.

And we were going back to New York.

Know what else I remember about Game 5? As happy as we were, I remember thinking that we couldn't keep winning that way, getting big hits at the last minute, cutting it so close. That's a dangerous way to play. Really good teams get contributions from everybody. The Yankees were a good team and we needed everyone to beat them—not just me—and we were making it hard on ourselves. We were pitching great and playing good defense, but we needed everyone to contribute because that was the only way you were going to beat the Yankees in a seven-game series.

And in Games 6 and 7, everyone did his part.

By now, I'm sure you know that we went to New York and won the last two games to eliminate the Yankees and win the series, coming all the way back after losing the first three games. In Game 6, Mark Bellhorn hit a big three-run homer against Jon Lieber, who shut us down in Game 2, and Schilling came back to pitch on a bad ankle and shut down the Yankees. He was gutsy, bro. On the next night, in Game 7, I hit a two-run homer in the first inning—I was killin'—and we scored four more runs in the second. The Yankees never really had a chance. We won the game, 10–3, and nobody was asking questions about whether we could come back and beat the Yankees anymore. No team in baseball history had ever come back to win a seven-game series after losing the first three, but we did it, against the Yankees, in New York, and we beat Rivera twice to get there.

After Game 7, people were calling our series win against the Yankees the greatest comeback in the history of team sports, and I wasn't about to argue. I don't know enough about every comeback every team has ever made, but I don't know how any could be bigger than ours. Coming back from three games down, that was something no team had ever done in baseball. After Game 3, everyone thought we were going to lose. (Except us.) And this was against the Yankees, our rivals, in their house, after we had gone eighty-six years without winning a World Series. I mean, there was so much at stake. After the Yankees beat us in 2003, after we got Foulke and Schilling, after A-Rod went to New York, *we came back and beat them.* To the people in Boston, that meant as much as winning the World Series. Our owners were in the clubhouse celebrating with us and it was like we won the World Series, like we finally ended the curse. I think that meant as much to the people of Boston as anything.

I know it meant a lot to us.

For me, after the walk-off hits in Games 4 and 5, things were just starting to change, but I really didn't have time to notice yet. I got named the American League Championship MVP after hitting for a .387 average, with 3 home runs and 11 RBIs in the series, but I was still focused on other things. As happy as everybody was, we still had work to do.

We were going to the World Series.

We needed to win four more games.

We hadn't really beaten the curse yet.

THE ST. LOUIS CARDINALS WON 105 GAMES IN 2004 AND A LOT OF people thought they were the best team in baseball, better than even us or the Yankees. But looking back, I don't think it really mattered who we were playing against or where we played the games. At that time, I don't think anybody could have beaten us.

We were on a roll.

After Game 3 of the Yankees series—the game we lost 19–8—we didn't lose again. We took the final four games against New York and we won the first four against St. Louis—that's eight straight against two of the best teams in baseball—and we won the World Series. I hit another homer in the first inning of the first game against the Cardinals—it was my first career World Series at-bat—and there was no looking back. In the four games against St. Louis, we never fell behind. Not once. We batted .283 and the Cardinals hit .190. We scored twenty-four runs and they scored twelve. Schilling, Pedro, and D-Lowe all won games for us, and Keith Foulke pitched in all four games of the series. Manny went 7 for 17 (a .412 average) with one run and four RBIs, and he was named the Series MVP.

It's like I told you, bro.

Everybody did his part.

We couldn't lose.

In my first World Series, I batted .308 with my Game 1 homer and four RBIs. I walked four times. For the whole post-season, I went 22 for 55—a .400 average—with 6 home runs and 19 RBIs in fourteen games. I had three walk-off hits, two of them homers. I walked thirteen times. I had the best year of my big-league career and my team won the World Series, and I got to be a part of history. I waited my whole life to get a chance like that, to play in the World Series, and I felt like I didn't have to prove anything to anybody.

We were the world champs, bro.

And I was pretty sure I didn't have to worry about getting released.

STEPPING OUT OF THE BOX:
TERRY RYAN AND THEO EPSTEIN

I n baseball, as in physics, Isaac Newton's third law of motion holds true: For each and every action, there is an equal and opposite reaction.

But for the Boston Red Sox, it took eighty-six years of wretched history to prove that point.

When the Red Sox signed David Ortiz on January 22, 2003, the news hardly qualified as a lead story in the pages of either the *Boston Herald* or *Boston Globe*, the two city dailies that regularly cover the Red Sox throughout the year. During the winter months, baseball goes dormant in many places in the country, but Boston is one of the remaining few cities—New York is another—where baseball is regarded as a twelve-month-a-year obsession and, in some cases, addiction. One of the ironies of following the Red Sox, in fact, is that the team frequently makes bigger news in the winter than in the summer, something that does not reflect especially well on Boston's on-field pursuits during the team's considerable history.

In Boston, as the story goes, the winter generally serves as that time when the Red Sox clean up the mess they made in the preceding months.

By the time Ortiz signed a one-year contract for $1.25 million, however, much of the annual Red Sox housecleaning already had taken place. Though the Red Sox had won ninety-three games in what was otherwise a generally successful 2002 campaign, they had fallen six games short of their simplest objective: the playoffs. The Red Sox had operated during the 2002 season with an interim general manager, respected baseball veteran and executive Mike Port, a fact that proved symbolic in every way imaginable. The Red Sox were in a state of transition. Less than a year earlier, the team had been sold. The roster and front office were about to undergo a dramatic and radical overhaul, the latter of which took place when the team named then-twenty-eight-year-old general manager Theo Epstein the permanent replacement to Port, who had previously worked under former general manager Dan Duquette.

Even then, Epstein was not the club's first choice. Despite considerable efforts, Red Sox owner John Henry and president Larry Lucchino had failed to lure away general manager Billy Beane from the Oakland A's, for whom Beane was consistently building playoff-caliber teams despite a significantly smaller payroll than many other major-league clubs.

In retrospect, had Beane landed in Boston, there is no telling how the Red Sox might have changed.

Or whether things might have changed at all.

Of course, Red Sox history was filled with crossroads of the like, places where the Red Sox invariably made the wrong turn. How many times could things have been different? In 1978, despite having one of the best teams in their history, the

Red Sox lost a historic one-game playoff to the rival New York Yankees, who went on to win their second consecutive world title; in 1972, when a labor dispute between players and owners erased a chunk of the regular-season schedule, the Red Sox finished a seemingly impossible half game behind the first-place Detroit Tigers, who (for whatever reason) were allowed to play one more game during the season; and then there were the seasons of 1946, '67, '75, and '86, when the Red Sox lost the World Series in the maximum seven games. In the last instance, the Red Sox did so despite having a 5–3 lead with two outs, the bases empty, and two strikes on the batter (New York Mets catcher Gary Carter) in the bottom of the tenth inning in what proved to be an apocalyptic sixth game.

Still, in Red Sox history, all of those occasions were nothing more than spin-offs to Boston's decision to sell Babe Ruth to the Yankees prior to the 1920 season, a literal and proverbial fork in the road that forever altered the history of both franchises.

What if Boston had kept Ruth?

What might have happened then?

Over the years, the decision of then–Sox owner Harry Frazee took on enormous significance, helping to spawn both a clever, creative book by author and longtime *Boston Globe* columnist Dan Shaughnessy as well as an explanation of the fate that befell the Red Sox in the twentieth century. Thus was born the Curse of the Bambino. In reality, theories differed as to why Frazee sold Ruth to his chief rivals in the American League, though the most popular and accepted version always has been that Frazee sought to finance a Broadway play, *No, No, Nanette*. Regardless, the simplest truths were two: Frazee sold Ruth because he needed the money—Ruth's price tag was a reported $125,000—and during Ruth's fourth season in New York, 1923, the Yankees won the first of their twenty-six world titles, in an eighty-six-year period in which the Red Sox did not win a single one.

By the winter of 2002–03, with the Red Sox having gone (at the time) *only* eighty-four years since their last world championship (in 1918), nobody imagined that the Red Sox would turn the tables and capitalize on someone else's blunder.

And no one ever could have guessed that David Americo Ortiz would become, in some ways, retribution for Babe Ruth, that Ortiz would be the key to lifting the Curse of the Bambino.

FOR AN ETERNITY, IT SEEMS, THE MINNESOTA TWINS HAVE BEEN LOOK-ing for power hitters. Even now, in a cynical age when baseball has endured skepticism about everything from steroid use to smaller ballparks to souped-up baseballs, the Twins have not had a player with forty home runs in one season since 1969, when eventual Hall of Famer Harmon Killebrew clubbed a team record of 49.

Still, what the Twins lacked in power, they frequently made up for in shrewd decision making and an emphasis on fundamentals. Minnesota won the World Series in both 1987 and 1991 with relatively young, sound, and aggressive teams that stressed the little things. And even when the Twins were at their worst during an eight-year stretch in which they failed to finish even once with a winning record, opposing teams frequently traveled to Minnesota expecting to compete against a scrappy Minnesota team that played good defense, ran the bases both well and aggressively, and, above all else, placed a premium on that most endearing athletic quality: hustle.

While Twins general manager Terry Ryan had put value on all of those things since taking over Minnesota's baseball operation in 1994, he also had acted with commendable judgment. When the Twins traded away All-Star second baseman Chuck

Knoblauch to the New York Yankees in 1998, for instance, Ryan acquired (in addition to $3 million in cash) four young players in outfielder Brian Buchanan, pitcher Danny Mota, pitcher Eric Milton, and shortstop Cristian Guzman, the latter two of whom would become staples in Minnesota's lineup for several years; in 1999, Ryan worked a deal with the Florida Marlins in which the Twins ended up with the rights to young left-handed pitcher Johan Santana, who would go on to win two Cy Young Awards as the best pitcher in the American League; and in 2003, Ryan executed the kind of trade on which careers are built, sending catcher A. J. Pierzynski to the San Francisco Giants for a trio of young pitchers named Joe Nathan (who would become a dominating, All-Star closer), promising right-hander Boof Bonser, and an oft-injured prospect and left-handed pitcher named Francisco Liriano, who took baseball by storm during the summer of 2006 and established himself as a candidate for the American League Rookie of the Year Award.

But for all of the good decisions that Ryan has made during his tenure as Twins GM, one will forever follow him: He is the man who released David Ortiz.

"To be up front with everything surrounding the scenario, this wasn't an economic decision. I'd be less than honest if I said it was," Ryan admitted shortly after the 2006 season, one in which the Twins qualified for the postseason while Ortiz established a Red Sox franchise record with fifty-four home runs. "I misevaluated him. There are other players we've had that we've shown more patience with, and that's where we made the mistake with David. That's the fact. I don't want to pretend that it was anything else. There's nobody that wouldn't want to pay for the production that David has given Boston."

Still, in modern baseball, especially, economics are at the core of almost every transaction. Under the terms of the collective bargaining agreement between baseball players and owners, teams have tremendous control over a player's salary during the first three years of his career. Most players with less than three years of service make less than $500,000 per season, significantly lower than the approximate $2.7 million average salary of all players during the 2006 season. That number then begins to escalate rapidly through the processes known as salary arbitration and free agency, the latter of which results when a player has completed six full years of service in the major leagues.

At that point, assuming he is not under contract with another team, the player can then peddle his services to the highest bidder. And depending on a player's value, the process can lead to excessive bidding that culminates with a familiar sound.

Cha-ching.

For a team like the Twins, however, baseball's salary structure and economic system frequently required them to make difficult decision at the most difficult times. In baseball, perhaps more than any other sport, the growth and development of players can be slow, gradual, deliberate. Players sometimes can spend several years in the minor leagues and two to three years in the majors before realizing their potential, which requires patience and money. Some major-league players are drafted and others are not, but they all are paid— and some more than others. And in the instances of many small-market teams like the Twins, players are just beginning to realize their potential when their salaries are due to begin escalating, forcing teams to make judgments not solely on their ability or potential but also on their *value*.

Frequently, the question is not whether a player is *good enough*, but rather whether he is *worth the money*.

In the case of Ortiz, Minnesota's ability to make a sound judgment was further clouded by another matter: injuries.

During his time with the Twins, Ortiz had injuries to his hamate bone, wrist, and knee, all of which required him to miss time on the field. The end result was a career during which Ortiz showed flashes of his ability in inconsistent bursts, though some of that had as much to do with Minnesota—at least in Ortiz's case—perhaps placing too much emphasis on defense and not enough on what was clearly a unique ability to hit a baseball.

And to hit one with power.

"We had a little problem as far as the stamina or durability, but the injuries David experienced here were not career threatening," said Ryan, who never has been shy about accepting responsibility for releasing Ortiz. "That's another issue. Things like hamate bones—that happens."

In fact, the Twins themselves acquired Ortiz for the same reasons the Red Sox did: They recognized in him a raw and natural ability to hit. Ryan recalls scouting Minnesota's minor-league affiliates when he saw Ortiz play for the first time for Wisconsin (an affiliate of the Seattle Mariners) in the Class-A Midwest League, and in 1996 Ryan traded veteran third baseman Dave Hollins to the Mariners for the slugger. The Mariners were in playoff contention and needed a veteran third baseman, so Seattle did what so many clubs do as a long and arduous baseball season reaches its critical stages: Sensing an opportunity to win a championship, the Mariners traded away a (very) young and promising player (Ortiz) for a more reliable, established veteran. Among most baseball executives, after all, it was understood that such trades were to be made if a championship was at stake.

A year later—the 1996 Mariners missed the playoffs, as it turned out—Seattle began paying the price. Ortiz blew through Single A, Double A, and Triple A to reach the major leagues by the end of the season, and the Twins fully believed that they had something special on their hands.

Of course, they did.

"We had some [scouts] in the Midwest League and we had a couple of people recommend [Ortiz]. I had to make room for Todd Walker [another prospect, to play third base in the major leagues] and that's how it started," Ryan said of the decision to trade Hollins. "He came over here and we got him to the instructional league [after the 1996 season], and I remember our people down there telling me that the ball sounded different coming off his bat [compared to most other players]. I remember that."

Nonetheless, for an assortment of reasons already mentioned, the Twins were still waiting for Ortiz to blossom when the moment of truth came following the 2002 season. Ortiz had four years of major-league service to his credit and his $950,000 salary was due to balloon to roughly $2 million, and Minnesota officials were frustrated by what they ultimately decided was insufficient development. Ortiz had been injured. Rightly or wrongly, they were skeptical about his defense. His production was too inconsistent for a team with limited resources that had to maximize every dollar spent—or so they felt—and so Ryan and his aides began looking for a solution. Twins assistant general manager Bill Smith called one of Ortiz's agents, Diego Bentz, and informed him that the Twins had reached a crossroads with their client. The alternatives were clear. The Twins could keep Ortiz, which seemed increasingly unlikely, or they could try to trade him. If neither option proved out, the Twins would be forced to unceremoniously release the player, though Minnesota officials were hoping it would not come to that.

At that moment, recognizing that paying Ortiz was unrealistic and that releasing him was particularly unappetizing, the

Twins set out to trade him. Twins officials went to baseball's annual off-season convention—the winter meetings—intent on exploring any and all deals that would allow them to send Ortiz to another club.

"Bill Smith had called me up and indicated that they didn't know what David's situation would be," said Bentz. "They said they were going to look for trades for him and, basically, they couldn't find one."

And when that happened, the rest of major-league baseball similarly received an indictment.

At one point, in fact, Ryan said he called the remaining franchises in baseball to see if any of the twenty-nine would be willing to trade a prospect for David Ortiz, and the proposed deals covered an array of scenarios and possibilities. In some of those instances, the team acquiring Ortiz would have to send the Twins nothing at all if they subsequently were unable to sign Ortiz to a new contract.

Not a single club took the bait.

Facing an annual deadline on (or about) December 20, by which date all teams had to decide which players to retain for the coming season—this *tender date,* as it is known in baseball, has since been moved up a week under the terms of baseball's latest bargaining agreement—Ryan and the Twins made a costly and inevitable decision. They released Ortiz on December 16, knowing that Ortiz would end up somewhere else, hoping that the decision would not come back to haunt them.

"I called him directly. I'm not going to hide from that [responsibility]," Ryan said. "I called David in the Dominican, and that wasn't a very [enjoyable] phone call to make. There was a lot of silence on the other line when I told him he'd been released. He came up to [the major leagues] with [Torii] Hunter and [Corey] Koskie and Jacque Jones and [A. J.] Pierzynski— all those guys. David was a part of that and I think he was comfortable in that group. I think he wanted to be a part of us and a part of that. And people liked to be around David for a good reason—he's a generous guy.

"I don't have a bad word to say about the guy," Ryan continued. "I think he's one of the good guys in the game. I don't know why it didn't happen here in a more rapid fashion, but it just didn't. For him to go on and be an icon in Boston, I'm happy for him."

As for the Twins, they continue to produce promising young talent. In 2006, first baseman Justin Morneau became the first Minnesota player since 1987 (Kent Hrbek) to hit as many as thirty home runs in a season. Teammate Hunter, a brilliant center fielder and charismatic personality, subsequently finished the season with thirty-one homers and inspired club officials to exercise a $12 million option on his contract for the 2007 season.

Still, with regard to Ortiz, the Twins can only wonder about what might have been.

"God knows what would have happened [over the last several years] if we had had that type of production [from Ortiz]. We've been looking for that type of home run and RBI production here for a long time," Ryan said of Ortiz, who *averaged* slightly more than 43 home runs and 131 RBIs during his first four seasons after leaving Minnesota.

"David Ortiz was out there for the taking, and no one grabbed him," Ryan concluded, with more than a hint of disbelief in his voice. "And Theo was good enough or smart enough or fortunate enough to give him a chance."

TRUTH BE TOLD, THEO WASN'T SO SURE, EITHER.

"It was a good move, but we weren't that prescient," a thirty-two-year-old Theo Epstein, the general manager of the

Red Sox, said following the 2006 baseball season, Ortiz's fourth in Boston. "We thought we were getting a guy who had the potential to be a hitter in the middle of our batting order, but we didn't see this kind of maturation or explosion."

How could they?

How could anyone?

The 2002 Red Sox, too, were at a crossroads, and in many ways it was fitting that the then-twenty-eight-year-old Epstein was given control over changing the face of the franchise. Though they had qualified for the postseason in 1998 and '99, the Red Sox seemed to grow stale during the summers of 2000, '01, and '02. The '01 season, in particular, had done considerable damage to even the most blindly loyal and masochistic Red Sox fan; it had culminated in an inglorious finish following the September 11 terrorist attacks. At several points, while baseball was shut down as America grieved, and after, the Red Sox were so dysfunctional and downright detached that their star players (Pedro Martinez, Carl Everett, and Manny Ramirez) were openly and disrespectfully undermining the authority of an interim manager, Joe Kerrigan, who had lost control of the team.

Following a 2002 season that was, if nothing else, a step in the right direction—for starters, the Sox fired Kerrigan during spring training and replaced him with the far more popular Grady Little—the young Epstein began giving the Red Sox the makeover they so desperately needed, on and off the field.

"A lot of research we had done on [Ortiz] showed he was an extremely popular player, not just with the Dominican players but with all players," Epstein said. "At that time, that was important to us, too."

Nonetheless, baseball is a business.

A smile only gets you so much.

Identifying those areas at which the Red Sox were getting

the least for their money—specifically, first, second, and third bases—Epstein made a series of maneuvers. In a trade with the Cincinnati Reds, he acquired second baseman Todd Walker (who by then had also become a Minnesota castoff) to displace the offensively impotent Rey Sanchez; he obtained first baseman and outfielder Jeremy Giambi in a trade with the Philadelphia Phillies; he signed free agent infielder Bill Mueller to a contract for relatively short money, a two-year, $4.5 million contract (an average of $2.25 million per season) with a club option that could keep Mueller in Boston for a third season.

And all the while Epstein challenged baseball protocol by pursuing infielder-outfielder Kevin Millar, a talented and underrated hitter who had resigned himself to the reality of playing in Japan. Placed on waivers by the cash-strapped Florida Marlins for the purpose of facilitating his trip to the Far East, Millar was unexpectedly claimed by the Red Sox, prompting him to rethink his position on Japan and to conjure up an amusing story about how his family was pleading with him to remain in the United States while America was at war with Iraq.

Had a team other than the Red Sox (or one like them) put in a claim for Millar, of course, the hitter would have spent the summer of 2003 eating sushi, presumably from a reinforced war bunker beneath his apartment near the home of the Chunichi Dragons.

And then, sitting on the open market like an unwrapped present, there was David Ortiz.

At that stage of the holiday grab served up as baseball's off-season, what could a box like that possibly hold?

"I was in the Dominican earlier that off-season and I was invited to a dinner at the Presidential Palace," said Fernando Cuza, another of the agents who represents Ortiz. "When I was down there, I ran into Larry Lucchino [the Red Sox president] and John Henry [the team owner] and I talked to them about two guys that I thought could help their team. I talked to them about David and I asked Pedro [Martinez] to make a call, and he did. I really thought Pedro's endorsement would help—and it did."

As for the other player whom Cuza recommended . . .

"Ramiro Mendoza," said the agent, citing a player whom the Red Sox also signed and whose career in Boston failed miserably.

But then, as it turned out, David Ortiz succeeded enough for both of them.

Like most baseball executives, Epstein was familiar with Ortiz. As an aide to San Diego Padres general manager Kevin Towers, who served as one of Epstein's most influential mentors during the young executive's development, Epstein was responsible for evaluating players in the minor-league systems of the other twenty-nine organizations in major-league baseball. Epstein had been working in baseball operations since only 1997, but he was regarded as something of a prodigy in an industry that, overall, was undergoing dramatic changes. Baseball always had been run by older men—the crustier the better—and the game had evolved over decades and decades. There was an accepted way of doing things. Evaluators and scouts were deemed the "lifeblood" of the game, and the only way to become a good evaluator was to spend years watching young players, attending games, driving from town to town, and staying in truck-stop motels or sleeping in the backseat of a broken-down car.

By the turn of the millennium, that routine earned scouts enough frequent-flier miles to travel around the world and enough hotel points to spend a winter in Fiji, but such perks tainted the image and made scouting out to be far more glamorous than it was.

The bottom line, as was the case in many things, was that there was no substitute for *experience*.

Yet, beginning with the ascension and success of Oakland A's general manager Billy Beane and a revolutionary approach to evaluation that came to be known as moneyball—the philosophy took its name from a Michael Lewis book about the A's and, in particular, Beane—that all began to change. Baseball evaluators began placing more emphasis on quantitative analysis, or sabermetrics, the study of statistics and their trends and less on the opinions of scouts and evaluators. By charting a player's production, tendencies, and strengths, teams believed they could more accurately forecast a player's performance. Subjective analysis (scouting) was being replaced with cold, hard facts (data), and the game was moving into a computer and Internet age where bright, young minds (who just happened to like baseball) could advance rapidly in a world that was starting to eye players as if they were stocks and bonds.

What was the value?

Was it going up or was it going down?

Would it be more prudent to buy or to sell?

A graduate of Yale University and the University of San Diego Law School, Epstein was just twenty-three when he began working in baseball operations, under Towers, during the 1997 season. That was the year that Ortiz blew through the Twins' minor-league system and eventually reached the major leagues. And two years later, when Epstein was in his second season evaluating the talent in other organizations, Ortiz was enjoying a 1999 campaign that was the best minor-league season of his career.

That year, in 476 at-bats over 130 games, the twenty-three-year-old Ortiz batted .315 with 30 home runs and 110 RBIs.

The executive and the player, it seemed, were on the same career path.

"My job in San Diego back in '98 or '99 was to keep track of the farm systems of other teams," said Epstein succinctly. "Back then, we had identified him, based on his performance, as a guy we'd like to acquire."

Now, several years later, Ortiz was available, albeit under far different circumstances: He had been released by his previous team, the Twins. Epstein felt confident in the acquisitions he had made and was hopeful the club would also be able to acquire Millar, but the Red Sox expressed interest just the same. "In a game like baseball, a team could never have enough talent or depth. Epstein had received calls on Ortiz's behalf from more than one player—along with Martinez, outfielder Manny Ramirez also urged the general manager to sign Ortiz—and Martinez's opinion, in particular, held weight with some Red Sox officials. During his first five seasons in Boston, Martinez had won two Cy Young Awards and finished second for another. He was coming off a twenty-win season. The Red Sox had yet to exercise a $17.5 million option on Martinez's contract for the 2004—that decision came a few months later—and there was still hope within the Boston organization that they could re-sign Martinez for the long term, thereby keeping the centerpiece of their starting rotation and pitching staff.

In short, the Red Sox had plenty to gain from signing Ortiz, not just Ortiz's abilities as a hitter, but also their relationship with Martinez, whose happiness and productivity (like that of most people) typically went hand in hand.

And rest assured, too, that Martinez knew his opinion meant something.

Still, Epstein had some concerns about what might happen if he succeeded in acquiring *both* Millar and Ortiz, thereby creating a glut at first base that might be difficult to resolve. In the end, the young general manager came to the conclusion that it would be a good problem to have. The Red Sox had several other holes—the team needed a major upgrade in its corps of relief pitchers—and Epstein reasoned that he could trade whatever surplus he had among Millar, Ortiz, and his other new offensive acquisitions for a relief pitcher at a later date.

"It was just luck and good timing," Epstein said. "The way we assessed the needs of the team, we needed at least a couple of corner bats. It was a good market to be aggressive on the lower- or midterm players, so we let [outfielder and first baseman] Cliff Floyd go [to free agency] and decided to spread the money around a little bit.

"We wanted to see if he could play first base," Epstein continued, speaking of Ortiz. "So we asked Dave Jauss [then a scout with the Red Sox who was managing in the Dominican winter league] to see if he could sneak Ortiz away and see if it was a realistic option. Jaussy did a great job, but I think it was really perfunctory at that point."

The doubters?

"At least one of our major-league scouts—who shall remain nameless—didn't want Ortiz at all because he said there was a hole in his swing," Epstein said.

Still, while the Red Sox were deciding to go forward, Ortiz similarly had decisions to make. Though the Red Sox pursued him most aggressively, his experience in Minnesota had taught him that there was a difference between the *best* place and the *right* place. He wanted to go somewhere he could play, but also somewhere he could excel. Bentz remembers some of Ortiz's friends and supporters advising him against playing for the Red Sox; they felt that Boston was too competitive a team and had too much talent to afford Ortiz consistent playing time. But Ortiz's agents, like his father, told him to trust in his ability and in their judgment.

Ultimately, reasoned Bentz, Boston was a place to play *and* be recognized, and in that way the Red Sox seemed like a perfect fit.

"I give David and his dad all the credit in the world because they remained confident," Bentz said. "His dad was a real big influence at the time because [David's] mom had passed away the previous year. I remember having a conversation where Leo said to David, 'If you think you're a medicore player, go to a mediocre team. But if you think you're a good player, go to a good team.'"

And so they all agreed.

It was decided.

Ortiz was going to Boston.

On January 22, 2003, with all parties pointed in the same direction, Epstein quickly worked with agents Cuza and Bentz to formalize a one-year contract that assured Ortiz would be playing for the Red Sox during the 2003 season. That the signing took place roughly three weeks before the start of spring training was an indication of how little interest there was in the player beyond Boston, though the timing hardly seemed to matter. Still, because many big-market teams had settled on their rosters for the approaching season, the signing was a little unusual. Big-market teams like the Red Sox, especially, did not typically hold job auditions during spring training; and if they did, they had long since settled on their candidates. That was especially true during the winter between the 2002 and 2003 baseball seasons, when there was a cluster of more affordable options for a team like the Red Sox. Epstein, in fact, also had inquired about another free agent that winter—designated hitter Brad Fullmer—to go along with his pursuit of Millar, Mueller, and Giambi. By late January, when most all of those players were signed, Ortiz was desperate, and the Red

Sox still had some uncertainty at first base, so both team and player had a need for each other.

In Ortiz's case, especially, he needed a job.

"When you have a player who is happy-go-lucky like David, with his natural ability, and his [professional] world caves around him, it's a wake-up call," said Cuza. "I had trouble getting him a job. I really couldn't find him one. And when that happened, I think something clicked with him. I think he sort of said to himself, 'If you put me in the right situation, that will never happen again.' "

Continued the agent: "David always had an incredible personality and he's always been a great guy to have in the clubhouse and I knew that meant something to [the Red Sox], too. He's always been a great teammate. Everywhere he's been, he's always had a major impact [on the people]. There are certain people that go to a big stage and that can handle it or thrive on it. David loves to go to the ballpark [in Boston]. Once David got on a roll over there and got going and got productive, he really felt good about that. And when that happened, I think people in Boston saw that personality. People in Boston are the kind of fans that really want to know their players. They want to know everything. They want to know if their players are good guys, things like that. They are so into that."

Of course, at the time, such matters seemed like unneccessary complexities. The bottom line, after all, was that the Red Sox still had a need. Ortiz did, too. And so, unsurprisingly, negotiations between the team and agent went swiftly, with Ortiz agreeing to a relatively modest one-year contract for $1.25 million that was, at the time, roughly *half* of the average salary of a major-league player.

For Red Sox historians, too, the number seemed terribly fitting.

Eighty-three years earlier, after all, the Red Sox sold Babe Ruth for one less zero—a tidy $125,000.

But then, after more than fourscore years of baseball, the game was bound to experience some inflation.

LIKE BABE RUTH, DAVID ORTIZ BATS LEFT-HANDED. LIKE RUTH, ORTIZ is a mountain of a man. Like Ruth, Ortiz has both an affection for and an appeal to children. Like Ruth, he has a nickname.

Papi.

Like Ruth, too, Ortiz had a profound impact on the history of the Red Sox, whose extraordinary drought without a world title came to an end in October 2004, thanks largely to the efforts of the man whom the Minnesota Twins deemed expendable. In the 2004 American League Championship Series between the Red Sox and New York Yankees, Ortiz batted .387 with 3 home runs and 11 RBIs, earning honors as the Most Valuable Player of a riveting seven games. Still, those numbers do not even begin to measure his importance to the Red Sox or to their history, the latter forever altered with Boston's historic comeback against New York (from three games down in the series) and subsequent sweep of the St. Louis Cardinals in the World Series.

Though Ortiz did not begin playing regularly for the Red Sox until roughly halfway through his first season in Boston— "Ortiz was getting a little bit of the short end of the stick," said Epstein—nobody could have denied him once he was finally afforded the opportunity to play every day; he was simply too good to take out of the lineup. In the final three months of the 2003 season, Ortiz had more home runs (27) than any other player in the American League. And over the long term, from July 1 of the 2003 season through the end of the 2006 campaign, Ortiz was the runaway major-league leader in both home runs (169) and RBIs (489), posting totals that rivaled those of Ruth during the Babe's peak years of production, though, at the time, the major league regular season consisted of eight fewer games.

Along the way, the Red Sox signed Ortiz to contracts worth $4.6 million (one year), $12.5 million (two years), and $52 million (four years), the latter of which was agreed to during the early stages of the 2006 season and all but ensured that Ortiz will remain with the Red Sox through at least 2010.

Before that final deal, even after Ortiz was earning multi-millions annually, Epstein once playfully admitted that he almost felt "guilty" that the Red Sox had hit the jackpot with their charismatic slugger.

"The goal of any contract is for it to work for both sides," Epstein said. "It's uncomfortable for the player when he signs a big deal and he doesn't perform or he gets hurt, and it can be just as uncomfortable for the club. To David's credit, he never brought it up. I think it ended up working out for both sides."

That is something even typically cynical Red Sox fans do not dispute.

THE LEGEND
GROWS

The 2004 season didn't end when we won the World Series. It just kept going, right into spring training, right into Opening Day, right into our home opener, when we got our championship rings. It was April, bro. And we were still celebrating.

It was one hell of a party.

Until we won the World Series, until people started going crazy and we had the parade in Boston, I don't think I realized what had happened, what I accomplished, what we all did. It was all moving so fast that none of us had time to think. But after we beat St. Louis and flew back to Boston, I think we all started to understand it better. There were people waiting for us as soon as we got off the plane and when we got back to Fenway Park. The whole city was going crazy. People were yelling out our names everywhere we went, and we all felt like heroes. It was unbelievable, bro. It really was. And after something like that happens, after you go home where it's quiet, you finally have the time to think and to understand. *We won the World Series.* That was something the Red Sox hadn't done in a long time. A lot of people probably thought the Red Sox would never win again.

The day we had the parade—I've never seen anything like it. I think more than three million people showed up. The weather was cold and rainy—it was a terrible day, bro—and the people were all out there, standing on the side of the road and on balconies, all kinds of stuff. They were carrying signs, calling our names, screaming like crazy. Next to beating the Yankees and the Cardinals, it was the best feeling in the world. I wish everybody could have an experience like that. You feel like you're on top of the world. I brought Tiff with me on the parade, along with my friends and my marketing agent, Alex Radetsky, who works with Fernando and Diego. There wasn't much space, but I didn't care; I wanted them all to feel a part of it. A lot of guys brought their wives, kids, girlfriends—whoever. We wanted everyone to enjoy it as much as we did. The way the Red Sox set it up with the city of Boston, we took these tour boats—they're called duck boats—through the streets of downtown Boston. These boats were unbelievable, bro. They had wheels like a regular truck, but then they could go in the water and float like boats, too. It actually made me a little nervous. When we drove off the road and pulled into the Charles River, I looked at everybody and I was like: "How is this thing going to float, dude?" Everybody laughed. But it was really cold outside and I don't really like the water, so I put on a life vest. Everybody cracked up.

The fans—they were great. When the boats pulled into river, some fans even got into the water, just to get closer to us. They had their faces painted and everything. During the parade, I was wearing a T-shirt—it said, "Who's your Papi?"—and the fans loved it. Those T-shirts were everywhere. After all of the stuff that happened with Pedro during the Yankees series—all those chants of "Who's your daddy?"—Alex, Diego, and Fernando approached this company in Florida with the idea for those shirts. That's how the whole thing started. And by the time the series ended—by the time I got all those hits and became the MVP of the series—it seemed like everybody was wearing one. And they all reminded me of when we came back to beat the Yankees in Game 7, when there were a bunch of Red Sox fans behind the third-base dugout while we celebrated on the field. They started chanting, "Who's your Papi?" the same way that Yankees fans did when Pedro on the mound in Game 2, only this time there wasn't anybody there to answer. The Yankees were gone, bro. Their fans had gone home.

I think that's why those shirts meant so much to people.

Right about that time, during the parade and after, I think I started to understand what I did, all the game-winning hits, what it meant. In a lot of ways, my career was just starting again. Even after the season I had in 2003—when I finished fifth in the Most Valuable Player Award voting—I don't think a lot of people knew who I was. I think they just looked at me as a guy who had one big year and who might never have another one, because that happens to a lot of players. Even after I had another big year in 2004, I think people saw me as a good player, as a developing player, but I'm not sure anybody really looked at me as a superstar. That all changed after the 2004 playoffs. There are a lot of good players and a lot of good hitters in baseball, but not many people make it to that next level. One of the ways you can really get there is to win a championship, and I was able to play a big part in the Red Sox finally getting one. That's just how it works. And once that happens, once you hold up that trophy or put on that ring, everybody starts to look at you a little differently, even if you still see yourself the same way.

For me, that all happened in the 2004 playoffs. The baseball playoffs are the time when everyone is watching, when the whole country—and the whole world, really—is keeping an eye on the game. And if you can step up on that stage, if you can come through and get the big hit, it's like the whole world wakes up and says, "Hey, where have you been, man?" And the truth is that you've been there the whole time, doing your thing, but that they didn't really notice because they were probably watching something else.

Once I got all those big hits in the playoffs, everyone started to notice. People started comparing me to Reggie Jackson, Mr. October, who was one of the best big-game players in baseball history. Jackson hit 563 home runs and played with a bunch of teams during his career before ending up in the Hall of Fame, but most people remember him for what he did with the Yankees in the 1977 World Series. Reggie hit five home runs in that series—three in one game—and he batted .357 with 10 home runs in 27 career World Series games. Reggie won World Series with the Oakland A's and Yankees, and he had 18 career home runs in the postseason. *Eighteen!* Most people looked at Reggie as being one of the greatest clutch players in the history of the World Series and now people were comparing me to him.

Big Papi.

Señor Octubre.

But seriously, bro. Not long after the 2004 World Series, my agents and I started getting calls from everybody. There were companies that wanted me to do endorsements and all kinds of deals, and we didn't know where to start. That's one of the reasons Alex came up for the parade. There were so many people who wanted to talk to me, who wanted to do business and get to know me, that we had to slow everything down. It all happened almost overnight. It wasn't even two years before that the Twins had released me, that the Twins couldn't trade me, and I had trouble finding a job. And now, after we won the World Series with the Red Sox, there were so many people who wanted to talk to us, who wanted do deals with us, that we had to figure out when to say yes and when to say no. In some ways, I think it was easier to step in the batter's box and get the hits.

Even after the parade was over, it was still crazy. I ended up on the cover of a Wheaties box and did autograph signings for them, writing my name on a cereal box. Pedro and I got invited to Disney World, where we got interviewed by Mickey Mouse and got to hang out with the whole case of Disney characters. I even went out to Los Angeles and did the *The Tonight Show* with Jay Leno, and even that was unbelievable. There were lots of shows calling my agents at the same time, and even after we committed to Leno, he and his people were still calling us, just to make sure we were coming. It was like *they* were checking on *me*. And when I finally did the show, Leno had on one of the "Who's your Papi?" T-shirts under his dress shirt. It was hilarious, bro. The whole place laughed. Leno is from just outside of Boston and he grew up a Red Sox fan, so I know the World Series must have meant something to him, too. And the more places I went, the more I started to understand that it meant something to *everybody*.

I mean, even the Ellen Degeneres show wanted us, and *Ellen* isn't the kind of show that really appeals to sports fans. The day I was on, I got introduced between Rachel Bilson, an actress who is on *The O.C.*, and Samuel L. Jackson, who is one of my favorite actors. And no matter where we went, no matter who else was there, I felt like the biggest star. The whole thing was incredible.

Of course, everybody wanted to know about the Yankees series, about the game-winning hits, about the walk-offs. That's what people focused on the most. In the playoffs, especially, the games are so important and so intense that when one of them ends, you start thinking about the next one. It's like you don't have time to focus on anything else. I remember saying a lot of things during the playoffs—that my teammates couldn't keep relying on me, that we all had to do our part—and I meant all of it. But you have to treat those clutch situations like they're just normal at-bats because otherwise you'll put too much pressure on yourself. And if you really get wrapped up in the game, if you stay focused on what you're doing, you don't have a choice. Your concentration is so high that you don't hear the crowd, the noise, anything. You just focus on the at-bat, the situation, and you do your job.

That's all it is.

People make fun of players saying this kind of thing sometimes, but it's true. You can only go one at-bat at a time, one game at a time, so you can't try to do too much. One of the things I like about our manager, Terry Francona—again, we call him Tito—is that he doesn't put too much pressure on us, that he understands how we feel. Tito is good like that, bro. In a place like Boston, most of the players are veterans who have been around, who know what it takes to win. We all have our own routines. Tito just lets us do our thing and tells us to have fun. He doesn't spend a lot of time calling team meetings and things like that, but when he does, there's always one thing he likes to tell us. *Don't let the game speed up on you.* And what he's really saying is that we all need to slow down a little, to just focus on things one moment at a time, one pitch. Players and managers and coaches talk about that kind of thing all the time, but it's really hard to do. The game starts to get exciting and the crowd gets into it, and the next thing you know, your mind is going a million miles an hour. When that happens, it can be hard to play. It can be hard to win.

For me, I think one of the big reasons I was successful during the playoffs in 2004 is because I was able to slow everything down. I didn't get ahead of myself too much. I don't know if that was because of the way my pop taught me or my experience—or both of those things. But I know that when it came time, when I had to focus on one situation, I was able to do it. And I think it's a big reason why I've been able to keep performing, keep succeeding, even after we won the World Series and things changed for all of us.

And believe me, bro, they changed.

Even when I left the United States, I noticed things were different. I was on the Major League All-Star team that toured in Japan after the 2004 season, and I felt like fans knew me there, too. During one of the games there, I hit this long home run—they measured it over 500 feet, bro—and I think the people there are still talking about it. There are fans in Japan now, even if they're not Red Sox fans, who know me just because of that home run. And even when I got back to the Dominican, where they know me, I felt like I couldn't go out. I guess that's why they call it the World Series, bro. I mean, it's true that the whole world is watching.

But not long after the season ended, not long after we'd won, some guys started filing for free agency and the Red Sox started to make changes—just like we did every year—and all of a sudden we had to deal with the things we always do, win or lose. That's the thing about baseball. No matter what happens, the game goes on. It's a business. The bad times don't last that long, and the good times don't, either. You have to go right back to work. It's like that time when I was with Minnesota, during spring training, when the Twins told me I wasn't going to make the club. I was devastated and I was ready to quit. Then my pop took me out to breakfast and I started feeling better about it, and the next day he knocked on my door and told me, plain and simple: *Time to go to work.* That's how you have to be when things are bad, bro, but that's how you have to be when things are good, too. Once the season ends—win or lose—it's over. You move on. You start getting ready for the next challenge and things start to change again.

For us, after winning the World Series, they started to change right away.

For me, the worst part was losing Pedro Martinez.

I don't want you to misunderstand, bro. I've been in this game awhile now. I know how it works. We all knew that Pedro's contract was up at the end of the year and we knew there was a chance he could go. We knew that about a lot of guys. Derek Lowe's contract was up, too, and so was Jason Varitek's. They were all a big part of our team. Nomar Garciaparra would have been going to free agency, too, but the team traded him at the end of July because we knew it might be hard to keep him. The trade worked out for us and we got Orlando Cabrera—he played great for us, right through the playoffs—but Cabrera was a free agent, too. So roughly two weeks after we won the World Series, even while everyone kept celebrating right through the winter, a lot of things about our team started to change.

In some ways, I never thought Pedro would go. I really didn't. There were a lot of rumors about Pedro, a lot of talk about him going to teams like the New York Mets, and when reporters asked me about it, I told them what I felt: Pedro wasn't going to the Mets. I didn't really know that, I guess, but maybe I just wanted to believe it. It's like I told you before: Pedro is one of the most important people in my life, and he's one of the most respected people in the Dominican. He helped me when I got released by the Twins and he helped me get playing time in Boston, and I have more respect for him than for anybody else that has ever played the game. For Dominican players especially, Pedro always took the time to help us out, build our confidence, push us to be better. He did that kind of thing for every player, really, but I think it's especially true for the Dominicans. I know it's true for me.

Of course, Pedro ended up with the Mets. They gave him a $53 million contract for four years and Pedro couldn't say no. He really wanted the four years. A lot of people in baseball thought the Mets were crazy to give Pedro four years because they didn't think he would make it through the contract, but they didn't understand. Pedro has been hearing that stuff his whole life, bro. He's still hearing it now, even after winning three Cy Youngs and a World Series. He'll probably hear it the day he goes into the Hall of Fame. The dude is one of the greatest pitchers who has ever lived—in the Dominican or anywhere else—but it seems like there have always been people focusing on the things he *can't* do. And because Pedro isn't that big, because he's smaller and skinnier than most pitchers, people always focused on the size of his body instead of the size of his heart. I never understood that. I never will. The guy is a great pitcher and a great person.

A lot of people asked me if I was mad at the Red Sox when Pedro signed with the Mets, but I really wasn't angry. I was more disappointed. The Red Sox have a business to run and they have decisions to make, and that's when this business can get tough for everybody. I think the Red Sox wanted to keep Pedro and I think he wanted to stay here, but negotiations are tough. They can be tricky, bro. And all it takes is for one team, like the Mets, to come in and make a good offer, to let a player know they *really* want him, and sometimes it's hard to say no. Sometimes you just feel like making a change.

Sometimes, too, a change is best for everybody.

Just look at me.

Still, when Pedro left, I was disappointed. It's hard to explain. To me, Pedro is more than just a pitcher, but on the field, that's the part we were going to miss the most. That's the part that people always forget. Negotiations can get so emotional—for everybody—that you can forget just how valuable a guy like Pedro is, especially in Boston, where it's not easy to pitch. It's not an easy thing to go into Yankee Stadium and beat the Yankees, or to go into St. Louis, during the World Series, and pitch the kind of game Pedro pitched. In Game 3 against the Cardinals, Pedro went seven innings and didn't give up a run. He gave up just three hits and had six strikeouts. Our pitchers dominated that series—they all pitched well—but they were all veteran guys. In a place like Boston, that's what it takes.

And Pedro wasn't the only one we lost.

The winter after we won the World Series, Derek Lowe ended up in another place, too. He ended up signing a four-year deal with the Los Angeles Dodgers for $36 million. D-Lowe was in the bullpen when the playoffs started in 2004, but he ended up winning some really big games for us down the stretch. He was pitching in relief when I homered to beat Anaheim in Game 3 of the Division Series—he got the win in that game—and he beat the Yankees in Game 7, on two days' rest. Then he went out and beat St. Louis in Game 4 of the World Series on the night we finished the sweep, and he gave us almost exactly the same game Pedro did: seven innings, three hits, no runs.

By the time we got to spring training in 2005, we'd lost more than just one our best pitchers from 2005.

We'd lost two.

Still, for everything that happened, we still knew we had a good team. Varitek re-signed and a lot of the other guys came back, like Curt Schilling and Johnny Damon. We signed Edgar Renteria to play shortstop and Kevin Millar was back, too, so we knew we were going to score runs again. Manny was back. I was back. We knew we could hit. Our front office was always good about making moves during the season, about getting us help to compete with the Yankees, so we all felt good about that. We had a lot of confidence, too, bro. After winning the World Series, we felt like we could go out and do it again. It had been a long time since the Red Sox had won, since people in Boston had confidence in the team, but I think we all sensed a change after we won in 2004. It was like everyone *knew* we could win now, that it was possible, that all we had to do was stay healthy and catch a couple of breaks. And by the time we got to camp in 2005, by the time all of the guys showed up and we started getting ready again, I think we all felt the same way.

We were ready to start playing ball again.

We were ready to show everyone that 2004 wasn't a fluke.

We were ready to go out and win again.

IN BOSTON, YOU HAVE TO UNDERSTAND: EVERYTHING IS ABOUT THE Yankees. New York is good every year and their owner, George Steinbrenner, spends a lot of money on the team. The Yankees always go out and get the best players. Nobody in baseball can spend the money the Yankees do—even if we come close sometimes—but there's a lot more to it than that. And because we beat the Yankees in 2004—because we basically have to fight them every year—fans ask us all the time if we hate them as much as they do.

Let me tell you, bro: We don't hate them at all.

In fact, we really respect them.

For all of the shit that has happened between us and the Yankees over the last few years, let me tell you what I remember the most. In 2005, after we won the World Series and after we came back to beat the Yankees in the American League Championship Series, we opened the season in New York. Losing to us bothered the Yankees so much that they went out and got Randy Johnson, who is one of the greatest left-handers of all time and who has won five Cy Young Awards during his career; Johnson beat us on Opening Day, 9–2. About a week after that, we finally got back to Boston to play our first home game since winning the World Series, and it was like a big party again. The Red Sox had all kinds of things planned—like they do every Opening Day—but this was different. There was a pregame ceremony to give us our championship rings, and some of the guys came back for it. D-Lowe came back from Los Angeles and Dave Roberts made the trip from San Diego—Roberts had that big stolen base for us in Game 4 against the Yankees—and I think the fans were really happy to see those guys. And with all of that going on, as luck would have it, the Yankees were the team standing in the third-base dugout getting ready to play us.

Can you believe that, bro?

After everything that happened in October, after having us come back against them before beating St. Louis for the world title, the Yankees had to *face us* in our home opener at Fenway Park.

They had to *watch us* get our rings.

Know what the Yankees did? They clapped, bro. They stood there and cheered just like everybody else. It was one of the classiest things I've ever seen a team do. As much as everyone thinks that we hate the Yankees and that they hate us, fans make a much bigger deal of it than we do. The games between us and the Yankees are always intense—we both want to win—but there's really not a lot of dirty play. I mean, we play eighteen or nineteen times a year, bro—and that's just during the regular season—and when you think about it, there really aren't a lot of problems. The Yankees play hard, just like we do, and they want to win, too. But because they're the Yankees and we're the Red Sox, because of all of that history, people sometimes think there's this big problem between us, that we hate New York as much as they do. I'll say it again: We don't.

In some ways, it's funny. The more you play a team, the more you get to know the other players and their personalities, the more you understand that they're no different than you. You respect them. The way the schedule is now, you play every team in your division an average of about two times a month, but sometimes you can play three or four or five series in a few weeks, depending on how the schedule goes. Sometimes you just get sick of seeing each other, of doing the same routine over and over again, and that can lead to problems, no matter who the opponent is. Since I've been with Boston, I don't think we've had as many problems with the Yankees as we've had with some other teams, like maybe Tampa Bay or even Baltimore. But if you look around baseball, if you look at all the fights that happen between teams during the year, I bet you'll find that most of them happen between teams in the same division. And they usually happen because teams are seeing each other too much, because even your family can get on your nerves if you spend too much time with them.

Why should baseball be any different?

But with the Yankees, I think they respect us. I know we

respect them. When we were getting our rings, I remember Joe Torre standing there in the dugout and clapping for us. I remember Derek Jeter doing it, too. That's the manager of the team and the captain, and that sets an example for the other players on the team. The Yankees have a lot of veteran guys, just like we do, so they all respect the game, their opponents, everything. That's just the way they are. And I know that every guy on our team felt the same way that I did that day, that the Yankees were very professional and showed a lot of class. That meant a lot to us, to see them there clapping for us even though we beat them. That's the way the big leagues are supposed to be. You play as hard as you can on the field and you try to beat the other guy's ass, but when the game's over, it's over. You have to respect the fact that they're trying to win as much as you are. That's what they're paid to do, too.

Know what else the Yankees impressed us with that day? Right before the game, when the starting lineups were announced, Mariano Rivera got a standing ovation from the crowd at Fenway Park. It was hilarious, bro. Because we beat Rivera in Game 4 and Game 5 of the American League Championship Series, our fans cheered him. It was like they were saying: "Hey, thanks for the help last year." A lot of players might get upset at something like that because they wouldn't know how to deal with it. For a closer, especially, blowing a game can be a hard thing to live with. But Mo—that's what they call Rivera in New York—he just laughed about it. He tipped his hat to the crowd and everybody started laughing— on both teams—and it was one of those moments when everybody forgot that they were the Yankees and we were the Red Sox, that we were supposed to be out there trying to beat the hell out of each other.

I mean, think about it: In 2003 and 2004, counting the playoffs, we played the Yankees fifty-two times. *Fifty-two*.

That's like one-third of a season, two months' worth of base-ball. That's a lot of games. We won twenty-seven games and the Yankees won twenty-five. Each of us won one American League Championship—in seven games. And in 2004, when we beat the Yankees, we scored 149 runs in the twenty-six games we played and they scored 146. Think about that for a minute. We played twenty-six games in one season—that's a lot of innings, bro—and we played extra-inning games, play-off games, every kind of game teams can play. We played games in New York and games in Boston, games at night and games during the day. And at the end of the year, when you added it all up, the difference between us and the Yankees was *three runs*, which you can get with one swing of the bat. That was the difference between us and the Yankees, between win-ning a World Series and feeling like you just blew the chance.

That's why, as a player, you have to treat every at-bat dur-ing a season like it means something.

Because at the end, when you add it all up, things might be a lot closer than you think.

After we got our rings that day, we went out and beat the Yankees, 8–1. It was the perfect way to end the day. Tim Wakefield shut down the Yankees and we got a big lead early, and the game was never really close. And when it was all over, after we got our rings and raised our championship flag and beat New York, I think we all felt like the 2004 season was fi-nally over. We'd played seven games and we were just 3–4, but we started playing better again right away. We took two out of three from the Yankees and then swept Tampa Bay, and it was like we were ready to defend our championship.

The 2005 season was here.

Finally.

FOR ME, IT DIDN'T TAKE LONG TO SEE THAT THINGS WERE GOING TO be different. Baseball is about adjustments, just like anything else, and if you keep hitting home runs and knocking in runs, people aren't going to pitch you the same way. They're going to change things up on you. As a hitter, you either have to change with them or they're going to start getting you out. Worse, you start getting yourself out.

If you look at my numbers during my first four years in Boston, my production has pretty much gone up every year. My walks have gone up, too. People started pitching around me more in 2005, after I had such a big postseason, and I guess that was to be expected. It was like everyone else was feeling as confident that I could hit as I was. So when teams pitched to me, they didn't want to make mistakes. That meant that I had to avoid swinging at bad pitches, take some walks, let some other guys on the team do their thing, too. One of the best things about playing for the Red Sox is that we usually have a deep lineup, so you can take your walks because you know the next guy is going to do the job. The more base runners we have, the better. And for me, the guy behind was usually Manny Ramirez, who is one of the best hitters in the history of the game. It's one of the biggest reasons why teams have had to keep pitching to me even when they didn't want to.

The bottom line is that pitchers either had to face me or face Manny. That's a good thing for the Red Sox. Either way, we feel confident about our chances.

As a hitter, taking a walk is always a good thing. It takes a lot of discipline and a lot of confidence. If teams are going to pitch around you more, it means you're going to get fewer pitches to hit. But if you can still put up the same numbers—or even better ones—it means you really have to take advantage of the pitches you get. You can't miss them when they come. So if you can take your walks *and* put up your numbers, you're helping your team even more than you did before. You're getting on base more and still knocking guys in, so maybe you're scoring more runs, too. And if you can do that, if you can pass on the bad pitches because you *know* you can hit the good ones, then it probably means your confidence is high. It means you don't *have* to swing at the bad pitches because you *know* you only need one swing.

Understand what I mean?

Look at a guy like Barry Bonds. In 2004, Bonds walked *232 times*—that's a record, bro—and he still hit forty-five home runs. He made every swing count. As a hitter, that's what you have to do.

With me, in 2005, I started taking more and more walks as the year went on. When I kept producing, teams started to pitch around me more and more. That's just how the game works. So as a hitter, you have to show discipline, be patient, swing at the good pitches and wait it out. Swinging at bad pitches isn't really going to help you because you're not going to be able to hit those, anyway. The pitcher *wants* you to swing at the bad pitch. He *wants* you to get yourself out. And the more you do in baseball, the more numbers you put up, the less pitchers are going to give you something to hit. So you really have to be patient, to wait for the times when a pitcher *has* to throw you a good pitch, and then you have the pitcher right where you want him. That's what good hitting is, bro. It's patience and discipline and strategy. It's knowing when to swing and when to let a pitch a go by. It's teaching yourself to stay focused and patient, even when all you're seeing is one bad pitch after another.

So, early in 2005, I just tried to stay focused and do my thing. In a lot of ways, our 2005 season went like 2004. We played pretty well in the early part of the year, then played

.500 for a long time. We had a lot of problems with our pitching, but we scored a lot of runs and won our share of games. By the end of June, we were having a pretty good year, and I was on pace for another big season. I was hitting .304 with 19 home runs and 66 RBIs—which put me on pace for about 40 homers and 130 RBIs over a full season. For the first real time in my career, I felt like everybody knew who I was, how well I was doing. Fans in opposing ballparks started calling my name when I came out of the dugout—"Papi!"—and even opposing players, guys I didn't really know, were coming up to me and saying hello.

And then I got even more proof.

The All-Star Game.

It's kind of funny, bro. Until 2004, I had never been in the All-Star Game. I got picked that year and had a great time. I even homered. As we got closer and closer to the 2005 All-Star break, reporters started coming up to me and asking again whether I wanted to go, how much it meant, things like that. Are you kidding? When I was a kid in the Dominican, I didn't even know they had an All-Star Game. I'm not joking. But then when you get signed and you start playing in the minors, when you go from Single A to Double A to Triple A, you learn that it's an honor. It means a lot. It means that fans look at you as being one of the best players in the game, one of the best in the world, and how could anybody be mad about that? Because the All-Star Game was in Detroit that year, an American League city, there was going to be a designated hitter in the game. So unlike 2004, when the game was in the National League and my name wasn't on the ballot, the manager didn't have to pick me. Fans had the chance to vote for me this time and they had a chance to make sure that I was going to be there.

Looking back, I guess they wanted me there as bad as I did.

By the time the All-Star Game came—it is always played in the middle of July—I had received more fan votes to play in the game than any other player in baseball. I was stunned. I got more votes than Albert Pujols, Ichiro Suzuki, Alex Rodriguez, or Derek Jeter—any of them. I really couldn't believe it. Those are all good players, bro—they're all *great* players—and some of them have been in the game awhile. They've done great things. And for me to get more votes than any of them—I really started to understand what my performance meant in the 2004 playoffs. I mean, *everybody* was watching those games, and sometimes, as a player, you forget that. You are so focused on your job, on what you're trying to do, that you forget there are 35,000 or 45,000 fans in the stands and millions watching on TV. But then, when something like the All-Star Game comes along and you have more than four million people voting for you—*four million*, bro—you really start to understand how many people were watching, how much they appreciated what you did, how difficult it was to do those things.

That's when you start to feel proud, for yourself, for your country and your people, for your organization and your teammates.

For everybody.

And when something like that happens, too, you have to be thankful, bro. People can't accomplish things like that by themselves. They need good families and friends, like I had, and they need good fans who notice. They need good teammates and a good organization. And then they have to go out there and keep doing their jobs, keep trying to get better, because the All-Star Game is an honor every time you make it. It's like they say: It's tough to get on top, but it's tougher to stay there. You have to work even harder the next time, and the time after that, and the time after that. That's why it should be feel like a reward every time you go.

Me? I had a lot of fun the first time. I had even more fun the next time. I got to be in the Home Run Derby, losing to Bobby Abreu, who was playing right field for the Philadelphia Phillies at the time. Abreu went crazy, bro. Nobody was going to beat him that night. I went 2 for 3 in the game and had a great time—the American League won again, just like we did in 2004—and that meant something, too. A few years back, Major League Baseball decided that the league which won the All-Star Game would have home-field advantage in the World Series, and that's a pretty big deal. I know it meant a lot to us in 2004 and it would have meant a lot to us again in 2005. For a designated hitter like me, that can be the difference between playing four games or playing three. I played first base when we played by National League rules against the St. Louis Cardinals in 2004—Tito wasn't about to take me out of the lineup—but there are some guys who don't play a position, who would have to sit on the bench if there was no DH.

Still, I think the bottom line is that the All-Star Game is supposed to be fun, that it's a chance for all of the good players in baseball to get together and put on a show for the fans, to say thank you for showing up every night and for buying tickets, for cheering us and appreciating us, especially when there are so many things that can happen off the field and that can take away from the things we do as players.

Me?

I don't know what to say, bro.

It was nice to know that fans saw me as the real thing, as the kind of guy who deserved to be there.

Four million votes.

That made me feel like I was on top of the world.

THE BASEBALL SEASON IS LONG, SO YOU HAVE TO PACE YOURSELF.
But right after the All-Star break, the feeling starts to change.
The trading deadline is coming—it's on July 31 every year—
and if your team is in contention, there's a pretty good
chance the general manager is going to make a move. That's
what Theo Epstein did for us in 2004, when he traded Nomar
Garciaparra for Orlando Cabrera and Doug Mientkiewicz.
Theo got Dave Roberts in another trade, too, and all three of
those guys made big contributions for us on our way to winning the World Series.

We couldn't have won without them.

So, once you get past the deadline, once you get into August and September, the games get much more serious. It's
time to play ball. The teams that win in August and September usually make the playoffs, and that means you have another chance at a championship.

Theo didn't make any moves at the trading deadline in
2005, but we didn't care. We had most of the same guys from
the year before and we felt like we could win with what we
had. That was one of the great things about that team, those
guys. We didn't make excuses. We just played and we won.
Our pitching had slipped a little since 2004—any team's
would after losing Pedro and D-Lowe—but we kept on winning games. If we had to win by scoring ten runs, we scored
ten runs. If we needed eleven, we got eleven. That's just the
way we looked at it. From the time I got to Boston in 2003—
that's when Theo brought in Millar, Billy Mueller, and a
bunch of other guys, too—we led the major leagues in runs
scored every year. We had the best offense in baseball in 2003
and 2004, and we were leading again in 2005, too. The one
thing we could always do was hit—and we could do it better

than anybody. So if that's the way we had to win games, that's the way it was going to be. We had no choice.

Looking back, I don't think I've ever played better than I did in the final two months of 2005, in August and September, for that long a period of time. Usually, when you get hot, it lasts a couple of weeks, maybe a month. Then you might cool off a little, even if for just a while, and wait for the next hot streak. That's the way the game works sometimes, so you have to take every hit you get when you're feeling good at the plate. But in the final couple of months in 2005, it seemed like I felt good all the time. I don't know why. But every time I stepped up to the plate, no matter what the situation was, I felt like I was going to do some damage. My confidence was really high.

And I think it showed.

As a team, too, we got hot in August. That can make all the difference, too. At one point in the middle of the month, we had won fourteen out of sixteen—or something crazy like that. It was almost like 2004. Our pitching wasn't as good, but we had one six-game winning streak where we scored 62 runs—*sixty-two*, bro—an average of more than ten runs a game. We won one game, 11–7, another, 11–6, and another, 16–5. It felt like nobody could get us out. And even though we were giving up a lot of runs, too, we were winning a lot and staying right there in the playoff race, where we needed to be.

When we got to Detroit in the middle of the month, I was really starting to catch fire. We had just won two games against the Chicago White Sox—they had the best team and the best pitching in the league that year—and I went 7 for 9 with two home runs, two doubles, and six RBIs. We lost the first game at Detroit, 7–6, and we were losing the second one, too, when I came up with two outs and the bases empty in the bottom of the ninth inning. Detroit was ahead, 3–2. The Tigers closer at the time was Fernando Rodney, a right-hander who I knew because he was from the Dominican. Rodney is a good guy. Because I knew him from the Dominican, I knew that Rodney liked to get guys out with his changeup, which he especially likes to throw against left-handed batters like me. So even when I got ahead in the count, I knew he had a lot of confidence in his changeup, so I told myself I would stay away from it, that I wouldn't swing until he threw me a fastball.

And when he did, I didn't miss it.

I homered and tied the game.

After that, our whole lineup went crazy. We went into the tenth inning tied 3–3, and we scored seven runs to take a 10–3 lead. I hit another homer. We ended up winning the game, 10–7, and a couple of reporters came by my locker and started asking me questions about my home run in the ninth inning, how I was able to lay off Rodney's changeup. Rodney had mixed up his pitches against me, throwing a changeup when the count was 2–0, but the count was 3–1 when he threw the fastball that I homered. The reporters asked me how I was able to be so patient, how I knew it was coming, and I told them: I didn't. But I knew that Rodney *wanted* me to swing at his changeup, that it was a pitch that would get me out, so I just sat on his fastball. And when he threw it, I made sure I was ready.

The team started to cool off over the next couple of weeks, but I stayed hot. And every time it seemed like the team needed a big hit, I got one. We beat the Los Angeles Angels with my walk-off homer on September 6 at Fenway Park and, about a week later, I had a bunch of big hits during a series in Toronto, where I went 6 for 12 with four home runs and seven RBIs. From there, we went home to play Oakland and then right back on the road to Tampa Bay—and I kept hitting. I was killin', bro. I had one homer against the A's and three more against the Devil Rays, giving me eight homers in nine games. We were fighting to stay in the playoffs, so every hit meant something, and after October 2004 and the All-Star Game and everything else, people were mentioning my name with something I never even thought about.

The MVP, bro.

The Most Valuable Player Award.

To tell you the truth, I tried not to think about it too much. I figured the odds were against me. No designated hitter has ever won the MVP, so I was pretty sure that I was going to have a hard time being the first. I just don't understand why. When reporters started asking me about the award, about my chances, I told them everything I felt: It was out of my control. I *wanted* to win the MVP—who doesn't?—but there are a lot of things about it that have to go right. There are a lot of politics involved—I told the reporters that—so I think there are a lot of guys who won't vote for someone like me, just because I'm a designated hitter and I don't play the field. I mean, is that my fault? No. I'd play first base if the Red Sox let me, but that's not the best thing for our team. My job is to *hit,* all the time, and that isn't exactly the easiest thing. Hitting is the toughest thing to do in baseball, no matter what anybody says, but then it comes time to give out the MVP award and a designated hitter can't win. I don't understand it. And in a lot of ways, it's even tougher for a DH like me, because sometimes you have to wait a long time between at-bats, which can really make it tough.

You know what you do during that time, bro? You walk up to the clubhouse and maybe get a cup of coffee. You sit on the bench for a while. Maybe you go down into the tunnel (behind the dugout) and take some swings in the batting cage or hit off a tee, just to stay loose. And then you have to step into the batter's, against some dude throwing 95 miles per hour, and try to focus like you've been in the batter's box the whole time.

And if it's late in the game and your team is behind, you have to come through.

At the same time, if people are talking about you as the MVP, you must be doing something right. It means people are noticing you. In a lot of ways, it's an honor just to be considered. At the end of the 2005 season, most people thought there were two real candidates for the American League MVP award—me and Alex Rodriguez, who was playing third base for the Yankees. I think that was the biggest advantage he had over me. A-Rod is a great player, bro, and he's a great fielder, too. He was having a great year. But I was getting a lot of clutch hits and I finished strong—I had 22 home runs and 60 RBIs from August 1 to the end of the season—and I think a lot of people voted for me because I kept getting big hits at a time of year when we needed them.

Of course, when the games are going on, you don't think about the MVP too much. There is too much else to worry about. We really struggled late in the year, and I think part of the reason is that everybody was tired. We were just worn out. Because we had some rainouts, earlier in the year, we had a stretch late in the season where we had to play something like thirty straight days without a day off, and I think that caught up to us. Mentally, it was just a tough thing to do. But where a lot of teams might not have been able to keep up, we managed to fight through it. We hung in there and kept fighting, which is what good teams do.

That year, like us, the Yankees had their problems. We had a chance to bury them early in the season, when they were really struggling, and we didn't do it. That was disappointing to me. For a while there at the end, I didn't think we were going to make the playoffs. We ended up winning ninety-five games—the same number that the Yankees did—but the Yankees won the division on a tiebreaker because they beat us head-to-head during the season series. Still, we both got into the playoffs. But instead of playing the first round against the Los Angeles Angels and opening the playoffs at home, we had to go on the road, to Chicago, where the White Sox finished with the best record in the league.

By now, I don't need to tell you what happened in the playoffs. The White Sox swept us, bro, three games to none. It was just their year. Chicago beat us in the first round and then beat the Angels in the American League Championship Series—the Yankees had lost, too—and then the White Sox went on to win the World Series by sweeping the Houston Astros, too. Chicago went 11–1 that October and they deserved to win. They were the best team. They had the same kind of year that we did in 2004, and I think that meant something to White Sox fans. Chicago hadn't won the World Series since 1917—until 2004, we hadn't won since 1918—and so maybe it was just their time. Maybe they were due.

Can you believe that, bro?

The White Sox won in 1917 and we won in 1918.

And then neither one of us won again until 2004 and 2005.

By the time Chicago won, we were already a few weeks into our off-season. I think everybody was enjoying the rest. Like I said, it felt like 2004 never ended in a lot of ways, so it felt like we'd been playing, nonstop, for two years. We didn't win the championship, but we had a good year. We made the playoffs again, and we probably had no right doing that. I remember being at the World Series to get the Hank Aaron Award in October—that's an award that goes to the best hitter in the league, as voted by the fans—and there were reporters asking me what went wrong, why we weren't able to repeat as champions. I told them that we never had that same feeling like we did in 2004, when we *knew* we were going to win. We just didn't have the pitching, I guess. And at the end of the day, no matter what anybody tells you, there's probably a part of you that knows that.

But I guess that's why those championships are so special.

A COUPLE OF WEEKS AFTER THE SEASON ENDED, I FOUND OUT THAT we finished second to the Yankees somewhere else: in the MVP voting. A-Rod won the award. A lot of people asked me about it and I told them the truth—I was disappointed—but A-Rod deserved to win, too. He had a hell of a year. I ended up finishing 2005 with a .300 average, 47 home runs, and 148 RBIs—the best numbers of my career. I scored 119 runs, the highest total in my career, and walked more than 100 times [102] for the first time, too. Any player will tell you that you don't get the chance to have too many years like that because it's hard enough to stay healthy. But I played in 159 games, more than in any other season, and I still felt strong.

We didn't win the World Series in 2005.

I didn't win the MVP, either.

So going into 2006, I still had a lot of reasons to be motivated again.

A BROKEN
RECORD

In some ways, the 2006 season was the best of my career. In others, it was one of my most disappointing. I had played four seasons in Boston by the time the year ended, and 2006 was the only one in which we didn't make the playoffs.

You have to remember: As much as you love what you do, as much as you are blessed to do it, it can be frustrating when you lose. You can put up big numbers and have a great year, but they don't mean as much if you don't win. That's obvious. Players always talk about how winning is the most important thing, and people sometimes think we're just saying the right things, but it's true. When you win, every contribution means something. A guy could put down a sacrifice bunt or turn a double play, and if it helps you win a game, everybody feels good about it. But when when you lose, people start focusing on the things you *didn't* do as a team, and that's not good for anybody.

After 2005, we had a lot of changes again. That's just the way the game works now. Most teams go through it. But with some of the changes we had after 2004, too, the team was really starting to look different. Johnny Damon ended up leaving as a free agent—he signed with *the Yankees*, bro—and that was tough for a lot of reasons. JD is a great player and a great leadoff man, but he's a great teammate and friend, too. It really meant a lot to have him in our clubhouse. I feel the same way about Kevin Millar, who left us as a free agent and signed with the Baltimore Orioles. Millar and JD were both big contributors to our team that won the World Series, but for me, it was a lot more than that. They were both really good guys who brought the whole team together and kept everybody loose, and that's really important when you play 162 games together. It's a long season. There are going to be ups and downs. You need to be able to laugh when things aren't going good, and Millar and JD always had a way of reminding us all that we needed to have fun, that we were playing a game we love and that things were never that bad.

Both of those guys were really good at that.

In a lot of ways, a baseball clubhouse is no different than any other place where people work together. You have people from all kinds of places, white players and black players and Hispanic players and anything in between. So on a lot of teams, it's not unusual for the Hispanic guys to hang out together or for the white and black guys to hang out together, just because they have a lot in common. It's only natural. When I'm with guys like Manny Ramirez or, say, when Orlando Cabrera was with us, we were comfortable around each other because we could speak Spanish to each other, things like that. That's our first language. So it's a lot easier to communicate, a lot more comfortable, and I think most people like to spend time with people who are more like them.

I mean, we all have friends we grew up with, right? And because you're from the same place, because you went through some of the same things, it's easier to understand each other. It's the same way in baseball.

But Millar and JD, they were special guys in the clubhouse, bro. They really were. They were guys that everybody liked, no matter where they came from, and they were guys that everybody felt comfortable talking to. I like to think that I'm the same way, that I get along with everybody on the team, and a lot of people say now that I'm a leader on the Red Sox, that I'm a big part of the team. I guess that's true. But to me, Millar and JD were guys who made sure everything was out in the open and that everybody got along, that could go around and make everybody laugh. They brought all of us together. They reminded us that we were a team and that we had to stick together, and that's really important in anything you do with other people, especially baseball.

Let me give you an example:

Since I've been in Boston, Manny hasn't talked to the media very much. He's just not comfortable doing it. It's not his personality. But because he's such a good player, because he hits all those homers and knocks in all those runs, reporters would like to talk to him more. It's only natural. So there was this one time in spring training when a bunch of reporters were near Manny's locker, and Millar came over and took over the situation. It was hilarious, bro. Millar brought over a chair from his locker and stood up on it, and he told the reporters that if they had any questions for Manny, they had to ask him and he would translate them for Manny. The reporters played along with it, too. So they would ask Millar things like, "Can you ask Manny how he feels at the plate right now?" And Millar would turn to Manny, ask the question, get the answer, and then repeat the answer for the writers.

A lot of times, Manny's answer and Millar's answer were totally different, so everyone would start laughing.

At one point, one of the reporters asked a question that was a little controversial, that Manny wouldn't have answered. I don't even remember what the question was. I just remember Millar listening to the question and looking at the reporter, then making everybody laugh with his answer.

"That's a stupid-ass question," Millar said, laughing. "Next question."

Everybody cracked up.

Even Manny.

By the time the reporters walked away, I think everybody was smiling and laughing. The whole thing was really funny, casual, and everybody was cool about it. Manny answered some questions. The reporters got to write their stories. Millar got to be a clown, which he loved to do, and nobody was stirring up any shit. For a guy like Manny, especially, that's what guys like Manny and JD could do. They could take a situation that might be tough and they could make everybody loose, get everybody to laugh about it. Both of those guys really liked to talk, so that kept the media happy. In a place like Boston, the reporters are around a lot. You have to have the right personality and approach to play there because the media in Boston are part of the deal. It's one of the reasons Boston is such a great place to play. The fans are interested in you, the media are interested in you, and they are very intense about the team. Everything matters to them. And like I've said before, I don't think there's any better place in baseball to play.

But the hard part, depending on your personality, is that

it's tough to get any privacy. So if you're the kind of person who's quiet, who doesn't like to be bothered, it can be hard to deal with sometimes. And on top of that, if you're a superstar like Manny is, it can be really hard to have your space. Sometimes you feel that you can't hide.

But when you have guys like Millar and JD on your team, guys who like talking to reporters and do it every night, a lot of the other guys in the team can just do their thing and not be bothered. The reporters get what they want and the players get what they want, and everybody goes home satisfied.

I really think all of that was a big reason why we won a lot of games during those years we were together, in 2003 and 2004 and 2005. It just worked. On the field and off, everybody had his role. We all fit together and we liked each other, and it's important to be comfortable when you're together all the time.

Let me get back to Manny for a minute. A lot of people ask me about him, about how important he is to our team, and let me tell you: He's been a really big part of our success. During most of my time in Boston, I've been the number-three hitter and Manny's been number four, and that's the way I like it. Manny's the kind of guy who can change the game just by being in the on-deck circle because the pitcher knows it when Manny's coming up next. If I step into the batter's box and there are two guys on base, the pitcher has a big decision to make. Is he going to pitch to me or is he going to pitch to Manny? If he pitches to me, he could give up a three-run homer. But if he decides to walk me, if he decides to pitch around me, now he has to face Manny *with the bases loaded*. That could be an even bigger problem.

Let me try to explain this some more: Since I've been with the Red Sox, I've had some really productive years. But if you look at intentional walks, Manny has twenty more than I do. *Twenty*. For intentional walks, that's a big difference, and that includes the final two months of the 2006 season, when Manny was out with a bad knee for a lot of the time and I got intentionally walked ten times. What it means is that no matter how many runs I knock in, no matter how many home runs I hit and how much I keep hurting pitchers, teams pitch to me more than they do to Manny. And that's all because Manny is right there behind me, standing in the on-deck circle with the bat on his shoulder, letting the pitcher know that there is no easy way out.

You have to pay now or pay later.

Over the last few years, there's been a lot of talk about Manny going somewhere else, about him maybe being traded, and I was always glad when it didn't happen. He's too valuable to me and to our team. I'll be the first one to tell you that. After the 2005 season, I was at the World Series getting the Hank Aaron Award as the best hitter in the American League when reporters started asking me about Manny, about whether the Red Sox were going to trade him. I was there with Andruw Jones, who plays for the Atlanta Braves and who got the Hank Aaron Award in the National League, and I remember pointing at Andruw and saying, "If the Red Sox trade Manny, they have to get someone like Andruw to replace him." I meant it. Andruw hit 51 home runs that year and he's one of the best players in the game, a guy who made his country famous. He's from Curaçao, an island in the Caribbean Sea not far from the Dominican Republic. Just like Manny, he's one of the best hitters in the game. And if you want to get the most out of me, a guy like Manny or Andruw is a big help.

And if you have to get Andruw to replace Manny, why not just keep Manny in the first place?

That's how I've always felt.

With Manny, a lot of people don't understand him. I think that's part of the problem. Manny can be kind of quiet and he doesn't really talk to the reporters, so he gets criticized a lot. But let me tell you, bro: He works his ass off. People have no idea. When I first got to the Red Sox, Manny kind of took me under his wing, worked with me on my hitting a lot. We worked together. On game days, most guys wake up late and have breakfast and maybe lunch later in the day, then go to the ballpark in the early afternoon. Not Manny. He goes to the ballpark in the morning and works on his hitting, then breaks for lunch and comes back. Then he hits some more. Manny is a really talented hitter and one of the best in the history of the game, but one of the biggest reasons is because he works at it. It's not like he just shows up and hits. In the big leagues, no matter how good you are, you have to work at it or you're not going to succeed. Other guys are working just as hard as you are, and if you slack off a little bit, you're going to get beat.

For a while there, I went to the park to hit with Manny almost every morning. Over the last couple of years, I've come up with my own routine. When the team is home, especially, I like to stay home with Tiff and the kids, try to spend some time with them. That's important to me. We're all different and have different ways to do things, different things that help us succeed, but that's what works for me.

Manny? He likes to hit.

A lot.

That's just how he prepares.

There's one more thing I should tell you about Manny, just because people ask me about him a lot. Because he doesn't talk to reporters a lot, because he avoids them, people come to me all the time and ask me questions about how he feels. It gets a little tiring sometimes. Manny can do what he wants, bro, and I support his decisions 100 percent. He should be able to do it however he wants. But I don't understand why reporters come to me, just because I'm his friend, and ask me to speak for him. No person can ever speak for anyone else. The same thing used to happen sometimes with Pedro when he was with the team, when he decided that he didn't want to talk to reporters. So reporters would come and ask me because they know I'm friendly and I won't chase them away, and that's when you feel like people are starting to take advantage of you.

It's like I said, bro.

We're all people.

Some of us like to talk and some of us don't.

But my relationships with my teammates always come first.

IN OUR GAME, PEOPLE TALK ABOUT CHEMISTRY ALL THE TIME, AND there are a lot of people who think that it's all bull. It isn't. As a player, especially, the guys you play with are really important. You don't need to be best friends with them, but you need to get along, respect each other, things like that. We spend a lot of time together, bro. The season is long. If there are major problems in the clubhouse, if people can't get along or communicate, it can make for a really long year. It makes everything harder, even on the field. We're all professionals, and we all do our jobs, but we're people, too. We're not perfect.

The good news, even though we lost Millar and JD, is that we brought in some really good guys in 2006, people like Mark Loretta and Mike Lowell. They're totally professional guys who have been around for a while, who know how to deal with people. They fit in right away. Our team was different, but our clubhouse was still a good place. Guys like JD and Millar weren't running around anymore, making guys laugh, but everybody got along. It was very professional. From the second you meet a guy like Lowell or Loretta, you can tell right away that he's a good guy just by the way he talks to you, shakes your hand, looks you in the eye. It means a lot. You can tell that he's been around, respects people, knows how to act. And when you have that, you know there aren't going to be any problems.

Still, it takes awhile for guys to get comfortable around each other, to get to know each other, to build relationships and chemistry. I mean, if you change jobs and go to a new place, it takes awhile to fit in, right? It doesn't happen in a week or two weeks. It can take months, sometimes years. In baseball, it probably happens a little faster because, during the season, we're basically together every day. There are no weekends and holidays, and there are only a handful of days off in the schedule, so relationships develop faster. They have to. The only way to get to know people is to spend time with them, and we spend a lot of time together in the clubhouse.

In 2006, too, there was also the issue of the World Baseball Classic, which was basically a World Cup for baseball. There were teams from all over the world—the Dominican Republic, Puerto Rico, Japan, China, Australia, and a bunch of others—and it was a chance for all of us to play for our countries. That was a lot of fun. Like I told you earlier, baseball in the Dominican is a big deal. It means a lot to the people there, and to a lot of people in the Caribbean, in places like Venezuela and Puerto Rico, too. It was the first time, really, that all of the players from the Dominican got to play together, and the first time for me to be on the same team as Albert Pujols and Miguel Tejada, Vladimir Guerrero, and all of the other guys. We've always had great pride in our country and we feel like we have the best baseball players in the world, and now we were getting the chance to go out and prove to everybody that we were right.

The other teams had that chance, too. That's what made it so much fun. Some of my Red Sox teammates, like Jason Varitek and Mike Timlin, got to play for the team from the United States. Alex Cora played for Puerto Rico. Lenny Di-Nardo pitched for Italy. I think we all had fun.

At the same time, the World Baseball Classic changed the spring for everybody. We all had to change our routines and our workout programs—everything. Because this was the first time they ever held the tournament, nobody was really sure how it was all going to work. For a guy like me, who was getting ready to play his tenth year in the big leagues, I wasn't sure if I was going to be ready. I like to get a lot of at-bats in spring training, get my timing down, get ready. I don't plan to play tournament games in March. But because the WBC was important to baseball, because it was a chance for us to show the whole world the game, people in the league office wanted us to take it seriously. They wanted us to put on a show. They wanted us to help the game grow to places it has never really been before.

The way I felt that spring, I was sure I was going to have a bad year. During the World Baseball Classic, I felt terrible at the plate. I ended up playing pretty well, and our team from the Dominican Republic made it to the semifinals, where we lost to Cuba, but I never really felt comfortable. I ended up going 3 for 20, which is only a .150 average, but all three of my hits were home runs and I walked eight times. I got on base a lot. Still, I was facing pitchers I had never seen before—a lot of guys who weren't in the big leagues and who probably never will be—so the numbers really didn't mean much. I can usually tell how I'm going as a hitter by how I feel at the plate—I think any hitter can—and I just wasn't feeling right. That's the funny thing about hitting. You can feel great at the plate and go 0 for 4, or you can feel awful and get four hits with two homers. The season is so long that those days usually even out, and most of the time you produce when you feel good.

But that year, during the spring, I felt terrible.

And I thought it meant that I might have a bad year.

By the time the major-league season started, things were starting to click for us. Even though we had all of those new guys, we won our share of games. We went 11–4 to start the season and we were playing good baseball, getting good pitching from Curt Schilling and Josh Beckett, who we picked up in an off-season trade with the Florida Marlins. In some ways, those two guys were both like new players on our team. Schilling had been with us for two years by then, but after he hurt his ankle during the 2004 playoffs, he never really got healthy in 2005. It basically took him a whole year to recover. But by the time he showed up for 2006, he looked like himself again. And with him and Beckett together, we had two guys who could really throw hard, one old guy and one young guy, and it was a good mix. We looked like we had a balanced team and it was nice to see things come together so fast.

And that was true for me and the team both.

I don't know what it was, bro, but as the season opened, I started hitting. I had three hits, including a home run, at Texas in our first game of the year. When we got to Fenway Park to play the Toronto Blue Jays in our first home series, I homered in all three games. And even when the team slumped—we finished 14–11 for the month—I kept hitting, getting four more homers in the final ten days of the month and finishing April with ten homers, which is a big number for someone like me. I mean, if you look at my history, I hit most of my home runs in July and August, like most power hitters do. That's when the weather is the warmest and the ball carries the best. And for someone like me, who grew up in the Dominican and always played in warm weather, the cold weather takes a little getting used to. It doesn't bother all that much, really, but any hitter will tell you that it's better to hit when it's warm.

Still, after how I felt in the World Baseball Classic, it was a good start.

I mean, there are six months in the baseball season.

If you hit ten homers a month, that's sixty for the year.

I don't care who you are, bro.

That's a lot of home runs.

But like I've said a million times already, the baseball season doesn't work that way. You have to play every game and stay focused for every at-bat. The numbers don't come by themselves. I hit only five home runs in May—that was fifteen for the first two months, which is a pace for about forty-five over a season—but we were still playing well as a team and winning some games. That's really all that matters. Because of all the changes we made during the winter, a lot of people thought we wouldn't be as good in 2006, that we wouldn't make the playoffs. But we were doing just fine. Our record was 31–20 at the end of May—that was a pace for 98 wins, the same number we finished with when we won the World Series in 2004—and we were in first place for most of the first two months. We finished May in a tie for first and we were still playing pretty good ball into the middle of June, when all of sudden something happened.

We caught fire.

We couldn't lose.

From June 16 to June 29, we played twelve games and won them all. A lot of those games weren't real close. Because we had lost Millar and JD, a lot of people thought we'd have trouble scoring runs, that we might lose some low-scoring games. But when we started to hit in the middle of June, we were winning games big. During the twelve-game streak, we won by scores of 11–3, 9–3, 10–2, 9–4, and 10–2. We won the close games, too. We had two games that went into extra innings and we won both of those, and that's when I started to get some walk-off hits again, which the fans in Boston were starting to get used to.

I don't know what it is, bro, but the walk-offs seem to come in bunches, too. We were tied against the Philadelphia Phillies when I came up against their closer, Tom Gordon—everybody calls him Flash—in the bottom of the tenth inning. I hit one out and we won the game, 5–3. A few days later—we were still playing the Phillies and we went into extra innings again—I came up against a guy named Clay Condrey in the bottom of the twelfth. We had blown a 6–0 lead in the game and the Phils had scored in the top of the inning to go ahead, 7–6, but we tied the game in the bottom of the inning when our first baseman, Kevin Youkilis, got an RBI single. Loretta then drew a walk before I got my chance, and I singled to score Youkilis and give us an 8–7 win.

Right after that, the New York Mets came in and we swept them in a three-game series. Pedro Martinez pitched the second game of the series—it was his first game in Boston since he left as a free agent—and we beat him pretty bad, winning 10–2. The fans loved that. I went 3 for 4 with a homer in the next game and we won, 4–2, and all of a sudden we had a four-game lead in the division and one of the best records in baseball. Everyone was starting to notice. Nobody was starting to overlook us anymore. I hit eight home runs in the month to give me twenty-three for the year—again, we were only about halfway through the season—and that's when people started to ask me if I thought I could hit fifty homers, which only one player in Red Sox history had done up to that time.

The player was Jimmie Foxx, bro.

He's in the Hall of Fame.

And even though I didn't know much about him at the time, I told people I wanted to learn a lot more.

BASEBALL IS A FUNNY GAME. THINGS CAN CHANGE FAST. YOU HEAR players say it all the time, but it's true: The most important thing you can have is health. You have to stay injury-free. Every player has to deal with aches and pains during the season—there's no way around it—but as long as you avoid the big stuff, you're usually fine. But if any team has too many injuries to too many key people—and I don't care who you are—you're not going to succeed. You're not going to win. The game is going to catch up to you.

For us, it happened at the wrong time.

Right after the All-Star break, we won five in a row and we were still in first place by three and a half games over the Yankees. I was having one of the best months of my career. In the first eight games of July—just before the break—I hit 8 home runs and had 16 RBIs. I was hitting everything in sight. I kept hitting after the break, but our offense really started to struggle and we had fewer men on base. We were having trouble scoring. We ended the month losing five of the last nine games we played, and we were lucky it wasn't more. In two of our wins I had walk-off hits—one against the Los Angeles Angels and the other against the Cleveland Indians—and those were against teams that we should have been able to beat more easily at home.

The game against Cleveland came second. We were losing 8–6 going into the bottom of the ninth inning, and it looked like we were in big trouble. Alex Cora opened the inning with a single against Cleveland's closer, Fausto Carmona, and then Youkilis walked. Then I came up and hit one into the center-field seats for a three-run homer that won the game for us, and all of a sudden Fenway started going crazy. I ran around the bases and took off my helmet right before I got to home plate—like I always do—and it was one of our biggest wins of the year. It allowed us to stay in front of the Yankees in the division and gave us some momentum at a time we really needed it, and it topped off a month when I hit 14 homers and had 35 RBIs, numbers that some guys don't put up in a whole season.

At that time of year, especially, it was a really big win for us. The trading deadline had just passed—and our front office wasn't able to make a trade that would help us out. There are usually a lot of rumors around the time of the trading deadline, and as a player you try not to pay too much attention to them. No matter what happens, you still have to play the game. The big thing that happened around the deadline that year was that the Yankees made a big trade and got Bobby Abreu from the Phillies—he's the same guy that won the home-run derby at the All-Star Game in 2005—and Abreu is a good player. We all knew he would help New York a lot. But as a player, like I've said, you can't worry about that stuff. You have to play and do the best you can. Our front-office people are up there working, trying to do their best, too. Making trades isn't easy. And if they end up not making a trade, for whatever reason, that's their decision. That's what they're paid to do. As players, we have to believe that they're making the right choices.

But after the Yankees got Abreu, I think that game against Cleveland meant a lot to us.

It was like we had that same attitude we had in 2003 and 2004, like we decided that we were going to win, no matter what.

We'll just win anyway.

The way things turned out, I'm not sure a trade would have helped us, anyway. What happened to us in the next couple of weeks—I'm not sure any team could have handled it. On the night we beat the Indians, Jason Varitek hurt his knee and ended up missing about a month. That was a big blow. Varitek is our catcher and our captain, and we rely on him for a lot of things. He's really important to our team. Right around that time, too, we lost Trot Nixon for about a month. That was another big blow. We already had two starting pitchers on the disabled list—Tim Wakefield and Matt Clement—and that didn't help, either. Our shortstop, Alex Gonzalez, was also having problems with injuries, and Loretta and Lowell were both playing hurt. We were really banged up. All of a sudden, when Varitek and Nixon got hurt, it felt like half of our team couldn't play. And when something like that happens, especially that fast, it's really hard to recover.

And we didn't know it, but things were about to get worse.

Right after we played Cleveland, we had series against Tampa Bay and Kansas City, two of the worst teams in the league. And at the time, Cleveland wasn't very good, either. We ended up going 3–7 in those ten games and we lost a lot of ground to the Yankees—they were three games *ahead* of us now—but we had some games coming up with New York, so we had a chance to pick up some ground there. Those games against Cleveland, Tampa, and Kansas City, I think proved something that players say all the time: You can't take anything for granted, bro. No matter who the other team is, you have to play well to beat them. In the big leagues, there's really no such thing as a bad team. Everybody's a professional. Everybody's a good player. And if you're not ready to play all the time, if you're not prepared, you're going to get into trouble.

After the Kansas City series—we lost all three to the Royals—we came home and straightened things out a little. We swept a series against the Baltimore Orioles and picked up a game on the Yankees, but then we lost two games in a three-game series against Detroit. We were still only one-and-a-half games out of first place when the Yankees came into Fenway Park for a big five-game series that started on August 18. It would have been really good for us to win three games out of the five and pick up another game, putting us right there with New York entering the final six weeks of the season.

By now, we all know what happened, bro.

We got swept.

We lost all five.

And for any player, after you put so much time and work into the season, that's really hard to take.

I DON'T LIKE TALKING ABOUT THIS TOO MUCH AND I WAS SURPRISED when it came out, but let me tell you a little bit about what happened to me when the Yankees were in town. On the first day of the series, a Friday, we played a doubleheader and lost both games, getting outscored 26–15. It was a long and frustrating day, and by the time we went home, I think

BIG PAPI

everybody was tired. Later on, I was at home just hanging out with Tiff when my chest started beating really fast, and Tiff noticed it, too. She had her hand on my chest. It made us a little nervous, but then it went away and we didn't think anything of it.

The next day, on Saturday, it came back.

I don't know if it was a coincidence, but we were losing badly again—the final score was 13–5 this time—and it was in the late innings when it felt like my heart started racing again. I wasn't sure what to do. I mentioned something to Tito, our manager, and we decided that I should I come out of the game and get it checked out. It was late in the game, anyway, and it was a good chance to get it looked at without anybody knowing what was going on. So I went up into the clubhouse and the team doctors started looking at me, examining me, just to make sure there wasn't anything major going on. One of our team doctors, Dr. Larry Ronan, decided we should probably go to the hospital and have some tests done, so he drove me over to Massachusetts General Hospital, which isn't far from the ballpark. We took a back way into the hospital so nobody would see us, and they took me and did some more tests. I spent the night there, just to be sure, and the next day they released me.

Know what the problem was?

Stress.

Before I say any more, bro, let me tell you something: We all want to win. Players are all different, just like other people, and we deal with things differently. Some players get frustrated faster than others and some guys show it more, but we all care. We all want to play and win. And when things don't go right for us—just like when they don't go right for any person—it can be tough to deal with sometimes. If you spend a whole season playing baseball, fighting to give yourself a chance, it's hard to accept when things start to slip away. You get stressed and frustrated and uptight, no matter who you are, until you finally accept that there is nothing you can do about it. After that, things get better.

I'm no different.

I don't like to lose.

When I got back to the team. Nobody knew much about my trip to the hospital and that's the way I wanted it. For me, once I found out everything was OK, it wasn't a big deal. I didn't miss any games and the next night, on Sunday, I was back in the lineup. I went 3 for 6 with a double and a home run, but we lost again, 8–5. By that point, I think everybody was frustrated. We had one game left with the Yankees, on Monday, and I think we played our best game of the series. David Wells pitched for us and he's a veteran guy who's been in a lot of big games. We ended up losing, 2–1, and the Yankees left town with a big lead in the division. We were six and a half games out. In four days, we lost five games in the standings. *Five.* I think that's when a lot of fans started to feel like our season was over.

To make things worse, Manny didn't play in the final game against the Yankees. One of his knees had been bothering him all year, and the problem was starting to get worse. A lot of fans and reporters wondered whether Manny was really hurt, and I guess they just don't know Manny the same way I do. He wants to win, bro. He's no different than anybody else. A lot of people think Manny doesn't care, that nothing bothers him, but none of that is true. He's a person just like anyone else. He cares. And when the team loses, when things go wrong, he gets as frustrated as anybody else.

After the Yankees left town, we went to Los Angeles to play the Angels and lost the first game of a three-game series there. But then we came back to win the final two games—I homered in both—and things picked up a little again. In baseball, that's all it takes. As bad as things get, all you need to do is to win a couple of games in a row, and all of a sudden your confidence starts to pick up. And then you start to believe in yourself again, you start to feel better, and you start to think that you still have a chance if things go right.

For us, that feeling didn't last long.

And it didn't last long for me, either.

Before one of the games against the Angels, a reporter came up to me and asked me about an Internet report that said I had gone to the hopsital during the Yankees series. I couldn't believe it. I didn't know how someone saw us. One thing you learn as a player now is that there is almost no way to hide anything because, with the Internet and everything else, somebody is going to find out sooner or later. That's how the world works now. So I told the reporter that I didn't want to talk about it much, that I was feeling fine now, but that the story was true. I didn't want to lie. Once we finished the Angels series and got to Seattle, some other reporters wanted to ask me about it, so I met with a bunch of reporters before one of the games there. I told them all the same stuff—that it was over and I didn't have to worry about it—and that was the last time I planned to talk about it.

We got swept in Seattle, losing all three games. We went to Oakland and got swept there, too. We were pretty banged up at that point, and just before the start of the first Oakland game, my heart started racing again. It started beating really fast. I hadn't been sleeping great and we were all tired and frustrating, and that's when the Red Sox decided that they were going to send a bunch of us back to Boston. We were losing ground fast to the Yankees. One way or another, it felt like half of our team was hurt. Because of that, the Red Sox told me that they wanted to get me completely checked out, that they wanted to make sure there was nothing wrong with me before they put me on the field again.

After the first Oakland game, Tito told the reporters that I was going back to Boston and that I was having the same problems again. I can't say enough good things about the Red Sox for how they handled it, how patient they were with me. Our season was slipping away and I was having a great year, but they told me they didn't want to risk my health for a baseball game. It was really unbelievable, bro. As a player, you want to keep playing and keep fighting, keep trying, until it's over. That's just the way we are. But the manager and the general manager and the rest of management, it's their job to make the tough decisions, to do what's right for everybody. And when they tell you that your health is more important than anything, that the games don't matter compared to that, you know you're working for really good people who care about you.

With the Red Sox, that's what I felt like.

When I left the team in Oakland, I was up to forty-seven home runs. Depending on when I came back, it looked like a I had a good chance to break the team record. I spent a couple of days at Mass General Hospital having a bunch of different tests, and by the time I got out of there, everyone knew there was nothing major wrong with me. Just the rest was probably good for me. I ended up missing about a week of games, and I got a standing ovation from the fans at Fenway Park when I came back. It was a great feeling, bro. I can't even explain it. We were eight or nine games behind the Yankees at that point and we were way behind in the wild-card race, too, so it was looking like we were going to miss the playoffs for the first time in four years. But we still had a month to play, still had time to get our act together, and I still had a few things to shoot for.

Jimmie Foxx's record was one of them.

And I thought I had another chance at the MVP.

A COUPLE OF DAYS AFTER I GOT BACK IN THE LINEUP, I HAD A BIG weekend in a three-game series against Kansas City. We lost two out of three games to the Royals, but I went 6 for 12 with a home run and six RBIs. I was closing in on Foxx's record. It looked like I was going to lead the league in home runs and RBIs. One of the writers who covers the team asked me about winning the MVP, and I told him I thought I was having a good enough year to win, that with all the injuries we had, I was still producing. A guy like Derek Jeter, who was also having a good year and was a candidate for the MVP, was on a Yankees team that also had injuries, but the Yankees had more depth than us. I thought that was something that might help me.

Somehow, that all came out wrong in the press.

And before I knew it, people were asking me why I thought Jeter shouldn't be the MVP.

As a player, that kind of thing can be frustrating. It can help me understand why Manny doesn't like talking to reporters sometimes. Derek Jeter is one of the best players in baseball and he could probably be the MVP every season. He's that good. It's not a coincidence that the Yankees have won all those championships since Jeter has been there because the guy is a winner. Every player in baseball knows it. There isn't a guy in the game who doesn't have respect for Derek Jeter and the way he goes about his business. He's one of the most professional guys in the game. But with the way things came out, I think Jeter was offended and the Yankees might have been a little pissed off. We were in Baltimore when it all happened and we were about to go to New York, so we made sure to call the Yankees and clear everything up. Tito called the Yankees manager, Joe Torre, and he told him that the way it sounded was not what I meant. By the time everything got settled, everything between me and Jeter, between us and the Yankees, was cool.

But let me say a few things about the MVP.

In baseball, the MVP is the biggest award you can get outside of being elected to the Hall of Fame. It really means something. There is only one guy in each league who can win the award, and it's usually a sign that you've had a really special year. For me, I felt like I was having one of those seasons. I felt like I had one in 2005, too. After finishing second to Alex Rodriguez in '05, I thought, in some way, that I was playing even better in 2006. But now there were other guys who were getting consideration for the award, guys who didn't have the same numbers that I did, and it was all a little confusing to me.

I mean, what does a guy have to do to win?

Is it about the numbers or is it about winning?

And can a designated hitter like me win it or not?

For someone like me, it's just hard to figure out. A few ago, when he was playing for the Texas Rangers, A–Rod won the award, even though his team finished in last place, because he had the best numbers. In 2006, when I led the league in home runs and RBIs, I ended up finishing third. Sometimes the MVP winner comes from a playoff team and sometimes he doesn't. Starting pitchers have won and closers have won, but a DH never really has. As a player, the only thing you can do is what your team asks you to do, every day. And if you do that better than anybody else, if you do that better than any hitter in the league, shouldn't that count for something?

Still, I don't want anybody to get me wrong. The guys who have won the MVP over the last few years, they all deserved it. The guy who ended up winning in 2006 was Justin Morneau of the Minnesota Twins, a first baseman who put up really good numbers and whose team won the division. That all counts for something. But as a player, when you feel like you're consistent, it's just hard to understand what matters sometimes. It's probably hard for the guys who vote, too. The rules seem to change every year, so you never really know what you have to do to become one of those guys that win one, that can hold that trophy and know he has done something really great.

But maybe that's what makes the MVP so special.

By the time we got to the final few weeks of the season, I was pretty sure I wasn't going to win the MVP. The team was way out of the playoff race and we were playing younger guys, and nobody was giving us much of a chance. With the MVP, the month of September is really important. That's when the races are decided. And if your team is not in contention, if you're not even close, chances are that people are going to forget about you and vote for someone else. I think that's what ended up happening to me.

Still, I had some other exciting things going on.

While we were in New York, I hit my forty-ninth homer of the season on Sunday, September 17, in the first game of a doubleheader against the Yankees. We ended up winning both games and splitting a four-game series—the Yankees had swept us in a doubleheader the day before—and that put me within one homer of Foxx's team record of fifty home runs. No other Red Sox player ever had hit fifty homers in a year— not Babe Ruth, not Ted Williams, not Jim Rice—and Foxx did it only once, in 1938. That was almost *seventy years* earlier, bro. That's a long time. A lot of good players have played for the Red Sox during that time, but nobody ever did what Foxx did. And as much as people talk about how Fenway Park can be a great place to hit—and it is—it can be a tough place to hit home runs, especially for a left–handed hitter like me. Foxx was right-handed, so he had the big left-field wall to shoot at. But for me, I either had to hit homers to the opposite field—and that is never easy—or I had to hit them to right field, and Fenway has one of the deepest right fields in the league. They don't give away home runs in Boston, bro. You have to earn them.

As much as it would have been nice to catch Foxx in New York, the good news was that we were going home after the Yankees series, so I was going to get the chance to break the record at home.

In a lot of ways, that was best situation, bro, especially when you think about who we were about to play.

The Minnesota Twins.

The team that released me.

Can you believe that?

After I went 0 for 5 against the Twins in the first game of the series, I started to get hot. I hit number 50, tying Foxx, against a young right-hander named Boof Bonser in a game we lost. The crowd gave me a standing ovation and it was one of the best feelings I've ever had in the world. After the game, we got the ball and auctioned it off for charity. One night later, against the Twins again, I homered in the first inning against Minnesota's ace, Johan Santana, to break the record. Fenway went crazy again. Santana was just a kid when I left the Minnesota organization, but now he might be the best pitcher in the game. He's a friend of mine, bro. He's a really good guy. And as I was running around the bases, Torii Hunter was clapping for me in center field and it was one of the most incredible feelings in the world, doing something that nobody in the history of the Red Sox ever had done before.

Doing it against the Twins, that meant something to me, too, bro.

But it ended up meaning more than I thought because I was able to share it with some of the guys I played with in Minnesota.

Later that night, I hit another home run, number 52, and I finished the game 3 for 3 with two homers. We won, 6–0. I hit two more home runs during the last week of the season, giving me fifty-four for the year, the most in the American League. In all of baseball, only Philadelphia Phillies first base-man Ryan Howard—a big left-handed hitter like me—hit more. My fifty-third homer of the year came in Toronto against a left-hander named Gustavo Chacin, and that homer meant something, too. It was my thirty-second homer of the year on the road, tying an American League record, and you'll never guess whose name is next to mine in the American League record book.

Babe Ruth, bro.

The Bambino.

Never in a million years did I think I would tie a record that would put me right there next to Babe Ruth.

LET ME ADMIT SOMETHING TO YOU: SOMETIMES, AT THE END OF A long day, I'll sit there by myself and I'll say to myself: "How did this all happen?" God gave me a lot of things, bro, and not just on the baseball field. He gave me good parents, good friends, people to teach me things, and the strength to deal with them. Life goes up and down. It can be really hard for everybody sometimes. I've been lucky enough that I could handle the bad times because I've learned to remind myself that those things are *temporary,* that things will improve again before long and that things will be fine.

But what about the people who always have the bad times? What about those people who can't look at it as temporary? How do they do it? How do they get by?

I look at people like that sometimes and I think, *I've got it easy.*

Of course, as you get older, you realize that it's not easy for anybody. We all have our challenges. I've had mine. I spent my whole life wanting to be a ballplayer and believing that I could be, but I didn't grow up with much. I got signed as a free agent when I was seventeen years old and I came to United States like a lot of other players do. Most of them don't make it. I got traded by one team and released by another, and all I ever wanted was a chance that I felt like nobody wanted to give me. I signed with the Boston Red Sox as a free agent in January 2003 and I was twenty-seven years old, and a lot of people thought I was never going to be more than what I was at the time, a part-time designated hitter who had some power but wasn't productive enough to play every day.

Now, four years later, even strangers know my name. The Red Sox have won a World Series. I was the Most Valuable Player of the 2004 American League Championship Series, and I got more votes than any other players for the 2005 All-Star Game. I'm proud of those things, bro—who wouldn't be?—but I'll tell you the truth: I still can't believe it myself sometimes. I feel like I've waited my whole life to get where I am now, but I've always felt like I have an obligation to remember where I came from. My mom and pop taught me that. And sometimes I feel that my life and career are just starting even though I know it's been a long trip that has had its share of ups and downs and problems.

That's why now, going into 2007, I laugh when I take the field and I hear people call out my name like I'm some movie star or heavyweight champion, or one of those dudes that makes *me* get excited.

I mean, my pop still calls me *Dah-veed*.

It's the rest of the world that calls me Big Papi.

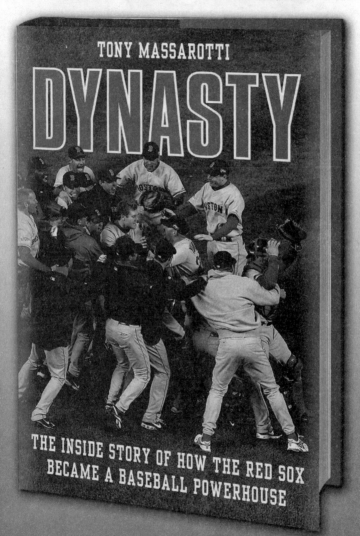